A special scar

'This book is written by a survivor of suicide. Alison Wertheimer lost her own sister by suicide, but she has not made the mistake of assuming that this makes her an expert on the subject. Her expertise comes from very wide reading and from the systematic interviews she has carried out with fifty other people who have been bereaved by suicide.... She is to be congratulated on drawing all these strands together into a volume which will be of value to caring professions, counsellors, and friends of those bereaved by suicide, as well as the bereaved survivors themselves.' – Dr Colin Murray Parkes, author of *Bereavement: Studies of Grief in Adult Life*, Routledge 1986.

Every year more than 8,000 people in Britain take their own lives. But what happens to their families and friends – the survivors of suicide? Because of the stigma attached to suicide, they have remained a largely hidden group, yet there are likely to be more than 80,000 new survivors annually, people whose lives have been profoundly affected by the suicide of someone close to them.

A Special Scar describes the experiences of survivors of suicide, including the parents, children, siblings and spouses of suicide victims. It reveals the particular problems which this group of bereaved people face: the stress of coping with the police, with post-mortems, inquests, and the resulting media publicity; the negative attitudes of friends and the community at large; the survivor's own feelings of shame and stigma; and the guilt and anger which many experience. A final chapter and resource section suggest how survivors can be helped and supported by those around them.

Alison Wertheimer, whose sister committed suicide in 1979, is former policy director of Mind and now works as a freelance writer and researcher. She has published many articles on bereavement; this is her first book.

A special scar

The experiences of people bereaved by suicide

Alison Wertheimer

London and New York

First published in 1991
by Routledge
11 New Fetter Lane, London EC4P 4EE

Simultaneously published in the USA and Canada
by Routledge
29 West 35th Street, New York, NY 10001

Reprinted 1992, 1993 and 1995

© 1991 Alison Wertheimer

Laserset by
NWL Editorial Services, Langport, England
Printed and bound in Great Britain by
Mackays of Chatham PLC, Chatham, Kent

British Library Cataloguing in Publication Data
A catalogue record for this book is available from the British Library

Library of Congress Cataloguing in Publication Data
A catalogue record for this book is available from the Library of Congress

ISBN 0-415-01762-9 (hbk)
ISBN 0-415-01763-7 (pbk)

For Anna Rosamunde
15 August 1942 – 26 February 1979

Clinical diagnoses are important ... but they do not help the patient.... The crucial thing is the story. For it alone shows the human background and the human suffering.

Memories, Dreams, Reflections
C.G. Jung

Contents

Contents

Contents

Part three: Looking to the future

Foreword

Why should it matter so much how people die? Surely what really matters is how they lived? Yet the way to death *does* matter. One of the saddest things about suicide is the fact that it may become the only thing that is remembered about a person, and remembered with fear. Part of the reason for this is the difficulty which we, the survivors (for we are all survivors), have in making sense of anything so senseless. Suicide calls into question the priority which we give to life, it outrages our basic assumptions. When life is all we know, how can anyone be anti-life?

This book is written by a survivor of suicide. Alison Wertheimer lost her own sister by suicide, but she has not made the mistake of assuming that this makes her an expert on the subject. Her expertise comes from very wide reading and from the systematic interviews she has carried out with fifty other people who have been bereaved by suicide. In fact she is very self-effacing and she avoids pontificating, theorising, and offering simple answers to complex problems. In much of the book she allows the survivors to speak for themselves, elsewhere she quotes the opinions of others, but they are always opinions offered for our consideration rather than holy writ. And because she shows us bereavement through the eyes of the bereaved, what we see is often direct and painful, but not without hope. Her witnesses are coming through one of the most painful and complicated types of bereavement. Little by little, in their own ways, they are picking up the pieces and assembling a new model of the world. Often, one feels, it is a stronger and more mature set of assumptions which is emerging and we, the readers, are privileged to share in this process of maturation.

There are, of course, many kinds of suicide and many different reactions to suicide which may be appropriate. There are suicides which come unexpectedly, as a bolt from the blue when some mental illness or aberration which should have been transient leads to a consequence that is anything but transient. Such suicides are a major trauma to the survivors. There are suicides that come at the end of a long and painful struggle, whose final outcome was never much in doubt. Some mental illness can be just as malignant as cancer and cause relentless pain, not only to the sufferer, but to the family as a whole. When, despite every effort to mitigate the pain, the illness ends fatally, we should hardly be surprised if our immediate reaction is one of relief. Our grief, when it comes, is more for the misery that preceded the death than for the death itself.

Occasionally a suicide can be a kind of triumph over death as when someone willingly lays down their life for the sake of others. To those of us who benefit from this largesse our gratitude is not unmixed with guilt. Do we deserve to benefit from the death of another, no matter how freely chosen this was? Yet if we refuse to benefit do we negate the very meaning of the gift?

Many bereavements are so painful that the survivors feel as if they are being punished. When the bereavement results from suicide, the imputation is much greater. Why did he (or she) do this to *me*? What have I done to deserve it? The fact that in most instances the lost person was only seeking their own quietus is of little account.

By its very essence suicide is an act against the self, and even those suicidal people who blame others may be simply seeking a vent for their own distress. How often do we find that people in the extremes of misery hit out at those they love; perhaps they too felt that they were being punished.

In this, as in many other ways, the survivors have something in common with the dead. Does this mean that we are all potential suicides? In the vast majority of cases the answer is 'no'. Suicide remains a very rare act. For every person who commits suicide there are 8,000 who don't and there is certainly no reason to regard a family as 'doomed' simply because one member has chosen to end his or her own life.

Even so, suicide does strike at the very nature of a family. Every family is a network of individuals who share a common need to protect and support each other. They do this by means of a complex set of rules, alliances, and assumptions which allow each to contribute to and benefit from the shared commitment of the whole. Family structure and functioning are always changed by bereavements, but bereavement by suicide is often seen as a rejection of the central supportive function. Leadership is undermined, alliances broken or devalued, and faith in the family as a source of love and security is called into doubt. People who normally communicate with each other and trust each other may find themselves unable to do so. Small wonder that suicide can come to be seen as the skeleton in the family closet.

The people who have assisted with this book have not been afraid to face the facts of suicide. They show us what has harmed them and what has helped them. They show us that, far from being destroyed by speaking of the unspeakable, a family which chooses to face the facts of loss can achieve a new identity.

Alison Wertheimer is to be congratulated on drawing all these strands together into a volume which will be of value to members of caring professions, counsellors, and friends of those bereaved by suicide, as well as the bereaved survivors themselves. She ends the book with a challenge to all of us. If we accept the evidence that one of the best ways to help people to communicate is to draw them together with others who share similar problems then there is a real need for us to find ways of creating a forum where people bereaved by suicide can meet.

Colin Murray Parkes MD FRCPsych
February 1990

Preface: a survivor's story

On a Monday morning in February 1979, my only sister, Rosamunde, took her own life. Ros was thirty-six when she died and she left a husband, a nine-year-old daughter, and a six-year-old son. Her death came as a complete shock to me; it was also my first experience of someone close to me dying. Having no other bereavements with which to compare this, it was some time before I realised how different and how particularly difficult the loss of someone by suicide can be. Over ten years later I am still trying to understand more fully what it means to be a survivor of suicide.

Although Ros and I had seen much less of each other since leaving our boarding school, I suppose her suicide should not have been the totally unexpected event that it seemed at the time; one of the things I've discovered since then, is that survivors only achieve understanding with hindsight. She had suffered serious bouts of depression since she was a teenager; the summer before her death she had been admitted to a psychiatric hospital, emerging with a diagnosis of manic depression. Ros never seemed to recover after that time in hospital, but although I had sensed that things were going badly when I spent Christmas with her two months before her death, the thought that she might commit suicide had never entered my head. Perhaps there are some things which are so dreadful to contemplate that we decide not to admit them into consciousness.

Fortunately, shock acts as a protective blanket. For the first few days after she died I felt too numb and exhausted to really take in the awfulness of what had happened. The fact that I neither saw her body, nor attended the preliminary inquest to hear what had happened, is something I now regret; at the time it just fed into that sense of unreality. Because I'd never seen a dead person before, let alone someone who had died violently, I think if I am honest that I was just too frightened. If only I could have talked this over with someone. Now it's too late, and I never did get to say a proper goodbye.

Although close friends rallied round immediately and were extremely supportive I still found it hard to face other people. I could see the horror in their faces. Even to people who had scarcely known her or who had never even met her, her death was deeply shocking. Re-reading the many letters I received at the time, I am struck by the fact that only two people actually felt able to mention that she had committed suicide. They neither condemned nor supported what she had done, but they didn't pretend either that it hadn't happened the way it did. I'm still grateful to them for that.

Talking to people other than very close friends was hard. Because most thirty-six-year-olds don't die suddenly, I felt I had to offer some sort of explanation and when I told them it was suicide, they inevitably wanted to know why she'd done it. Often I was tempted to reply, 'How the hell should I know! Ask her yourself!' I didn't know. No one really knew. Perhaps even Ros didn't know why she did it. Since then, of course, I've learned that this is the one big question that survivors come back to again and again. But it's also the question for which there isn't really an answer.

On reflection, I can't really blame other people for their awkwardness and confusion. After all, there are no norms for dealing with suicide. When, five years later, my seventy-year-old mother died of cancer everyone knew what to say; it was a more or less respectable age to die, and her death was a 'merciful release'. There is a language, however cliché-ridden, for that sort of death. But suicide? We don't seem to have the words for it.

I suppose, to be honest, some of the awkwardness was on my side as well. A part of me did feel ashamed, did sometimes feel rather freakish. After all, I reasoned, people in nice, normal families don't kill themselves, do they? So we must be a pretty weird bunch. I think if I'd been able to talk with other people who'd been through a similar experience I might have seen things differently. There was, in fact, one friend with a suicide in his family but we didn't really talk about it. With my newly acquired – and unsought – identity as a survivor of suicide I felt very isolated, very set apart from other people.

Suicide leaves the survivor with a ragbag of painful and conflicting feelings. Guilt was probably top of my list, although I think this only surfaced gradually. I felt guilty because I was the one who had survived. Ros had died but I was alive – was I to blame for this in some way? I felt I should have been able to stop it happening. The fact that I hadn't even thought her suicide was a possibility didn't make me feel any less responsible; survivor guilt can be pretty irrational. I was working for a mental health organisation at the time. Why hadn't I made sure she got help?

But wondering if somehow I could have prevented her death was a fruitless exercise. In a sense I didn't really have any choice. Ros had decided that she was going to have the last word. Guilt became overlaid with anger. OK, I was the one who was still alive, but being a survivor of suicide wasn't turning out to be much fun either. Why had she left me to cope with all this? I hadn't asked to be a survivor.

Almost from the day it happened, I felt a sense of relief. Often I wasn't sure who this was for – her or me? Perhaps it was for both of us. Even so I can still find it hard to admit sometimes that I'm glad I don't have to worry about her any more; her problems and crises don't interrupt my life. But we're not supposed to be glad when someone dies.

Although I had never in my life contemplated suicide, one of my biggest fears after Ros's death was that I'd kill myself too. Only a few weeks after Ros died a colleague at work also hanged himself. That made things even worse. The world began to feel very unsafe. Two people in two months? I remember lying in bed after hearing about John's suicide, looking at the curtain rail and thinking it would be quite easy to copy them. Ros died when she was thirty-six, and I breathed a sigh of relief when I reached my thirty-seventh birthday and found I was still alive. Those feelings have almost completely disappeared now, but at the time I kept them to myself, and there was no one to tell me that this is a common reaction to suicide.

Ten years ago, searching through the bereavement literature I could find virtually nothing on the particular difficulties of survivors of suicide. I turned to writings on suicide, books like Alvarez's *The Savage God*, but they tended to focus on the suicidal person rather than on those left behind. Some years later, I came across Cain's rather scholarly *Survivors of Suicide*, but I found nothing written this side of the Atlantic and nothing that was really accessible to survivors themselves.

When I started talking to other survivors and to bereavement professionals, people often assumed that I was going to come up with the answer to why people committed suicide. Some of them assumed I had a set of preconceived theories about the causes of suicide and its impact on survivors which the book would prove; others hoped that if suicidal people read my book it would prevent them from killing themselves.

The truth was that I set out with none of these aims in mind. I simply wanted to describe the experiences of some survivors – to tell their stories, as I have told mine. I think I did have an idea that as I talked to survivors some common threads would emerge, that there would be some shared experiences, thoughts, and feelings. I also thought that each person I saw would be very different. If it doesn't sound too paradoxical, I was right on both counts.

This book has been written for survivors as well as for their relatives and friends. I hope they will feel some common bonds with the people whose stories are told in this book, and that this will help them to feel less isolated. There are many hidden survivors, hidden because the fact of suicide has been concealed; the true nature of their loss remains a closely guarded secret; I hope they will realise that their secret is not so dreadful, and that secrets do not have to be kept for ever.

This book is also for people who in one capacity or another care for, advise, support, and counsel those bereaved by suicide. They may be doing this as volunteers, or it may be part of their paid work. They include general practitioners, health visitors, social workers, psychologists and psychiatrists, counsellors and therapists, members of the clergy, police, and coroners' officers. This does not purport to be a textbook or manual on working with survivors, but I hope it will help them reach a better understanding of what it is like to be a survivor and so enable them to meet survivors' needs more effectively.

Coming to terms with a suicide is a unique process for each survivor. Each of us has to find our own way through. Writing this book has been a part of my healing process, but I also hope that it will enable more survivors to realise that they are not alone, that we do not have to hide the truth, and that, painful as it may be at times, we can learn not just to survive but to live.

February 1990

Acknowledgements

I would like to thank the following: the King Edward's Hospital Fund for London who provided financial support to meet the interviewing costs, and the Nuffield Foundation whose grant financed the transcription of the interview tapes; my agent, Gloria Ferris, particularly for her encouragement in the early stages of this project; Gill Davies and Edwina Welham of Routledge; CRUSE, The Compassionate Friends, and the Editor of *New Society* for putting me in touch with people willing to talk about their experiences as suicide survivors; Douglas Chambers, Phil Clements, Libby Insall, Colin Murray Parkes, Barbara Porter, and Susan Wallbank for their advice on particular issues; and John Costello who helped me stay on the journey.

A legacy from my father (who died while I was researching this book) enabled me to take time off from other work and write this book without interruption. For that I wish to thank him.

Above all, I owe an enormous debt of gratitude to my fellow survivors who shared their stories with me. I am grateful for their openness, their willingness to share thoughts and feelings which were often painful and difficult to talk about. They taught me a great deal, not only about survivorship in general, but about my own particular experience of being a survivor.

Acknowledgement is due to the following for permission to quote from 'The Guide' by U.A. Fanthorpe, Peterloo Poets (*Standing To* 1982) and King Penguin (*Selected Poems* 1986).

Part one

Introduction

Chapter one

Suicide: an introduction

The act of suicide, which represents both personal unhappiness and the implied belief that the victim's fellow-men are powerless to remedy his condition, can never be viewed with indifference.
(Carstairs 1973: 7)

The idea that a person chooses to die creates in us a profound sense of unease. Suicide challenges some of our most deeply held beliefs. It defies the cherished notion that all human life is sacred; it challenges the value of life itself, and places a question mark over the taboos against the taking of life. The suicide of another person forces us to question the value and meaning not only of life in general but of our own individual lives.

For many people, the contemplation of apparently self-chosen death hardly bears thinking about and yet, over the centuries, they have found it impossible to ignore the subject. There have been persistent attempts to categorise and compartmentalise suicide and, in doing so, perhaps we have been trying to make ourselves a bit more comfortable with it. It has been examined from many angles. Lawyers, doctors, novelists, poets, philosophers, and theologians have all contributed to the debate.

But the fruits of that continuing quest for understanding are not only to be found in the pages of legal, medical, and philosophical journals. We have inherited a varied collection of images of suicide, and our reactions to the act of suicide do not occur in a vacuum. Historical images have helped to shape society's attitudes and feelings towards those who take their own lives, and towards the survivors of suicide – the victim's family and friends who are bequeathed such a painful legacy. This introductory chapter will explore some of

1

the most common images and attitudes, as well as setting out some of the facts at our disposal – such as they are. This chapter and the one that follows form the backcloth to Part two which will be looking at the experiences of some individuals bereaved by suicide.

Facts and figures

Every two hours someone in Britain commits suicide. Translated on to a global scale, an estimated one thousand people a day take their own lives or nearly one a minute (Staudacher 1988). In many countries today, suicide is one of the ten leading causes of death, and it is almost impossible to estimate the number of people across the world who will be affected by these sudden and often violent deaths.

These offical statistics, however, only tell part of the story. The annual rate of around 4,300 suicides in England and Wales (1988 figure) is almost certainly a considerable underestimate (Stengel 1973; Office of Health Economics 1981; Chambers and Harvey 1989). The same is true for other countries such as the USA (McIntosh 1987a). But why is there this apparent disparity? The main reason in Britain is because official statistics are based on coroners' verdicts.

It is not always clear whether the person actually intended to commit suicide. In the case of a suspected suicide, an inquest will be held, but the victim's intention to commit suicide must be strictly proven, and, according to Douglas Chambers, coroner for Inner North London, 'The common-sense or balance of probabilities approach will get short judicial shrift' (1989: 181). In the absence of any clear proof of intent, the verdict cannot be suicide; instead it is likely to be classified as 'death by misadventure', 'accidental death', or there will be an 'open' verdict.

Some coroners may be less inclined than others to pass verdicts of suicide (Keir 1986) and they will seek to protect relatives from what is sometimes considered to be a distressing and unwelcome verdict. In certain circumstances, the evidence must be heard before a jury, and juries, like some coroners, can be reluctant to return a verdict of suicide. An examination of inquests in Inner North London found that juries hearing cases of deaths on the London Underground returned suicide verdicts in only some 40 per cent of these cases, despite the fact that 'the common assumption must be that all such deaths are suicidal' (Chambers and Harvey 1989: 184).

On other occasions, a verdict of suicide will never even be considered. Take the case of a car in which the driver is the sole occupant. On an empty road, in apparently good weather conditions, the car goes off the road, and the driver is killed. There are no witnesses to offer possible explanations, and faced with an apparently inexplicable event, the verdict will almost certainly be 'accidental death'. No one is likely to state publicly that the driver could have deliberately driven off the road with the intention of killing himself, and the death will not be included in the suicide statistics.

Various attempts have been made to estimate the true rate of suicide in Britain. Professor Norman Kreitman, an expert on the epidemiology of suicide, speaking on a radio programme in 1986, suggested that the actual rate was probably about 60 per cent higher than the official statistics. A recent study by Chambers and Harvey (1989) indicates that it may be more than double the published figures. Alvarez (1974) suggests between a quarter and a half as many again.

The official suicide statistics for other countries are equally unreliable (Stengel 1973), and the lack of universally agreed criteria for determining suicide makes accurate international comparisons virtually impossible. In countries where suicide is strongly condemned for religious or cultural reasons there will almost certainly be underreporting of suicides, the nature of such deaths often remaining closely guarded family secrets. Perhaps it was a desire to avoid international scandal that led the seventeenth-century Scot, Robert Blair, to describe suicide in Britain as 'our island's shame that makes her the reproach of neighbouring states'. High suicide rates were obviously not something to boast about.

But despite the unreliability of international statistics, suicide does seem to be more common in more affluent, industrialised countries, which tend to have comparatively high rates (Stengel 1973). Suicide is not necessarily an escape from material poverty, and wealth does not act as an insurance policy against suicide.

Although suicide rates may vary between countries, the rate within individual countries tends to remain reasonably stable, although sudden major fluctuations tend to occur during periods of major social or political upheaval. Britain offers a good example of how major disturbances can affect the suicide rates (Keir 1986). During the First World War the rate fell, only to rise again in peacetime, a rise which became more marked during the economic depression of

3

the 1930s with its high levels of unemployment. The number of suicides fell again during the Second World War and gradually rose again after 1945. War may provide an outlet for aggression which otherwise can be turned inwards in acts of self-destruction. The correlation between suicide and unemployment is not fully understood, but the Dean of the Royal College of Psychiatrists claims that unemployment has contributed to the increase in suicide rates among men (The *Independent*, 20 April 1987).

So who is the typical suicide victim? Recent publicity has drawn attention to the increasing number of young people in Britain who are taking their own lives, but although this is indeed the case, suicide is no particular respecter of age. For example, in 1986 there were 303 suicides of people aged 65–69 and 331 among 20–24 year olds. However, these figures mask some important differences; suicides account for 0.5 per cent of all deaths of 65–69 year olds but nearly 14 per cent of all deaths in the younger age group. After accidents, suicide is the most common cause of death among young men. The impact of these deaths on surviving family and friends is also likely to be greater because the victims are younger and their deaths are untimely (see Chapter 2).

There are marked differences in the suicide rates of men and women. The ratio of male to female suicides has fluctuated considerably during this century, but although the proportion of female suicides is now somewhat greater than it was in the early 1900s, men still account for approximately two-thirds of all suicide deaths, and the proportion is likely to increase as the number of male suicides is increasing. According to the Samaritans, male suicides increased by 38 per cent between 1975 and 1987. Female suicides, on the other hand, decreased by 20 per cent over the same period.

There are significant differences in the methods men and women use to commit suicide. Women tend to opt for less violent methods so that nearly half of them will die as the result of an overdose, a method used in less than a quarter of male suicides. The more violent method of hanging, though, is the single commonest choice for men; nearly three out of ten male suicide deaths are the result of hanging, whereas less than one fifth of female suicide victims die in this way.

Suicide is often assumed to be a winter problem, when the bad weather and long hours of darkness can cause even the most cheerful person to feel depressed, but the patterns of suicide suggest a different picture. The numbers start to rise in March and peak around May (Alvarez 1974). Springtime, welcomed by most people, may be unbearable for people who are feeling suicidal and hopeless. As the husband of one suicide victim said: 'I showed her the new buds in the garden, but I sensed she wasn't going along with that new life.' The contrast between feelings of inner deadness and the outer growth of spring can and does lead some people to commit suicide, an argument which is given added weight by the fact that suicide rates in parts of the southern hemisphere tend to follow the same seasonal patterns (Stengel 1973).

Suicide has weekly as well as annual patterns, and more people kill themselves at weekends or immediately afterwards than on other days of the week. After all, weekends are supposed to be for fun and relaxation, for enjoying oneself in the company of family and friends. To the suicidal person it can seem as though everyone out there is having a marvellous time, or, as someone said on the radio recently, 'even if they aren't, they'll pretend they are anyway'. For some people, going out to work during the week may, at least temporarily, obliterate their sense of isolation and depression. Weekends remove that protection.

The loneliness and depression which some people face at weekends can be magnified during holiday seasons such as Christmas. There is a pervasive myth that the so-called festive season is just that for everyone. Perhaps, though, realism is beginning to creep in; we now seem to hear a bit more about family stresses and about the loneliness of many individuals during the Christmas season.

Lastly there will be times which are stressful and difficult for individuals, and when some people may be more at risk of committing suicide. Anniversaries of all kinds can be a problem for the suicidal person, whether they commemorate seemingly happy occasions such as weddings or birthdays, or sadder events such as death or divorce. As one young woman said, after making a serious suicide attempt on the anniversary of her father's death: 'It was the time when all the hurts came out' (Shneidman 1982).

Images of suicide

The facts and figures discussed above present a rather one-dimensional picture. When it comes to trying to understand something of society's attitudes towards suicide victims and their families, we need to examine some of the images relating to suicide and how these have helped to shape our views.

If a group of people were asked to describe their individual pictures of the sort of people who commit suicide, they would almost certainly come up with a number of different images. They might mention ill-fated lovers such as Romeo and Juliet, the writers Sylvia Plath and Virginia Woolf, Marilyn Monroe, IRA hunger strikers, Japanese *kamikaze* pilots, people who jump off the cliffs at Beachy Head, or *Eastenders* star, David Scarborough. War, drama, opera, newspaper stories, television programmes – the sources are many and varied. As one woman said, after her father's suicide: 'It's amazing how often the mention of suicide crops up ... almost every day.'

Certain suicides seem to be considered more acceptable than others. Captain Oates, who walked out into an Arctic blizzard to save his fellow explorers, is usually considered a hero. In fact, altruistic suicides go back a long way. In the sixth century, elderly people were jumping off Beachy Head when crop failures led to insufficient food supplies. It could be argued that these deaths are acts of martyrdom rather than suicide, but the distinction is somewhat blurred in the sense that both are self-chosen deaths.

Society may no longer expect sick or elderly people to dispose of themselves when times are hard, but there are still people who commit suicide believing – rightly or wrongly – that they are an unacceptable burden to others. As the mother of one suicide victim speculated: 'He might have been trying to say it was better for us without him.' Victims may sometimes make statements to that effect in their suicide notes. For families who have lived with someone who has made repeated threats or suicide attempts, sometimes over many years, the suicide can leave them feeling that a burden has been lifted.

Sometimes, though, the person may see suicide as a means of saving themselves rather than others – as literally saving themselves from 'a fate worse than death'. In Japan, the Samurai had complex ritual codes for different methods of suicide which would bring them 'death before dishonour'. The Japanese railwayman who committed suicide recently after he was found to have caused a fatal train accident was not really acting that differently from his ancestors. This sort of suicide may be less common in Western society but it can still occur; remand prisoners facing the prospect of a public trial, for example, are a known high-risk category for suicide.

There are many examples in history of imitative or 'copycat' suicides which have, on occasions, reached epidemic proportions; one such epidemic occurred in Budapest in 1928 when, in the space of two months, over 150 people deliberately drowned themselves in the Danube. The authorities finally sent out a patrol boat to drag would-be suicides from the river which put an end to that particular epidemic (Chesser 1967). More recently, there have been reports from the USA of 'cluster suicides' involving several teenagers from the same town (Lukas and Seiden 1987). There may well be some truth in the idea that 'the first one makes it easier for the rest' and publicity can draw attention to methods which work. At least twenty people a year jump off Beachy Head (described by one journalist as 'the world's favourite suicide spot'), not because Britain is short of cliffs but because it is known as a place for successful suicides. However, although research on copycat suicides is inconclusive, there is some measure of agreement that people who apparently commit imitative suicides have almost certainly already contemplated taking their own lives. In other words, publicity may be a trigger for the already suicidal, but is not likely to be a cause.

Political suicides, which can be traced back to events such as the mass suicide of Jews at Masada in AD 73, have been a regular feature of the news in recent years. IRA prisoners on hunger strike in Northern Ireland and Arab suicide bombers in the Middle East have died for causes which they believed to be worth the personal sacrifice involved. In society's eyes they may be martyrs, murderers, or madmen. Alvarez suggests that with political suicides of this kind, the victims are caught up in magical thinking: 'my death will result in the enemy's death', a view which he does not share: 'There seems to me to be nothing to justify such optimism' (1974: 68).

Reporting of political suicide presents one of many different images of suicide featuring in the media today. Most people probably encounter suicide through radio, television, and the newspapers. The reporting of real-life suicides is often accompanied by dramatic, eye-catching headlines – 'Fireball suicide of lovesick businessman' and 'Would-be MP leapt to his death' – reinforcing the idea that the person committing suicide is making a dramatic public statement. But at the same time, we are presented with selective images based on a tiny proportion of suicides – the more sensational or bizarre, the more public suicides, and the suicides of the famous.

The stories are often as atypical of most suicides as the headlines.

To quote one recent example: a Sunday newspaper carried two brief stories about suicide on the same page. The first concerned the discovery of a man's body beside that of his mother. He had just committed suicide – she had been dead for a year. The other story reported how seven Japanese women had set fire to themselves after the death of their religious leader. Hardly typical cases of suicide, but typical of the news coverage of suicide. But even if we are proud of our ability to distinguish between fact and fiction, what did television viewers make of the following recent episode of a popular detective series? A young man has committed suicide. His spirit returns to haunt the family home, leading to the death of his father. Is this a twentieth-century version of the medieval belief that victims of suicide return to haunt the living as an act of revenge?

Sometimes the media will go to the other extreme, adopting a much more reticent approach. The Press has many euphemisms for cases of suspected suicide – 'foul play is not suspected' – 'tablets were found near the body' – 'no one is being interviewed'. Death announcements in the personal columns usually carry the same cloaked messages; it is rare to read that someone 'died by his own hand' (*Guardian*, 3 October 1986); instead people die 'suddenly' or 'tragically' – though perhaps this is hardly surprising when a newspaper like *The Times* does not even permit the words 'dead' or 'died' in its death announcements!

Images of suicide are sometimes mixed up with other quite different images. Many people will remember that Marilyn Monroe supposedly committed suicide, but she is also remembered as a glamorous film star and sex symbol. Janis Joplin was a successful rock star but she also died from an overdose. Suicide is never a pleasant business, but sometimes it becomes linked with glamour and success.

Local newspapers have a large readership, and are an important source of information for many people. Most carry regular reports of local cases of suicide, and this is discussed in some detail in Chapters 7 and 15, but here is just a final – if slightly flippant – point on imagery. There is sexism even in suicide: Shepherd and Barraclough's study of one newspaper's coverage of suicide revealed that men 'kill themselves', but women (or should it be ladies?) 'take their own lives' (1978).

Attitudes towards suicide

Unlike the weather or the latest cricket test-match score or football results, suicide does not crop up that often as a topic of conversation. Even thinking about the fact that some people choose to take their own lives can leave people feeling deeply uneasy. They avoid the subject, not because they feel it does not concern them, but rather because it can arouse such powerful emotions. 'We do not, in truth, really want to know...', Keir suggests; 'Contemplation of the deed itself, the manner of its execution – the overdose, the drowning, the hanging – fills us with horror' (1986: 13).

My personal experience bears this out. I recently attended a conference where the programme included a session on suicide and bereavement. The speaker started by asking those present to share their thoughts and feelings about suicide with the person sitting next to them. My neighbour was distinctly uncomfortable with the subject; she expressed feelings of horror at the very idea, and was at a loss for words when I told her about my sister's suicide some years ago and my plans for writing this book. I don't think her response was that unusual: feelings of unease, horror, and general embarrassment.

Despite our reluctance to discuss the topic of suicide, scratch the surface and, more likely than not, people will be found to have some very strong opinions. They may approach it from a religious or legal standpoint; or they may judge it in moral terms – as a question of right or wrong. Others will view it as a scientific or sociological issue for which a solution or cure must be found; and finally, there will be those who claim they find the whole idea quite incomprehensible.

Despite a lack of clear biblical evidence, Christianity has, in the past, generally condemned the act of suicide, seeing it as a failure to uphold the sanctity of life, and, according to Alvarez, providing the victim with 'a one-way ticket to eternal damnation' (1974: 70). However, this century has seen the emergence of a generally more tolerant and sympathetic attitude (at least among some individual members of the clergy), both towards the victims and their families; Christian funeral rites and burial are no longer withheld from those who take their own lives (Alvarez 1974).

Judaism, likewise, has generally not supported the act of suicide, although neither the Talmud nor the Bible include any specific prohibition. However, some Jews today do make a distinction between premeditated or 'wilful' acts of suicide – which are considered unacceptable – and those carried out when a person is of unsound mind or under extreme physical or mental stress (Keir 1986).

The views of the other major world religions – Islam, Buddhism, and Hinduism – are even less clear-cut and writers such as Stengel (1973), Alvarez (1974), and Keir (1986), all of whom discuss religious attitudes to suicide in some detail, put forward a range of views, some of which appear to conflict. Keir, for example, makes the point that while Buddhism forbids suicide, Buddhist monks were setting fire to themselves during the Vietnam war.

Religious opposition to suicide was largely responsible for the growth of laws which made suicide a crime. England was the last European country to repeal its anti-suicide legislation and as recently as the 1950s people were still being sent to prison for attempting suicide. The 1961 Suicide Act finally repealed the law under which both actual and attempted suicides were held to be criminal acts, although the Act did introduce a new offence – that of aiding or procuring the suicide of another person (which carries a penalty of up to fourteen years' imprisonment).

Although suicide victims are no longer committing a criminal offence, to some extent the legal framework remains in place. We still talk about a person 'committing suicide', with its overtones of committing a crime. The inquest has replaced the criminal trial, but all the legal accoutrements remain: evidence is heard in a court, witnesses are summonsed to appear, and a verdict is pronounced. It is hardly surprising that for many families, attending the inquest on their relative feels like being on trial (see Chapter 7).

While the Church and the courts have, to some extent, moved from the centre-stage position they previously occupied, researchers have moved in; suicide has become a major area of research. A new breed of academic – the suicidologist – has appeared on the scene and the number of publications on suicide is growing rapidly, particularly in the USA. According to Alvarez, scientific research may have helped to dispel some of the fallacies and misconceptions about suicide, but with the result that: 'modern suicide has been removed from the vulnerable volatile world of human beings and hidden safely away in the isolation wards of science' (Alvarez 1974: 93).

When someone dies it is usually considered bad manners to start pointing out the person's weaknesses or misdeeds. In fact, the opposite tends to happen with the deceased commonly acquiring the status of a saint. When someone commits suicide, though, these niceties often fall by the wayside, and other people's judgements about the suicide victim can be added to the survivor's burden. As the mother of one young victim commented: 'When you say that she took her own life, people think she was a no-gooder; but', she added, 'she was a daughter anyone would have wanted'. Another parent had to listen to her daughter's suicide described as 'an act of cowardice'.

Not everyone will make such punitive judgements. Some people maintain that, whatever others may think or feel, individuals have the right to end their lives if they decide so to do. As a psychiatrist said of one of his patients: 'If her life is so unbearable, who are we to say she should live it?' But this emphasis on individual freedom and choice can be hard on those left behind; as someone once described it: 'suicide is a social right with a built-in social deterrent'.

Some people find the idea of a person choosing suicide genuinely puzzling and incomprehensible; they will say things like, 'I can't understand why on earth he did that' or 'she had everything to live for'. They may try to relate the idea of suicide to their own situation, only to conclude that they could never contemplate doing anything so terrible. In fact there are probably very few people who could honestly say they have never considered the possibility of suicide, however fleetingly, though only a minute proportion of them will go on to take their own lives.

Suicide is still largely a taboo subject, but beneath the silence lie deep-seated anxieties about people who take their own lives. Unless we understand these feelings, unless they are brought out into the open, we may find it hard to help those who have been bereaved by suicide.

The language of suicide

Finding the right words can be a problem, as many of those bereaved by suicide have discovered:

> I couldn't say 'suicide' for years. I always said 'taken her life'. It's awful isn't it? (Pam)

> I usually say 'she took her own life' ... because that gives her the dignity of having made a decision and taken the action herself and I think she needs that – I need her to need that anyway; it's my need I suppose. (Francesca)

> 'Killing oneself' is pretty raw and 'committing suicide' I don't
> like because you commit sins and crimes. (Bridget)

It can be difficult to find an acceptable language for suicide. Too often, the words we use carry messages about (committing) crime, and even about murder (by killing oneself). Indeed, the Oxford English Dictionary includes 'self-murder' among its definitions of suicide.

Attempts to find an alternative vocabulary can produce equally distressing messages. 'She took her own life' may sound preferable to 'she committed suicide', but taking your own life, although it somehow decriminalises the act, implies a degree of conscious choice, and hence a conscious rejection of other people.

People who attempt suicide are often referred to as having 'failed', the implication being that those who die are 'successful'. But as Dunne and Dunne-Maxim point out: 'From the perspective of suicidologists, the person who completes suicide is considered "successful" .... From the perspective of family members and friends, the suicide itself represents failure' (Dunne 1987a: xii).

Perhaps it never will be possible to find the right words, and in starting to write this book I have somewhat reluctantly chosen to use the term 'committing suicide', although from time to time I do also use the expression 'taking his (her) own life'. I realise, however, that for some readers one or both of these terms may not be wholly acceptable.

If those who commit suicide are no longer viewed as criminals or self-murderers, how should we refer to them? They are often described as 'victims', a word which has many different dictionary definitions; two in particular, though, seem to reflect with some accuracy the suicidal person's situation: 'somebody that is adversely affected by a force or agent' and 'a person ... made to suffer'. I have, accordingly, chosen to use the term 'victim'.

Albert Cain, an American suicidologist and editor of one of the first published works about people bereaved by suicide, called his book *Survivors of Suicide* (1972). In the USA, where support for those bereaved by suicide is more widely developed than in Britain, this has become the most widely used term. It is the term I have adopted here.

I realise that in Britain, the word 'survivor' is sometimes used to describe people who have survived a suicide attempt; I hope my decision to use it in a different context will not confuse the reader, but there were positive reasons why I chose to use it, other than simply adopting Americanese. I believe the word has positive connotations: for example, the survivor can 'continue to live or exist in spite (of an experience, condition, etc.)' (*Longmans English Larousse*).

I believe that those bereaved by suicide also have affinities with other survivors. The word 'survivor' is used to describe those who have been through a major trauma such as the bombing of Hiroshima or more recent disasters such as the King's Cross fire or the Zeebrugge ferry sinking. We also talk about survivors of the Holocaust. Writing about Hiroshima, Lifton describes the survivor as 'one who has come into contact with death ... and has himself remained alive' (1969: 479); like those Japanese survivors, recognised everywhere by their keloid scars, the survivors of suicide also feel they carry permanent scars. The experience of surviving the suicide of a close relative has been described as 'a personal Holocaust'.

Finding a language for suicide is not an easy task. But perhaps, as we talk more about those who take their own lives and those left behind, we shall find that we have the right words. 'What one truly understands clearly articulates itself, and the words to say it come easily' (Boileau, quoted by Cardinal 1984: 6).

Chapter two

Survivors of suicide

Until the 1960s, the needs of survivors were largely ignored. Attention was focused almost exclusively on the suicidal person and efforts were directed mainly towards suicide prevention. Survivors remained a hidden group, isolated from one another, scarcely considered by researchers and receiving little or no help in coming to terms with their loss.

It was the development of 'psychological autopsies' which drew attention to the particular needs of suicide survivors. These autopsies began in the late 1950s, when staff at the Los Angeles Suicide Prevention Center were asked to interview relatives, friends, employers, and doctors of suspected suicide victims in an attempt to reconstruct the person's background, personal relationships, personality traits, and character (Litman *et al.* 1970). The official purpose of the exercise was to provide the coroner with additional evidence in equivocal cases of possible suicidal death (Shneidman and Farberow 1970). What the Center's staff discovered, though, was that survivors badly needed to talk – about their grief, their guilt and anger, and often about their own suicidal feelings. 'It was usually the first time [they] had been given the opportunity to talk about the suicide, and they frequently found the interview therapeutic' (Colt 1987: 14). It was also found that the experience could help to lessen the survivor's guilt and make acceptance of the death easier (Litman *et al.* 1970).

It is less than twenty years since Cain's book appeared which included some individual case studies and reports on a limited number of small-scale research projects. Since then, though, both research and support services for survivors have developed much more extensively in the United States. Bibliographies on survivors have appeared

(McIntosh 1985–6) which list the growing numbers of research projects and over 150 survivor support groups have been set up across the USA.

In Britain, however, the special needs of suicide survivors have continued to be largely overlooked. With the notable exception of Barraclough and Shepherd (e.g. 1976, 1977, 1978), researchers have virtually ignored the issue; a review of the literature on survivors (Henley 1984) draws almost exclusively on material published in the USA. Until recently the only help available to survivors has been through organisations offering general bereavement support such as CRUSE and the Society of Compassionate Friends or by crisis services such as the Samaritans. The Survivors of Suicide network, which was started by members of the Compassionate Friends, now offers support to parents bereaved by suicide but this, together with a handful of local suicide bereavement groups (see Appendix A), remains virtually the only nationally available resource specifically for those bereaved by suicide.

Who are the survivors?

'Suicide appears to be the most personal action an individual can take yet ... it has a profound social impact' (Stengel 1973: 13); a single act of suicide can affect a wide circle of people.

Take the case of a young man who has committed suicide by carbon monoxide poisoning, after driving the family car to a local beauty spot. His death will have a major impact on his immediate family, his parents, brothers, and sisters, some of whom may still be living together in the family home. There will almost certainly be other relatives: grandparents, aunts, uncles, and cousins, perhaps young nephews and nieces. Then there are the neighbours who had known him since he was a baby and who had watched him grow up. There are his friends, too, some of whom he had known since starting school nearly twenty years ago. Perhaps he had a girlfriend. Then there was the owner of the garage where the young man had worked since leaving school, and the family doctor who had been treating him for depression. Suicide also touches the lives of complete strangers: the children who were playing nearby and found the car; the police who were called to the scene, who had to go and tell the young man's parents that their son was dead, and who then had to investigate the death; the coroner and coroner's officer who were responsible for the inquest; and the pathologist who carried out the post-mortem.

In recent years, various attempts have been made to calculate the total number of survivors. Bernhardt and Praeger (1983) have estimated that each suicide will involve, on average, a minimum of five family members or 'significant others'; McIntosh (1987a) suggests at least six other people will be affected, and Lukas and Seiden (1987) calculate that between seven and ten people will be 'intimately affected'. On the basis of these estimates, there are likely to be anything between 40,000 and 80,000 *new* survivors in Britain each year.

This book focuses on the experiences of those most directly affected by suicide – the parents, children, spouses, and siblings of suicide victims. But others who have been involved with the victim in some capacity will also be affected and some of them are likely to experience very severe reactions (Cain 1972). A policeman told me how he still has nightmares several years after entering a blood-stained flat where the victim had committed a particularly messy suicide. Many of the reactions experienced by family members which are described in Part two of this book may be shared by these 'secondary survivors'.

Teenage suicide, for example, can involve many such secondary survivors. The suicide rate among teenagers and young adults has been increasing in recent years, and these deaths will often have a serious impact on other young people. Adolescence is a time when intense relationships are often formed, as young people experiment with making adult relationships; the needs of these young survivors should not be underestimated.

Sometimes those outside the family may be very directly involved in the death. A friend or colleague at work may have been the one who heard the person threatening suicide; they may even have discovered the body. An American study found that one in five of those who witnessed the actual suicide or who found the body were friends or workmates. Strangers found the victim's body in another one in five of cases and in one in twenty cases the actual suicide was carried out in front of a complete stranger (Andress and Corey 1978). Strangers may have found themselves trying to persuade someone not to commit suicide, only to watch helplessly as the person carried out the threat.

The impact on those who witness a suicide can be serious and long-lasting. In 1987 over 300 people died on British Rail tracks, and between 1984 and 1988, deaths on the London Underground increased by nearly 50 per cent (Finney 1988). Drivers who have witnessed suicides have reported a range of subsequent problems including insomnia, sexual difficulties, recurrent nightmares, and heightened stress and anxiety (Finney 1988). The impact of suicide on this particular group of witnesses has finally been recognised, however, and train drivers are at least now eligible to claim compensation under the Criminal Injuries Compensation Scheme.

There is one further group of people whose identity as survivors may remain permanently hidden from the rest of the world: they may have been the partner in a gay or lesbian relationship which family and friends may not have known about; or they may have had a lover who was married to someone else so that their relationship was a closely guarded secret. These 'hidden' survivors may be at particular risk because their sense of loss and their needs cannot be openly acknowledged.

Features of suicide bereavement

While survivors of suicide have certain things in common with other bereaved people, some aspects of their bereavements are unique. Like all those bereaved, they are faced with a major loss, and with having to accept that the loss is permanent. Anger and guilt are common bereavement reactions, but are often more intense and long-lasting among survivors of suicide. Like those bereaved as the result of a road accident or an unexpected heart attack, survivors face additional difficulties. There are no farewells. The fact that suicidal deaths are often violent bequeaths an added legacy which the survivors share with the relatives of murder victims. Only in the case of suicide, though, does the survivor have to live with the thought that the death was self-inflicted and may have been self-chosen.

Suicide can affect people in many different ways (Bowlby 1985). There is certainly no single set of reactions which will be experienced by everyone bereaved in this way, and individuals will be affected by the death in varying degrees. Nevertheless, there are some common threads. In 1982, when a group of survivors in the USA began meeting together to share their experiences they discovered that their

> reactions were not universal, nor did they describe any one person's experience all the time. Yet there seemed to be enough to suggest a syndrome of sorts – a set of behaviors, attitudes and emotional reactions which both typified us in our responses to

the world and separated us from it. (Dunne and Dunne-Maxim 1987: xiv)

It is these behaviours, attitudes, and reactions which are discussed below, drawing on published case studies and research reports. Part two of this book describes the experiences of fifty survivors, and their stories illustrate directly and in greater detail the more theoretical discussion in this chapter.

The nature of the death

The survivor of suicide is faced with a death which is, more often than not, unexpected, untimely, and possibly violent.

Survivors who either witness the person committing suicide or, more commonly, find the body, are left to come to terms with a shattering experience. Memories of the scene are likely to remain with the survivor for many years to come, and may never disappear completely. Even when a person has not actually discovered the body, being told about the circumstances of the suicide can leave the survivor with horrific images of the scene of the death (Shneidman 1982), making it hard for them to think about anything else at first. Where the victim died in a violent manner such as jumping in front of a train, this reaction is likely to be intensified.

People who commit suicide frequently announce their intentions to other people, sometimes in quite explicit terms. Nevertheless, even when there have been threats, 'it usually wreaks havoc among the survivors because the mind is not prepared for such a destructive event' (Hauser 1987: 62).

Initial feelings of shock and disbelief are likely to be more accentuated and to last longer than is usually the case with other bereavements. It is not uncommon for survivors to receive news of the death from a complete stranger; it is possible that the death occurred away from the victim's home. Both these factors can increase the likelihood of survivors experiencing feelings of disbelief or denial (Bowlby 1985).

The immediate and very direct involvement of total strangers such as the police and the coroner's officer creates an additional source of stress. Private and personal grief comes under public scrutiny, and the victim's family may even find themselves under suspicion of murder.

Britain has virtually no cultural guidelines for viewing the dead except in the case of certain religious or ethnic groups. In the absence of any norms, deciding whether or not to view the body may be even more difficult. Survivors are often advised not to visit the mortuary or the undertakers. However, not only does this deny them the opportunity to confront the reality of the death, but it can leave them with disturbing fantasies about the state of the body – fantasies which may be much worse than the reality.

Events leading up to the death

Suicides do sometimes occur totally unexpectedly, apparently coming as a complete surprise to family and friends who genuinely seem to have had no idea that anything was seriously wrong. But for many survivors, even if the possibility of suicide has been consciously denied, the death occurs after months or years of stress (Hauser 1987).

Survivors may have been living with a person who not only made repeated threats but who attempted suicide, sometimes on numerous occasions. Two thirds of people who commit suicide have communicated to others their wish to die and one third have a history of previous attempts (Litman 1970a). Even where this was not the case, the victim may have had many years of mental health problems, sometimes resulting in considerable stress and disruption of family life.

Because of these various stresses, relations between the victim and the survivors often will have been fraught with difficulty. But when someone commits suicide the chance to work on any unfinished business is denied to the survivor (Hauser 1987) and there is no chance for a proper farewell.

Faced with overt threats of suicide, some survivors will become caught up in a power struggle, the suicidal person determined to die and the survivor equally determined to prevent that happening (Lake 1984). For other survivors the thought of suicide is too horrifying to contemplate and they may attempt to deny the possibility – while not always succeeding completely: 'I knew that she meant it', said the daughter of one suicide victim, 'I just never thought she'd do it'.

The search for understanding

Suicide can seem a particularly meaningless act and one of the most common reactions is 'the endless search for why' (Hauser 1987: 64). It has been described elsewhere as a search with two separate, but linked, concerns (Calhoun *et al.* 1982): first, the need to understand the reasons why that particular person committed suicide, what led up to the event, and what triggered it; and second, the search for a more general understanding of suicide.

The death of an elderly person (and even perhaps the death of a younger person from a disease like cancer) may cause great anguish to the bereaved, but timely death or death from an unasked-for illness can usually be more easily accepted. But when someone commits suicide, death will appear to have been deliberately chosen, and the survivor will almost invariably want to know why the victim made that choice. Trying to understand why can preoccupy survivors for months and even years although 'the most important informant can no longer be questioned' (Stengel 1973: 46).

Survivors will seek to answer the question 'why' in many different ways; they may go over and over again the days and weeks leading up to the suicide, searching for clues that were missed at the time; their own relationship to the victim will almost certainly come under the microscope; where a note was left, it may be endlessly re-read in the hope of discovering fresh clues or further answers; survivors will often scour books on suicide in the hope that these will yield the answers.

Ultimately, though, survivors may have to accept that the only way they can cope is by acknowledging that they will never have all the answers since, according to one eminent suicidologist, 'the causes of any suicidal event can never be fully fathomed' (Shneidman 1982: 17).

Suicide and the law

Suicide is no longer a crime, but as soon as the suicide is discovered the law steps in, and the survivor's personal loss becomes a matter for public scrutiny. All cases of sudden death must be investigated by the police. Alongside the survivor's own personal search for explanations, a legal inquiry has to be carried out.

Where the death has occurred in the family home, evidence must be gathered for the coroner; photographs are taken and personal items belonging to the victim may be removed. The suicide note, though legally the property of the person to whom it is written (Barraclough and Shepherd 1976), will also be taken away as evidence. However necessary these procedures are, for the survivors the whole business can feel extremely unwelcome and intrusive.

A publication on suicide and attempted suicide illustrates how legalities can permeate the whole business: 'Once death has been recognised as unnatural, the perpetrator of the fatality must be identified as the victim himself and it has also to be established that demise was the consequence of an intentional act' (Office of Health Economics 1981: 5). For many survivors, the full inquest is an important but distressing event (Barraclough and Shepherd 1977). They may have to attend the coroner's court, not knowing what to expect, what distressing evidence they may have to see or hear, or what may be expected of them as witnesses. Once more, their private tragedy becomes exposed to a wider audience; inquests take place in public – 'justice must be seen to be done' – and anyone is entitled to walk in off the street and sit in the coroner's court.

The frequent attendance of press reporters at the inquest is a further source of stress for many survivors. Subsequent press reporting can fuel their distress and survivors may particularly resent the fact that the coverage is frequently sensational or inaccurate (Barraclough and Shepherd 1976).

Suicide and religion

Regardless of whether survivors hold any formal religious beliefs, they may be looking for reassurance that their relative has not committed an unforgivable sin; they may be anxious to know if the victim is 'at peace', or whether they are being punished. They may be afraid that because the death was a suicide they will be denied the normal funeral rites (Rubey and Clark 1987). It is usually the clergy who will be expected to deal with these anxieties.

Members of the clergy are frequently in contact with a bereaved family immediately after the death and are, therefore, a potentially important source of support to survivors. Like anyone else, though, clergy may have difficulty in coming to terms with their own feelings about suicide. As Rubey and Clark point out though (1987), bereaved families will need support at this time, not judgement – whatever the clergy may feel.

Parkes's suggestion that 'the funeral is usually regarded as a last gift to the dead' (1986: 175) may be particularly relevant to survivors. In the past, they may have felt helpless to prevent the suicide occurring; now, although they have failed to keep the person alive, this is something they can do for the deceased.

The funeral can fulfil several other important functions: it can bring together a network of people to express their support for the bereaved relatives (Worden 1983) and acknowledge their own sense of loss; it allows the bereaved to experience the full reality of the death (Parkes 1986); and the ritual of the funeral enacts a separation of the living from the dead (Raphael 1985). All these functions are important for survivors of suicide, and some particularly so. In cases of suicide, survivors have often not seen the body; the funeral may be the first (and only) time they come face to face with the reality of death by seeing the coffin, and by hearing publicly words of farewell.

Facing suicide as a family

Suicide has been described as 'the most difficult bereavement crisis for any family to face and resolve in an effective manner' (McGee, in Cain 1972). Stigma may be attached to the person who commits suicide, and families will frequently feel themselves to be stigmatised by association. Wrobleski, herself a survivor, describes this as embodying 'the twin myths that "nice" people don't kill themselves, and that suicide does not happen in "nice" families' (1984–5: 179).

The impact of a suicide on individual survivors may be such that family members are unable to offer one another any support; Cain suggests that this may be because they are 'too deeply preoccupied with their own grief to be helpful to one another' (1972: 15). But even when someone wants to share their grief in the family, they may refrain from doing so, worried that their grieving will overwhelm others (Hildebrand 1989).

There are other reasons why communication in families of survivors can be difficult. According to Bowlby, 'the tendency to apportion blame is likely to be enormously increased' (1985: 184); there may be silent accusations about who was thought to be responsible for the death; sometimes family members will openly point the finger of blame at each other.

Individual family members are likely to respond in very different ways to the suicide. One person may cry openly while another may prefer to cry alone; one person may want to talk compulsively about the dead person while another cannot bear even to hear their name mentioned; time scales of grieving are different for everyone, and the person who is still grieving acutely may resent someone else in the family who appears to be getting on with life again (Cain 1972). The process of bereavement is highly individual, but when those differences emerge in the family setting, they can generate feelings of bitterness and hostility.

Sometimes a family may seek to avoid completely the pain and distress involved, and any mention of the manner of death will be taboo. Carried to extremes, the dead person may no longer even be mentioned. As a result, family myths or secrets may be created where the truth becomes denied or distorted as families attempt to avoid their feelings of guilt and the pain of their loss (Pincus and Dare 1978). This is particularly likely to happen where the survivors include children, and when communication in the family often becomes distorted as attempts are made to hide the truth from them (Worden 1983).

Some aspects of suicide bereavement may be linked to the family relationship of the survivor to the deceased. Other factors will also play a part, but there is sufficient evidence from research studies and other publications (reviewed by McIntosh 1987b) that particular family relationships are likely to intensify particular reactions. So whether the survivor is the parent of a suicide victim, or the spouse, the child, or the sibling, this is likely to have some bearing on the way they will react.

Facing the world: other people's reactions

Like anyone who has suffered a bereavement, survivors of suicide can be helped and supported by those around them including relatives, friends, neighbours, and colleagues at work. But when the death was a suicide, survivors commonly find that they have less social support than other bereaved people (McIntosh 1985–6); contact with other people may become fraught with difficulty because:

suicide is not a socially acceptable way to die under any circumstances ... without socially acceptable reasons for the death, how can the loss be socially acceptable? The survivors have no available rationale to ease acceptance, their friends have no socially acceptable words of comfort, no special rituals or ceremonies can be invoked to mobilise support and no tradition helps filter the remembrance. Bereavement from suicide, like the suicide itself, is without social acceptance, without institutional patterns. (Wallace 1977: 44–5)

Surveys of community reactions to suicide, summarised and discussed by Rudestam (1987), suggest that there are, in fact, strong norms for what other people should *not* do when someone has committed suicide. But because people are unsure of how they *should* respond, total avoidance of the survivor may be the preferred solution. Given society's highly ambivalent attitudes towards suicide, it is perhaps not surprising that we lack appropriate social norms and rituals for this sort of death. It would be hard to find acceptable ways of expressing feelings such as blame and horror.

However, problems of talking about the suicide can be mutual. The survivors themselves may have difficulty in facing other people. They may be reluctant to discuss the suicide with friends and may even resort to lying about the cause of death (Rudestam 1987). If survivors already feel guilty, believing they are in some way to blame for the death, they may assume that other people see them as deserving of blame; they may feel that ostracism is what they deserve. Whether or not this is true, the survivors' own shame can sometimes make it hard for them to accept support from other people.

Support services for survivors

Some survivors will be able to get all the help and support they need from family and friends, but in some cases, perhaps for the reasons discussed above, survivors may turn for help to those outside their immediate circle.

Often the survivor will have been the one who coped, who supported the suicidal person, and who generally held things together in the family. Relinquishing the coping role and acknowledging their own need for help and support can be difficult. If survivors also feel that they failed to cope because the suicide occurred, they may also feel themselves to be undeserving of any help or support.

Many victims will have been in contact with their family doctor shortly before they committed suicide; they may also have been seen by mental health professionals including psychiatrists. Approaching these same people for help after the suicide can be difficult if the survivor feels that these professionals failed their relative by 'allowing' them to die (Dunne 1987a: 183). As a result, according to Lukas and Seiden (1987), survivors will often express considerable anger towards the medical profession.

It can be difficult for survivors to obtain the right sort of help where professionals lack the appropriate knowledge and/or skills. General practitioners, often the first port of call for a bereaved person (Parkes 1986), may know little or nothing of the particular problems of bereavement by suicide. They may also lack the knowledge to refer survivors elsewhere.

Because so few specialist services exist for survivors of suicide, the only available support may be a general bereavement support group. But apart from the fact that survivors often feel uncomfortable alongside people bereaved by non-suicide deaths, such a group may fail to address the unique problems of suicide survivors (Battle 1984; Wrobleski 1984–5). Where a local bereavement service can also offer individual counselling, this may be more appropriate.

So what are the needs of suicide survivors? Workers in one survivors' support programme (Rogers *et al.* 1982) found a range of needs. People wanted to talk about the suicide and put it into some sort of perspective; they wanted a safe place to express their feelings, which included anger and guilt, and to be able to feel better about themselves; they also wanted help with family problems arising from the suicide. In addition to help with emotional problems, they were also looking for information and advice: they wanted to find out more about typical reactions to suicide and were seeking factual information about suicide in general; they were also asking for advice on practical and social matters.

Although some survivors will seek help immediately after the suicide, many people will struggle on for years before deciding to seek help (Dunne 1987b). This may reflect, in part, the lack of services which recognise the extreme vulnerability of survivors at the time of the death, and their need for 'psychological resuscitation' (Resnik 1972). If this kind of psychological first aid were more readily available, it could not only support survivors through the immediate crisis but could enable them to embark on a healthy process of bereavement; families could be helped to begin sharing their grief with one another which, in turn, might prevent the development of family secrets (see p. 23). Immediately after the death, significant family members are usually gathered together for some days or weeks; if help is only offered at some later date, the family network may already have dispersed.

The reactions of survivors

The earlier chapters in Part two focus on the experiences and reactions of survivors in relation to other people, including family and friends, as well as the police, the coroner, the Press, and members of the helping professions. The particular reactions described in Chapter 13, though, have more to do with the feelings that survivors will face on their own, for as Storr reminds us: 'the loss of a loved one ... can only partially be shared ... the work of mourning is by its very nature something which takes place in the watches of the night and in the solitary recesses of the mind' (1989: 31–2). Storr is writing here about bereavement in general, but survivors of suicide often have particularly intense feelings such as anger, guilt, or relief which cannot easily be shared with others since 'There are few socially acceptable outlets for these feelings. Relief cannot be shown and anger towards the dead is frowned upon' (Augenbraun and Neuringer 1972: 178).

Any attempt to describe bereavement reactions can easily fall into the trap of becoming a rather mechanistic exercise, reducing the complex and difficult process of grieving to a formal checklist. Nevertheless any attempt to communicate something of the experiences of surviving a suicide must tackle this issue. Many of the survivors whose experiences are described in Part two of this book had felt their reactions to be abnormal, signs of illness, or insanity rather than aspects of a normal grieving process. For some, it was only after meeting and talking with other survivors that they could begin to understand that their thoughts and feelings were typical reactions to suicide.

Each person's bereavement will be unique and the reactions of the fifty people whose experiences are described in Part two of this book testify to that. Nevertheless, from existing research and clinical studies, as well as anecdotal material, it does seem that survivors of suicide may experience particular reactions such as anger and guilt with greater frequency, and that these feelings may be more intense and possibly more prolonged (Cain and Fast 1972a and b; Hauser 1987; Rudestam 1987).

Surviving suicide bereavement

According to Lake, the survivor of suicide faces a stark choice: 'it is up to you ... to decide whether to be hurt permanently by the last act of a free individual or not.... This option is yours' (1984: 126).

Survivors of suicide share some common tasks with all those who have been bereaved: they must accept the loss as final, give up the attachment to the dead person, and learn to live in a world without them: 'Only mourning can bring about transformation; it enables us to really take leave and prepares the individual for new relationships' (Kast 1988: 145). This involves, Kast adds, 'making a commitment to life while living with leave-taking' (1988: 123).

Sometimes these tasks of mourning will seem very hard. Survivors may be forced to accept that they will never understand why the other person chose to die; it can mean acknowledging that they will never have an answer to the the question 'why'. For those who lived through many years of stress and upheaval before the death, and witnessed previous attempts at suicide, recapturing good, positive memories of the dead person may be a long, arduous process. Where death was violent, horror may blot out the good memories for a very long time.

The hurts may always be there, and people whose lives have been touched by suicide are changed irrevocably, but those bereaved by suicide can and do survive. Indeed they may do more than just survive; they may emerge from mourning to live more fully than ever before. As Jean, one of the survivors in Part two, said:

Life will never be the same again. I accept that and I look on that as a challenge. Life is all I have, and life is what my Anna didn't want. So, in a way, I will live to the full for both of us.

Part two

Aspects of suicide bereavement

Chapter three

Meeting the survivors

When planning this book, I hoped to be able to interview between forty and fifty people, although several people had expressed doubts as to whether that number of people would be willing to talk about such a difficult issue as suicide. In fact, nearly a hundred people contacted me; there seemed to be no shortage of people wanting to talk about their bereavement. In the event, I saw fifty of them, and it is their stories which are told here.

I have used the word 'stories' deliberately. Although I set out with a tape-recorder and notebook, I decided that, as far as possible, I wanted people to be free to relate their stories in the way that they felt most comfortable. I had a subject guide to hand, but even this was frequently discarded as people began to tell their stories – on some occasions for the first time. I saw my role as listener rather than interviewer, and my decision not to undertake formal, structured interviews reflected Cain's comment that, 'given the clamorous needs of many survivors for psychological assistance, survivor research will often acquire a strong action research flavour' (1972: 24).

Contact was made with survivors through a number of different channels: one group of people came forward in response to a letter placed in *New Society* (now *New Statesman and Society*). Most of the others made contact as the result of letters circulated by two bereavement organisations – CRUSE and The Compassionate Friends. The remainder were identified through personal contacts, and through other survivors.

These fifty people are a self-selected group, so how representative are they of survivors in general? Are they typical survivors of suicide or are they a group who have had particular problems in coping with their bereavement? I do not happen to believe that the typical survivor exists, and as the rest of the book will make clear, their experiences and reactions to the suicide varied. I believe that the fact that they offered to be interviewed does not indicate that their problems were any greater than those of survivors who did not come forward. (Only a relatively small proportion had felt the need to turn to specialist sources of help.) The common denominator was a wish to talk to someone – to tell their story – and this, I believe, is something which all survivors of suicide share with one another.

Perhaps this need to talk is one of the reasons why, although I also suggested that some people might prefer to write about their experiences, only one person chose to do so. However, one or two people who were interviewed did also share poems, letters, or diaries they had written around the time of the suicide.

The interviews were confidential. Only first names have been used, and just over a third of people asked to have their name changed. For some, this guarantee of anonymity was very important, reflecting the continuing need of many survivors to maintain confidentiality.

The length of interviews varied between one and three hours, the average length being about one and a half hours. With three exceptions, the interviews were conducted in the survivors' own homes.

Background to the survivors

The fifty people interviewed comprised fourteen men and thirty-six women. The fact that fewer men than women were apparently willing to talk about their bereavement matches the experiences of Lukas and Seiden (1987); looking at the situation of survivors in the United States, they found that men were generally less willing to talk and they suggested that possibly this was because men thought they had less need to talk to other people.

The ages of the survivors at the time of the suicide varied widely. The youngest person had been four when the death occurred and the oldest had been sixty-eight. Almost half, though, had been in their thirties and forties, many of them being the parents of young adults who had committed suicide.

At the time of the interviews (which were carried out between February 1988 and February 1989), seven people had been bereaved for less than a year, and a further twenty people for between one and four years. At the other end of the spectrum, six people had been bereaved over twenty years ago, all except one of these being adults who had experienced the suicide of a parent during their childhood.

The biggest single group of survivors consisted of parents (21), followed by almost equal numbers of siblings (10), children (9), and spouses (9). One person had lost a former lover. Two people had been bereaved twice by suicides in their family.

By occupation, the survivors included: doctors, teachers, social workers, civil servants, journalists, nurses, factory workers, shop assistants, clerical workers, students, housewives; others were currently unemployed or had retired from full-time employment.

The victims of suicide

The fifty survivors had experienced a total of forty-five suicides – twenty-three men and twenty-two women. (There are fewer suicide victims than survivors because in some cases more than one family member was interviewed.)

The youngest suicide victim was eighteen and the oldest seventy-five. By far the biggest single group (13) was aged between twenty and twenty-five. Forty-seven per cent of the victims were under thirty, and less than 7 per cent were over sixty.

Almost half the victims had left some sort of note behind – a far higher proportion than normal (see Chapter 6).

The single most common method used by the victims was overdosing on pills (13), sometimes in combination with alcohol. Information on the method used was only available in forty-one of the forty-five cases, but of these forty-one victims, twenty had used a method which could be described as 'violent' (e.g. jumping or lying in front of a train, jumping from a tall building, using a shotgun, setting fire to oneself, or hanging).

Appendix B summarises the information on individual survivors and victims.

Survivors' reasons for being interviewed

Survivors were asked why they had agreed to talk about their experiences, and a number of different reasons emerged. Some of these related to the survivors' own needs: they thought that talking to another person might help them in some way.

Liz, whose brother died four years ago, was someone who felt that the interview might be personally helpful. She hoped it would provide a means of overcoming her inability to talk about Tony, and before we met she wrote:

> it will be of therapeutic value to me as I've never talked about it.... Although other members of the family refer to him in conversation, I cannot. I suppose partly for selfish reasons I thought maybe it would help me to talk about it.

In some instances, people had not even been aware that they still needed to talk about the suicide. Hilary, who was eighteen when her mother committed suicide thirty-five years ago, was surprised to find herself crying during the interview. Afterwards she wrote: '[the interview] helped me, even though I didn't know I needed helping'.

For other survivors, the interview provided a welcome chance to talk about the person who had died; as Heather admitted: 'I guess I just like talking about Alastair'. This was something which survivors often had little or no opportunity to do after the first few weeks or months; the victim was often no longer a topic of conversation for other people.

Suicide can seem a very senseless act, and for some survivors, sharing their experiences with a wider audience was seen as a way of injecting some meaning and purpose into what could otherwise feel meaningless. Peter, for example, felt that by being prepared to talk about his sister's suicide, perhaps the subject would become less of a taboo, and that suicide would begin to carry less stigma.

For Kevin, who was ten when he discovered his mother's body, the interview was a chance to talk about the person who he was only now, twenty-five years later, beginning to understand and cherish. He talked of wanting to honour her memory, but, like Peter, he also saw it as an opportunity to help counteract some of society's more negative attitudes towards suicide.

So as well as meeting their own needs, many survivors hoped that by taking part in the interviews they would also be helping to lessen the taboos which surround both those who commit suicide and those left behind. Denise, whose father hanged himself when she was four, hoped that contributing to the book would help lessen the isolation of 'people who live in their own little hell, trying to sort it all out for themselves'.

It was encouraging that so many of the survivors said that they had found the interview helpful. I had been concerned that people would find it too distressing, and that the experience might harm them in some way; however, my anxieties were somewhat allayed by learning of the experiences of other researchers in this field such as Shepherd and Barraclough (1979), and Solomon (1981), all of whom reported that survivors had found it helpful to talk openly and at length to a non-judgemental and uninvolved person.

The fact that people knew they were talking to someone who had experienced a similar bereavement was particularly important to some survivors. Several people made it clear when we met that they had only agreed to be interviewed because they had been told in the introductory letter that I was also a survivor of suicide. Miriam was one of these: 'I feel strongly', she said, 'that such a study should only be undertaken by a researcher who has shared the experience.'

Finally, after the suicide, many survivors had scoured their local libraries and bookshops, searching for information on suicide and trying to find out how to cope with being a survivor. Having found nothing that could really meet their needs, they were eager to contribute to something which they felt could perhaps help other survivors in the future.

Chapter four

When the suicide happens

Even now what I can't really bear to think about is how he must have felt when he was taking the aspirin, what despair he must have been in, those awful thoughts he must have had. (Suzy)

It was just the worst day of my life. (Jennifer)

Finding out

Whatever has gone before, it seems that nothing can prepare the survivor for the suicide when it happens:

> It was 3rd December, the day my son died. [A friend] dropped me off at the bottom of the road. It was quite dark. As I walked up the road I saw a figure standing at our gate; it walked towards me and I saw it was [her husband]. He took hold of my arm and I could feel waves of shock coming from him. 'You'll have to prepare yourself', he said, 'Jon is dead.' I stumbled into the house and then I screamed 'No! No! No!' (Carole)

Like Carole, most of the survivors I met had been told the news by other people. But those who had actually discovered the body still had vivid memories of an event which, in some instances, had taken place many years before. Often the memory of what was seen remains with the survivor for a lifetime (Lukas and Seiden 1987). It is over twenty-five years since four-year-old Denise and her mother came home from shopping one day:

> [My mother] sensed there was something wrong. She went whipping through the house and got to the foot of the stairs and started to scream and then ran out; and so I followed to see

what she was screaming at – and he'd hung himself on the staircase; and I do remember quite vividly; I remember standing there looking; I haven't blotted it out. I haven't been told that either ... it's a memory that's always been with me.

It is not unknown for the victim to actually commit suicide when other people are in the house. Betty sat watching television one evening, unaware that, in an upstairs bedroom, her son lay dying from an overdose; he had even waved the bottle of pills at her as he left the room, but she had not understood the significance of this, nor had she understood the reason why, earlier that day, he had quite uncharacteristically hugged her and told her how much he loved her. That afternoon she had watched him writing letters, not realising that they were suicide notes. Now she is left with the distressing feeling that she was virtually a witness to his suicide – albeit an innocent witness.

Even when survivors hear the news from other people, they will often retain clear memories of the circumstances. Bad news has a way of etching itself permanently on to the mind. Fifty-two years after her brother died, Ann can still picture herself standing on the staircase of the office where she worked, and being told that Giles had committed suicide.

However, the fact that the death was suicide does not always emerge straight away; survivors are sometimes left uncertain as to the exact circumstances of the death. When the local police came round to tell Jennifer her brother was dead, all they had was a message from the police in another part of the county who had been called to the scene of Tim's death. They told her that Tim had been killed on a railway line, and the possibility of suicide did not even enter her mind at that point: 'it didn't register that he could possibly have done it himself. I thought it must have been an accident.' 'It was only later that day', she says, 'that it started to click that he'd done it himself.' She believes that even if the police were not sure what had happened, they should have mentioned the possibility of suicide. As it was, having begun to take on board the fact that Tim had been killed in an accident, a few hours later she then had to readjust to the fact that he had taken his own life.

Some victims disappear without trace, perhaps wanting to protect relatives from the shock of finding the body, perhaps wanting to guard against the possibility of being found to be still alive. For the survivors, though, this can mean days or even weeks of not knowing

– or at least not being sure – what has happened. Tony's body was eventually found in a pond which had frozen over in an unusually cold spell, and it was seven weeks after his disappearance before the family finally knew what had happened to him. Others may not have to wait quite so long, but it can still be a distressing time for relatives. Richard's body was discovered after nine days, but although Susan felt sure she knew what had happened, and told the police she suspected suicide, she still had to face comments from the police that her husband had probably gone off with another woman. The police, as the saying goes, have to keep an open mind, which can be hard for survivors who, because of what they know about the missing person, are more or less certain of what has happened. They may feel the police are not listening to them.

Sometimes the survivor will seem to know instinctively that the other person is no longer alive, even when there is still no proof. After her son disappeared, Lois reported him missing to the police, but knowing, at the same time, that Simon was already dead:

Everyone said, 'Oh, don't worry, he'll turn up', but something went inside me, and I just knew and it wasn't because of all these threats [of suicide], I hadn't really believed them, but it was just something inside me went; I no longer had that closeness.

Not everyone will be so sure. Sometimes, when the victim's body is not discovered immediately, the survivors will be unsure when the death actually occurred. Janice's elderly mother had lived alone and her body was not discovered for several days. The fact that she does not even know which day her mother died is something which Janice has found particularly upsetting. For other survivors, anniversaries are made more difficult than usual because the death has been registered with a date which the survivor knows to be wrong. When talking about her husband's death, Susan several times made the point that the police insisted Richard's death had occurred on the date he was found, a date which she knows to be wrong; but, as she says, 'You're in such a state of shock that it seemed irrelevant at the time to make a fuss and I just let it go.' Fifteen years after Richard's death, though, this is still something she feels strongly about.

A person will sometimes commit suicide when those closest to them are away from home. When this happens, survivors may wonder whether this was a deliberate choice on the victim's part: were they doing it to protect people they knew would be upset, or did they decide to wait until there was no one around who might stop them? Whatever the reason, it can leave survivors like Carol with inevitable 'if onlys'. A single parent, she had organised a weekend away, but had made arrangements for her ex-husband to be around. (Alan's brother was also living at home.) When Alan's father came round on Sunday morning, he discovered that Alan had hanged himself. Now Carol is left wondering – 'had I been there, I feel Alan wouldn't actually have died that weekend ... [but] I'm not sure whether that would have been putting off what would have happened anyway.'

Jean was on holiday when her daughter committed suicide after walking out of the psychiatric unit where she had been taken as an in-patient. Jean knows she badly needed the holiday to recharge her own batteries and in order to cope with looking after Anna when she came out of hospital; but despite this, she still felt guilty when she had to tell the coroner she had been away at the time of Anna's death, particularly when she was not able to explain why she had needed that break.

First reactions

A sense of numbness, of bluntness of feeling, is common among bereaved people (Parkes 1986), and can serve to protect them from feelings which may be too overwhelming to face immediately (Kast 1988). The shock of hearing about the suicide can be so great that survivors may find it impossible to believe what they have been told. A vague sense of disbelief can turn into denial. Three days after his wife's disappearance, John still felt sure that Averil would return home at some point. When her body was eventually washed ashore the coroner's officer gave him the news, and asked if he would identify her from clothes and jewellery found on the body: 'I still couldn't believe it, and I said "Yes, I'll be over; I'll show you that it's nothing to do with Averil."'

The fact that John was advised not to see his wife's body, well-meaning advice which he accepted at the time, only added to his sense of disbelief. He began to think:

perhaps it's someone else's body. He [the pathologist] ... said don't look didn't he? She could have changed her clothes with someone – she was a very generous person – and all the while nobody has officially told you, except for this bit of paper, that that's your wife.

Where the survivor has been in contact with the victim only hours before, and everything had seemed to be perfectly normal, news of the death can seem totally unbelievable. When Joan was woken by the phone one night, and told that her sister had been found dead in bed she just couldn't believe it: 'I'd only just been talking on the phone. I just thought, I'm still dreaming, and I said out loud, "You're just pulling my leg."'

The numbness experienced by many survivors in the first few hours can last for days. Pat remembers waking up the morning after her daughter had committed suicide, 'trying to believe, trying to accept. You don't; you can't. It's like someone giving you a pill that's big and saying "swallow that". It's impossible, it won't go down. You've got to chip away a bit at a time.' This numbness persisted, even after the funeral when everyone came back to the house and Pat found she was able to chat to everyone without breaking down or even crying. As she subsequently realised, it took some time for the reality of Caroline's death to sink in.

The period immediately after a death is often a busy one for families; other relatives and friends have to be informed, and funeral arrangements made. In cases of possible suicide, there will also have to be a post-mortem and preliminary inquest before the body can be released for burial or cremation. Numbness helps some survivors to deal with these tasks more or less automatically, but it can leave people incapable of doing even that. This state of immobility was vividly described by Leonard Woolf, writing of the days following Virginia Woolf's suicide:

> the long drawn out horror of the previous weeks had produced in me a kind of inert anaesthesia; it was as if I had been so battered and beaten that I was like some hunted animal which, exhausted, can only instinctively drag itself into a hole or lair.
> (Woolf 1969: 95)

Nichols has suggested (1981) that families should have a 'no decision' period of up to thirty-six hours after a sudden death, an idea which would seem to have many advantages. Survivors often talked of having made decisions immediately after the death which they subsequently regretted, including the decision not to see the victim's body (see pp. 46–50).

The involvement of strangers

When a death occurs, the bereaved person, Parkes suggests, 'needs time and protection from intruders' (1986: 173). But when someone is thought to have committed suicide, and particularly if the death occurs in the family home, survivors will lose the right to any such privacy, as Carole found after her son's body was discovered at the family's home. Their doctor came round, she remembers, but 'then the police came, and the CID, and the photographers, and an undertaker'; suddenly their house was filled with strangers.

After Janice's mother committed suicide, strangers had already entered the house before Janice arrived; the police had had to break in, and when Janice and her sister reached the bungalow, their mother's body had already been taken away. The body cannot be handed back to relatives until the coroner has issued a burial order, and for survivors, it can feel as though other people – strangers to boot – have completely taken over. Anne Downey described what happened after her son's body had been found: 'Two strangers in black took you away ... people filled the house ... then someone took the note away and talked about inquests and evidence' (1987: 13).

Survivors of suicide have little chance of nursing their wounds in private, as Victoria Alexander, an American survivor, discovered when her mother committed suicide: 'I was angry at my exposure, at having my open wounds and those of my family available for inspection by the police, by the medical examiner, neighbors and passersby. *Their spectacle was my nightmare*' (1987: 110) (my italics).

Conley (1987) has suggested that 'first responders' such as the police and the coroner's officer have three main areas of responsibility to fulfil: to satisfy the requirements of the law, to meet the needs of the survivors, and to secure the dignity of the dead person. It can be hard to meet all these requirements simultaneously. For example, the need to carry out a legal investigation can cut across the need to support relatives (see Chapter 15).

It is highly unlikely that survivors will have had to face this sort of situation before, and, in a state of shock, they are unlikely to realise that the police need to rule out any suspicion of foul play on the part of relatives. Being subject to what one survivor described as 'quite a grilling' by the police is an unpleasant experience at the best of times, but survivors might find it easier if the reasons for this were explained to them (Danto 1987).

Some survivors did comment positively on their dealings with the police: 'very very sweet; couldn't have been nicer' (Eileen); 'helpful, kind, and compassionate' (Robert). But not everyone had found the police so helpful. Maureen came home after hearing that her son had shot himself to find not only that her house was full of strangers but that she was not allowed back into her own home, and no one would tell her why:

> No one would tell me anything, see? And that was the hardest thing. If someone had just got hold of me, brought me in here, and sat me down and said, 'Look, Paul's shot himself, he's still upstairs, we can't move him yet', I would have known.

As it was, no one would tell her where Paul's body was. Sitting in a neighbour's house, she could hear the police 'banging about' in *her* house. And all the police would say was that they were 'just tidying up'. It was some time before the police even confirmed officially that Paul was dead. As Maureen commented: 'they don't know how to tell you your son's killed himself [but] they should come out with it just the same'.

As Maureen realised afterwards, the police were probably trying to protect her from the mess; Paul's bedding, his clothes, and the carpet all had to be burnt because of the blood. But not being told anything, not having anything explained, can leave survivors with fantasies which may be worse than reality. When Alastair's body was found in the local forest his parents wanted to go over there immediately, but were told by the police not to. 'So we didn't go', Heather recalls, 'but maybe that sowed the seed of "this is too horrid".'

Giving people bad news is never an easy task, but some survivors had been on the receiving end of considerable insensitivity. Mark described how: 'the police blundered in and did their blundering thing'. When a policewoman came round to interview his wife about their daughter's suicide, Francesca, who is a trained counsellor, found that:

> instead of interviewing me, she ... sat down at my feet, took her hat off, and told me how she understood because this had happened to her close relative and she started to tell me all about this, using me as a counsellor and I was sitting thinking ... what exactly is this all about, what's happening to me? I'm being made to listen to this policewoman who needs some help and

I'm a helper – I'm not a helper in this situation and can't be, so I just sat ... and eventually she went. It was quite bizarre.

Several survivors commented on how young the police were who had been sent round to see them, and how awkwardly they behaved. Like Francesca, Susan found herself in the anomalous situation of being the one who ended up doing the looking after:

[They sent] the youngest policeman in the [local] police force ... together with the youngest policewoman. They hadn't the faintest idea what to do. They were really frightened. I found myself trying to mother them ... and they gave me the phone number of the police station [in the area where her husband's body had been found] and they didn't even help me find the code. It sounds incredible to tell you that fifteen years later, but it really stands out in my mind.

Jane's experience was not dissimilar: '[There were] two of them. They both looked about fourteen years old and incredibly embarrassed.' Age does not automatically confer greater sensitivity or ability to handle difficult situations, but perhaps more experienced members of the police force would be more comfortable in this sort of situation and more able to support relatives. Training could also place greater emphasis on talking to relatives (see Chapter 15). The behaviour of the police and other emergency services at the time of the suicide is a matter of considerable importance, as these examples show; survivors will often remember how they were treated for a long time afterwards.

Unlike the police and the coroner's officer, ambulance crews are not there in an investigatory capacity, which may make their job somewhat easier; some survivors were particularly appreciative of the way that the ambulance staff behaved. Carol described the ambulance crew who took Alan's body away as 'superb', and she was particularly touched to receive a card from them the next day saying how sorry they were about his death. In contrast to the way the police behaved, Francesca found the ambulance crew who came to the house particularly kind and sensitive. Not only did they take the trouble to explain to her why it was not possible to try and restart Patricia's heart, but when they arrived at the hospital she was allowed to remain in the ambulance alone with the body and say goodbye to her daughter in private.

Farewells

Sudden death leaves the survivor no opportunity to deal with any unfinished business in the relationship, and no chance to say a proper goodbye (Hauser 1987). Indeed, what subsequently turns out to have been the last conversation between them will often seem quite normal to the unsuspecting survivor. Pat talked to her daughter only hours before Caroline jumped from the top of a multi-storey car park, and heard her say, 'I'm fine'; in Pauline's case her son went off 'happy as a sandboy', she remembers, saying 'cheerio, and see you next week'.

But not all survivors have such apparently normal partings. Some people were left with memories of an angry farewell exchange and having to come to terms with that. Melanie was living apart from her husband and had recently applied for a legal separation. Ian's last words to her before committing suicide were 'you'll have blood on your hands'. That was seven years ago. She still cannot forget those words, but she has reached the point of being able to acknowledge that she was not responsible for his death; at the time she felt less sure.

Facing the horror

As some of the initial numbness begins to wear off, survivors will often experience overwhelming feelings of horror, thinking about how the person actually died, and wondering what they went through at the end. Lois, whose son killed himself with a knife, found that particularly shattering:

> the horror of a loved one choosing to murder themselves is
> quite horrendous ... I thought if he would do such a thing, he'd
> go for a walk along the river, that's what I thought – that he
> would just slip away, but he chose a very dramatic death really.

Sometimes, just the thought of such violence makes it almost impossible fully to accept the manner of death – let alone talk about it – however hard the survivor tries. Marie, whose husband Oliver died on the railway line near their home, has found that although 'it's something you talk about, work through, come to terms with ... I think there's a limit to what you can talk about accepting'.

While some people manage to push any thoughts about the actual death to the back of their minds, others may find themselves unable to do so. Two months after her daughter committed suicide on the London Underground, Jean found she was becoming totally obsessed with thoughts of how Anna had died:

> I just spent the whole time thinking about the death ... the whole time. I thought, you're going to get totally obsessed like Anna, you've got to stop this ... that's all I thought about – her jumping and her looking, and how she looked in the funeral parlour. I just went over and over it, and how she felt and whether it hurt. I was in a terrible state ... so yes [a year after her death], I am still very obsessed with the way she died.

Wondering what the person was going through at the time they died preoccupies many survivors, though being given information by other people about what is likely to have happened can help to lessen that preoccupation. For several days after Tim's body had been discovered on the railway line, Jennifer found that all she could think about was how violently he had died, and so she was glad to hear from the coroner that Tim would almost certainly not have felt anything. Heather too, was helped by discovering that the way her son had chosen to end his life would almost certainly have meant a painless death.

Not having been there when the suicide happened, and realising that the person had died alone can be a cause of considerable anguish to survivors like Phyllis whose daughter, Julie, died of an overdose. Nearly four years later she still asks herself: 'Why didn't I ring her? Why didn't she phone me? Could I have done anything? Was she scared? Was she frightened? When she was dying, did she call out? It's awful.'

Survivors can blame themselves for not having realised how bad the victim must have been feeling. They may feel that they should have known what was going on, even when the victim had not shown any particular signs of distress. As a mother, Pat found that particularly hard:

> I find it hard [to live] with the knowledge that she was going through all this dreadful pain and I didn't know. And that's the overriding thing that's painful to me. I mean she killed herself and she's dead and she's gone and that is a dreadful pain but the worst thing for me to cope with is the knowledge that before she

died she was in such terrible pain and going through such torment and I didn't know.... To think that we were here for those two days before she died ... and I'm her Mum and I didn't even know and I couldn't help.

This sort of questioning may also be the survivor's way of trying to understand what led the other person to take the final step. Tim's death left Jennifer with many questions:

What must you be thinking that minute before you do it? If you're going to do something like that, what must you be thinking, what must you be doing? You wonder all kinds of things: whether he sat there a long time ... thinking, whether he experimented with something on the line to see how fast the trains were going, or if he cried.

Trying to understand why the person committed suicide is an extremely common reaction among survivors (see Chapter 6), but one of the greatest puzzles can be – what happened at the very end, what was the final trigger? Things may have been going badly wrong for the victim for some time, but why that day, what was it that finally tipped the balance? This is a question which the survivor may never be able to answer.

Seeing the victim's body

Bereavement experts frequently stress the importance of being able to view the body. By seeing the dead person, the bereaved must come face to face with the reality of the death, accept what has happened and acknowledge that they will not see that person alive again (Raphael 1985; Staudacher 1988). For someone like Maureen, going to see Paul's body at the undertakers did help her towards acceptance.

If I hadn't gone, I would never have believed he was dead. I had to go to prove to me that it was Paul [or] I'd have been out looking for him.... I had to see that he was actually at peace.

Even Irene, who described her dead husband's face as being 'so full of pain you could almost touch it', still feels glad that she was able to see him.

For some of the survivors, there had been a desperate need to touch and hold the person, a need that they were sometimes denied.

Pat and Robert were told by a policeman that they couldn't see Caroline's body straight away. Like any mother, Pat badly wanted to hold her daughter at that moment. Now she feels she has been left with a dreadful gap and wishes she had insisted, but as she now says, over a year later: 'I didn't really know that I had the right to; perhaps if I had I would have insisted.' At moments of crisis like this, though, when survivors are in shock, standing up for their rights may be the last thing they feel able to do.

By the time the body has reached the undertakers and has been placed in a coffin, the chance to hold the body for the last time has often passed, something which Jean still regrets. Having been told by her brother that Anna's body was 'viewable' she went to the undertakers, and although she was relieved that Anna's face was unmarked,

> what really distressed me about it was that I couldn't hold her.
> They'd done her up, I suppose because of the post-mortem; it was
> just her face and she was all done up in a kind of white parcel ...
> like a cardboard box .... when you've had your own child, you
> need to hold them, and I needed to see her body ... [I] wanted to
> see Anna's hands but I thought I had just better not look.

Because of what her brother had told her, Jean knew that Anna would look all right, but survivors may need more specific information. It is possible that Jean could have seen and touched Anna's hands, but she refrained from doing what she instinctively wanted to do because she did not know what to expect.

Where survivors have no information about the state of the body, what they are left with are fantasies which may be so horrendous that the survivor decides they could not possibly bring themselves to see the body. But fantasies can be much worse than reality (Raphael 1985), as David discovered when he went to see Paul after his son had shot himself: 'When I saw him, he was so perfect and so normal I was sort of quite relieved.'

Not all survivors will want to see the body, of course, but sometimes they may not even feel that they had any choice in the matter. Other well-meaning family members may put pressure on the survivor, with comments like 'best to remember her as she was'. As Raphael points out, being able to remember the person when they were alive is important, but the bereaved need to acknowledge them as dead too:

> The experience of seeing ... the dead person as a dead person
> makes it possible for the bereaved to develop an image of the
> person as dead ... different and altered from the living image.
> This image may then be held alongside the living image in the
> processes of separation and mourning. (1985: 36)

Other people will often feel they are being helpful by suggesting to
relatives that they should not see the body. Nancy, who was abroad
when her daughter committed suicide, was advised by her vicar not
to see Clare: 'He said "don't: better remember her as she was", and I
thought, well [he] knows what he's doing and I abided by that. But
I've regretted it ever since.'

Sometimes survivors have to face not only discouragement but
outright disapproval. When Suzy's father committed suicide, she
knew that going to see his body was something she both wanted and
needed to do, but other people in the family did not see things in the
same way:

> I'd already decided I'd go and see my father; my mother was very
> shocked at that and my sister thought it was revolting.... I felt it
> was important. I wanted to say goodbye.... I hadn't seen him the
> day before [when he had died].

Janice was faced not only with her sister's disapproval, but with being
strongly advised by the undertaker not to see her mother's body. Fortunately, though, she was able to talk this through with a therapist,
and looking back, is glad that she did in fact go to see her mother at
the undertakers, despite pressure being placed on her not to do so.

Having someone to talk things over with can help survivors sort
out what it is they want to do and can help them reach a decision
which is based on their own feelings, rather than on the wishes of
others. When Christine's husband committed suicide, she recalls
how 'everyone – the police, my parents, the undertaker' tried to stop
her seeing Graham's body which had been badly damaged and, after
three weeks, was also decomposed. Only the bereavement counsellor
who she had started seeing understood her need to go and accompanied her to the undertakers.

In many cases, survivors will not see the body until it reaches the
undertakers, but several people said how much they had wanted to
see the body before that. Not being sure what to expect, not knowing
what is 'allowed', and not having things explained can prevent sur-

vivors from doing what their instincts are telling them is right. Heather did not see Alastair when his body was in the hospital mortuary but admits: 'I wish I had gone. I had visions of bodies in drawers and I didn't want to see Alastair being pulled out [of a drawer] like you see on television.' In fact when her husband went to the hospital, Alastair was lying in a bed looking as if he was asleep. Now she regrets not having been to the hospital because:

> that was really [my] chance to say goodbye which I have never done.... When he was in the chapel of rest I didn't want to go because I thought they would have put make-up on him and combed his hair wrong and dressed him in something funny and I didn't want to see him in a coffin ... I'm glad I didn't go then. I only regret not going to the hospital. *I think if somebody had explained to me that it would be alright, persuaded me to go, I'd have been better off* because I haven't seen him dead, and I think that's important. I think I would have been further along if I had actually seen him dead.

The fact that their child's hair was combed the wrong way was something that several parents mentioned; it obviously mattered to them. Of course there is no reason why undertakers should know how the person wore their hair when they were alive, but there may be ways of overcoming this problem. Relatives could perhaps be asked for a recent photo. Or they could be invited to come and help to arrange the person's hair themselves.

This sort of measure is not always practicable, of course. Sometimes the body has been so badly mutilated, that there are virtually no recognisable remains. Faced with this, survivors may find it hard to accept that the person is actually dead. When Brian's wife committed suicide he was only able to identify Judy by her wedding ring and watch; though he is glad to have been spared the ordeal of seeing her remains, he has found it hard to accept her death, and in his dreams, Judy is often still alive.

> In Judy's case there was a funeral, there was a coffin ... [but] I didn't know where Judy was; I mean, maybe she was there.... Sometimes I wonder whether there's a part of me that hasn't accepted that she's not here any more because, although there was a funeral, I can't actually say that I felt she was involved.... I found the service very remote.

Raphael suggests that where there are no recognisable remains, the bereaved 'may still need to say goodbye and may need to talk through his or her feelings about what remains of the person' (1985: 36). But some survivors may need to do more than this. When Jennifer's brother died on a railway line, his body was very badly mutilated. As a result, not only were the family told it would be best not to see Tim's remains, but they were also advised not to look at the photographs used as evidence at his inquest. At the time of his death, Jennifer felt strongly that she needed to know that what had been found was indeed Tim's body, and that feeling persisted. But it was only months later that she discovered that she could see Tim's file at the coroner's office. So nearly a year after the death she went to the coroner's office and spent time looking at those photographs. She did not find it easy to do, but seeing them gave her the sense of acceptance she needed and she has no regrets about what she did. Not everyone would choose Jennifer's way of confronting the death, but survivors who are left with no recognisable body to see may have to find other ways of saying goodbye.

The time immediately after a death is rarely easy for the bereaved, and survivors of suicide face additional stresses, not least the legal investigations which have to be set in train. These, combined with the sometimes violent nature of suicide death, can leave the survivors in a particularly vulnerable state. Sensitive attitudes and behaviour on the part of the police, the coroner's officer, and others who may be involved can, however, help to minimise the survivor's distress.

Chapter five

Looking back

*He was talking about suicide all that week and had actually
threatened suicide ... that was the most terrible thing of all and I
just couldn't cope with it, I just couldn't handle it at all.... I can
remember saying, 'But you couldn't love me if you're saying you're
going to leave me' ... and to me it wasn't a reality, you see, that's the
awful thing, to me he was just talking, I never really believed it,
that's the terrible thing. (Lois)*

*You think, well, how could you be there and ... it happen despite
you being there? On the other hand, you're not almighty, and can't
control everybody and everything. (Marie)*

At times, people will commit suicide seemingly unexpectedly. Survivors may have been aware that the victim had problems, but the
death still comes as a complete surprise, as was the case with
Caroline's family. To Robert and Pat, their daughter was 'a twenty-
year-old who thought she should have a boyfriend and thought she
should be thinner'; the weekend before she died, Caroline had said
she felt unwell and had spent time in bed, but, as Robert explained,
it never entered their heads that 'she was in trouble that way'.

For other survivors, though, despite the fact that the suicide is
unexpected, when it happens it is as though all along they had been
half expecting something like that. When Jane heard the news from
America that her brother, Christopher, had died she remembers
thinking that it had probably been a stroke or something similar: 'I
was bracing myself to hear "coronary thrombosis" or "stroke" ... I
was summoning all my strength to hear something coming from a
direction I expected it to come from.' But what she heard was that
Christopher had taken his own life with a gun:

and it had never entered my head. He had never mentioned anything of this sort, never mentioned suicide. It was never a thought I had entertained in relation to Christopher, ever, and simultaneously I thought, yes, yes, I can see that.

Living with a suicidal person

Parkes has suggested that 'the greater the area occupied by A in the life space of B, the greater the disruption that will result from A's departure' (1986: 138). The strength of reaction to a death may be related less to love and more to the intensity of involvement between the two people (Marris 1978). At the point when many young adults are leaving the family home and parents are anticipating a well-earned breather, Mark and Francesca found themselves embarking on what turned out to be ten years of frequently intense involvement and caring for their daughter. They coped with the suicide attempts and the other crises; like many informal 'carers' they became the backstop when the official services failed, and it was to them and to the family home that Patricia always returned.

For many such survivors, the final act of suicide is the culmination of years of difficulty, often marked by previous attempts, threats of suicide, and repeated crises (Hauser 1987).

Frank and Ursula spent five years trying to care for their daughter before Josie finally died as the result of an overdose. Labelled 'schizophrenic' by the psychiatric services, Josie's adult life was punctuated by crises: admission to hospital would be followed by discharge and the inevitable readmission; there were other times when her parents had no idea where she was living; on one occasion they found she was serving a prison sentence; twice she attempted to commit suicide. Ursula often felt torn: mental health professionals told her that she should not let Josie return to the family home; her instinct was to want to look after her daughter. At the time of her death Josie was living in a bedsitter nearby, but frequently returning home in the day-time when Ursula would look after her.

Sometimes the suicidal person's difficulties can threaten to disrupt totally the lives of those around them. Andrew was a partner in a busy general practice when his wife's problems began. Although Gwen had suffered from intermittent depression for some years, her brother's suicide three years before her own death seems to have upset a fragile balance. Andrew can remember those last years clearly:

the vicious circle of the depression and the booze and the attempts at killing herself ... in and out of psychiatric clinics, repeated attempts at suicide, codeine tablets, barbiturates ... putting her overcoat over her dressing-gown and going down to the off-licence to buy her whisky in the morning.

Try as he could, and despite being medically qualified, Andrew admits that in the end he was powerless to help her.

It has been suggested that as many as one third of all suicide victims have made previous attempts (Litman 1970a), and four out of five will either have made a previous attempt or threatened suicide (McIntosh 1987a). Living with the knowledge that someone has attempted suicide and may do so again adds to the stress of what is often already a fraught situation. Isabel's husband took two overdoses during fifteen years of severe depressions, which led to unemployment and periods of in-patient psychiatric treatment. After the second attempt, Eric's doctor told Isabel that if her husband made no further attempts in the next four years then everything would be all right. His prediction was somewhat over-optimistic. Seven years later, Eric finally killed himself with another overdose.

Facing threats of suicide

It is estimated that as many as three quarters of all suicide victims will have announced their intention to commit suicide, either directly or indirectly (Litman 1970a; Stengel 1973; Keir 1986). They may have told someone outside the family such as their general practitioner, but they are equally likely to have told a relative.

Bridget was seventeen and in the middle of taking her A-level exams when her older sister Catherine committed suicide; their mother had died some years before, their father (who committed suicide later that year) was not able to cope, and it was left to Bridget to try to talk her sister out of the suicide threats:

I eventually worked out that I couldn't stop her by persuasion; I couldn't talk her out of it because it wasn't a logical thing ... I'd try and talk her out of it but in the end she'd just say 'I've just got to do it and I will', and so I didn't feel I could stop her like that at all – I tried.

Sometimes survivors find they are on the receiving end of what is

53

tantamount to emotional blackmail. Melanie found herself in that situation with her husband. Because things at home had become impossible, she and her baby daughter had moved out and gone to stay with her parents. But Ian wanted her back and began threatening that he would kill himself if she didn't return; on one occasion he sent her a farewell note and when she informed the police, they discovered that it was a false alarm. When it became clear that she was not coming back, though, he did kill himself.

As a response to threats of this kind, some survivors become drawn into bargaining with the suicidal person. Miriam's son, Ben, had made it plain for some years that he had no wish to go on living; he often told her how he envied the dead. The year before his death, he announced that he had made up his mind to die. Faced with this threat, Miriam can remember saying to him: '"Well, let's have an agreement, not this year", and he said "OK". I was beside myself with anxiety and I said to him, "If you do this, you will finish me off" and he said "Well you come too."' Late into the night, Miriam was forced to sit and listen as Ben explained how he had to tell her of his plans to die because he didn't want it to happen out of the blue:

> the feeling that it gave me was that it was rather as if somebody
> in the family had announced their intention of committing
> murder, and the fact that the person he was going to murder was
> himself didn't take away the fact that it would have felt like
> betraying him.

Miriam found that any attempts on her part to intervene and try to get help only made her relationship with her son worse. When she wrote to Ben's college telling them that he was suicidal, he saw it as an act of betrayal. Miriam found herself trapped, living on a knife edge: 'It was like carrying something that was going to be spilled if you weren't very very careful.' She knew what was likely to happen, but felt powerless to prevent it.

That feeling of carrying round a precarious secret was something that Susan also had to live with during her husband's three crisis periods. She coped alone as Richard refused to go and talk to anybody or have any treatment; his problems had to be hidden from everybody except her. The strain on her was, at times, considerable; Richard would be pacing up and down all night, after which, Susan recalls, 'he would pick himself up and go off to work'; she, on the other hand, would be left feeling absolutely shattered and wondering how much longer she could go on coping without support. The final and worst crisis lasted about nine months and Susan began telling Richard that she did not think she could carry on supporting him alone; he would have to get outside help. Now she is left wondering whether that was what made him decide he would rather take his own life.

Not all victims will threaten suicide as explicitly as Ben or Catherine. Sometimes it seems as if the person is using coded language, and then the message may simply not be understood. After Heather and her son had been watching a programme on teenage suicide one evening Alastair remarked, 'Now I know how to do it':

> and I didn't take a blind bit of notice because it didn't mean anything to me, it just seemed to be a flippant remark that he threw at me ... and now I think he probably thought that he'd almost told me and 'why didn't Mum help me when I told her what I was going to do?' But I didn't pick it up.... It was only when he was missing, then it crossed my mind ... and I thought, that's it, he's gone to do it.

Attempts to find help

A substantial proportion of people who commit suicide will have been in contact with their general practitioner in the weeks before their death; it is thought that as many as 75 per cent of victims are 'in medical contact' shortly before the suicide occurs (Office of Health Economics 1981). Some will also have been treated by the psychiatric services; Stengel (1973) suggests that about one third of people who take their own lives are thought to have been suffering from neurosis, psychosis, or severe personality disorder.

Many survivors, realising that things were seriously wrong and that the other person needed more help than they could give, turned to professionals of one kind or another for assistance; but sometimes they were disappointed. When Josie was suffering from what the doctors decided was 'a drug-induced psychosis', a diagnosis which they subsequently changed to schizophrenia, Ursula recalls going to psychiatrists for help: 'I very naively thought "ah, the experts will know what to do. They will deal with everything", and it came as a great blow to learn ... that they really did not know much more than me.'

Some suicide victims have problems which refuse to fit into any one psychiatric classification, and mental health services often seem to be as much at a loss as relatives when it comes to explaining what is wrong and deciding what treatment should be given. When Carol's son was seen by psychiatrists, nobody could decide what was causing his difficulties. Guesswork seems to have been the order of the day; they thought he might have schizophrenia, or possibly a personality disorder. He was given large quantities of medication and offered a day-centre place but no one ever seemed sure what was wrong. Lois had similar problems when Simon was referred to the local mental health services. There was mention of 'a psychotic episode' but the only advice she remembers being given over the years was 'be firm but kind'.

Faced with mental health services which may be unable to meet the needs of the suicidal person, relatives inevitably become the backstops – the ones who end up providing the care and support. Over a period of ten years, Mark and Francesca (see p. 52) tried to get help for their daughter from a range of services and professionals including psychiatrists, social workers, psychotherapists, day centres, and hostels; but as Mark recalls: 'there came the slow realisation that the so-called medical authorities ... [and] the social workers, had nothing to offer, no understanding, no genuine caring for the individual.... The worst thing [was] that Patricia was on her own.' This realisation that no one could really help was, Mark believes, one of the reasons which in the end led Patricia to take her own life.

Psychiatry in Britain is often described as the 'poor relation' of the NHS, something which Jean recognised when she tried to get help for her daughter. Even though she managed to get Anna admitted to the psychiatric unit of a large London teaching hospital, she soon realised that that was not going to be sufficient to really help her daughter. 'I was doing the best I thought I could do for her', she says, 'but it wasn't good enough. It didn't begin to address the problem.' Even with the resources of a large teaching hospital, for example, Anna only saw her consultant for ten minutes each week.

The impact on survivors

The strain of knowing that a close relative is suicidal can be intolerable. In a recent newspaper article, a mother described her feelings after fifteen years of her daughter's repeated attempts at taking her own life:

I wished it could be over. Ended, for ever ... I can't take the continued uncertainty.... I have to try and save myself, to cocoon myself against the day when the voice on the 'phone will say 'I'm sorry'.... The awful thing is, I long to hear that phrase. I wish it could be over and I could mourn for the daughter I used to love. (James 1988)

Faced with this situation, survivors may decide that if someone else in the family is not coping, then, whatever the stresses, they must be the ones that cope; they must remain on an even keel – or at least give the appearance of doing so – if the suicidal person is going to remain alive. Miriam felt that whatever was happening to Ben, and whatever her own distress she at least had to give the appearance of coping:

I actually thought, if he's going to be saved, then I have to control myself because it's not fair to beat him over the head and [to] have a mother that's distressed is something else that makes him feel that life is not worth living.

Lois found her life becoming dominated by constant worrying about her son, and she remembers begging Simon, 'just give me one day without my having to worry about you because I do so desperately need it'. The strain of caring for someone who is distressed and suicidal day after day, and sometimes for years, is bound to take its toll. In some cases, relatives may also be having to provide basic physical care; there were times when Ursula had to do everything for her daughter, when Josie could not even make herself a cup of tea or wash her hair. She recalls how Josie just drained her utterly, physically and emotionally.

Survivors can become suicidal themselves. Both Christine and her husband had been under considerable stress when Graham committed suicide. Graham had been having problems with his college lecturer's job, and their son had developed leukaemia and was extremely ill; as Christine admits: 'I'd been thinking in terms [of suicide] the previous year anyway, because things were so dreadful ... it could have been either of us quite honestly.' She managed to cope, despite her own suicidal feelings. When Irene's husband Bill hanged himself, though, she was already in hospital being treated with ECT for severe depression; as she admits: 'it was me that wanted to die ... not Bill'.

Survivors who are feeling under stress may find themselves caught between trying to balance their own needs with those of the other person. Janice lived with this dilemma for many years. During childhood she was somewhat protected from her mother's problems, not really aware that her mother was being treated for depression. But she can remember the university vacation when she decided she could not face going home, she just could not cope with her mother. When her mother attempted suicide some years later, Janice again began to feel that she was going under herself: 'I knew that I couldn't go and live with her and make it all right – for my own sanity – and I knew really that writing letters and ringing weren't enough ... I just felt myself going down and down.' Faced with this dilemma, survivors can feel that their own survival is under threat. Like Janice, they may be forced to make difficult choices.

Other stresses in the family

For some families, threats of suicide may be only one cause of stress in their lives. Like Christine, who was also coping with her son's leukaemia (see above), Paul's family had also been struggling with the impact of cancer. The day that Paul shot himself, his mother was staying with relatives, recovering from a course of radiotherapy. Looking back, though, Maureen still feels that despite her own needs at that time, she somehow failed her son by not being there when he needed her. 'Once you're a parent', she says, ' you're a parent for life and that is it ... I should have been there. My son needed me and I wasn't.'

For families like those of Paul and Graham, the suicide occurred at a time when they were already facing other life-threatening situations. For John, however, his wife's death came at a time when he was already trying to come to terms with other major losses. Two years before, Averil's son (by a previous marriage) had murdered his grandfather, for which he had received a life sentence. For John and Averil, it was, effectively, a double bereavement. When Averil's body was washed ashore, John found himself utterly alone.

Power in relationships

When a person decides that life is not worth living, they are saying, in effect, 'I have this right. I am responsible for my own actions.' But others are not likely to see it that way, and the result can be the emergence of a power struggle, but one in which there are no winners.

> We have created a power relationship between ourselves and that person. We have made him or her dependent on us. We have also given that person the power to threaten us – to threaten suicide, so that we dare not end the relationship and relinquish our power over that person for fear of failing. The result is that the two of us are locked into the classic power relationship of jailer and warder. Both are equally prisoners ... power and love are not compatible. Fighting replaces feeling. (Lake 1984: 125)

The jailer's job is to guard the prisoners, and survivors may find themselves continually watching over the suicidal person. When Betty's other children told her about Jonathan's two previous attempts she found herself watching him constantly. More than three years after Jonathan's death, Betty is still angry; despite her vigilance, it feels to her as though he slipped through her fingers. She thought she could have saved him: 'I know I could have done it. It's too late. I'm very angry.'

Trying to stop someone committing suicide can be highly disruptive for all those concerned. When Judy became suicidal, Brian found he was caught up in a sort of cat-and-mouse game, trying to watch his wife constantly and finding this meant he could not even go to work. When this strategy became impossible he tried getting friends and neighbours round to keep an eye on her. Eventually she was admitted to a psychiatric clinic. Despite all these efforts, Judy still managed to attempt suicide several times, and Brian finally had to come to terms with his own powerlessness in the situation:

> I think by the time [she died] I'd sort of realised that if she was going to make that many attempts when we'd had good professional help, she was just determined ... I obviously find it hard to accept that there was nothing I could have done which could have stopped her.

Bridget's sister had developed paranoid thoughts, so that Bridget's attempts to watch over Catherine became virtually impossible: 'Basically we were torn between wanting to make sure that she didn't damage herself and also not wanting to reinforce her delusions of being watched.'

Survivors may try to prevent the suicide happening by taking steps to ensure that the person is forcibly protected from harming themselves. For some survivors, though, the prospect of seeing a relative detained in a psychiatric hospital against their will is something they find unacceptable (Lukas and Seiden 1987). (It also does not necessarily guarantee protection as recent publicity about hospital suicides has shown.) Frank realised that long-term compulsory hospitalisation would have been his daughter's future life, had she remained alive: 'she would obviously have been detained somewhere indefinitely', he says, 'and there was no way that Josie would have wanted that, certainly.'

Despite her misgivings, Jean had originally agreed to her daughter being compulsorily detained in hospital, but found the experience unbearable:

> She was on a section [of the Mental Health Act], we did get her sectioned because it was the only way to make her continue treatment, but when they did lock her up after she made the first [suicide] attempt ... she was only there for three days and I said 'I simply can't stand it'; she was standing there like a little bird, it was terrible, and I thought, she's going to get much more ill like that, she must have more freedom.

Faced with someone who is determined to end their life, survivors will sometimes have come to terms with their own inability to control events even before the suicide happens. Before his daughter's death, Mark had realised he was in a no-win situation: 'one felt powerless, one felt up against a force, a death wish if you like to mythologise such power; it's the life instinct inversed, such power that nothing you could do would stop it.'

For other survivors, though, it is only after the suicide that they can begin to come to terms with their own sense of powerlessness. As Ursula discovered, this can be a painful and confusing struggle as the survivor wavers between feeling they should have been able to save the person and thinking that perhaps that would have been the wrong thing to do anyway.

> I'm a bit confused ... I feel I could have convinced Josie that life was worth living ... actually that's belittling her because it makes out that she would have been an idiot, because it wouldn't have been true and she wasn't unintelligent ... I do sometimes feel I

should have tried to convince her that things weren't as they were, but she would see through me, she would have known that I was lying.

In the end, though, she admitted that Josie did have the right to take her own life:

> if you deny someone that right, you're taking away something that is a vital part of them. You're imposing tremendous power if you deny that right. But I wanted to impose that power ... so it was a terrible conflict ... a complete contradiction.

For survivors, acknowledging their own lack of omnipotence also means recognising the other person's autonomy; as Francesca admitted: 'I have to give Patricia some responsibility for her own life, I can't take that all on myself.' Handing over the responsibility for running one's life can be very demeaning as Jennifer realised after her brother's death: 'Why should he hand over that power to me? Why should he? He wouldn't want to feel that small.'

Denying the possibility of suicide

Even when survivors are faced with overt threats of suicide, they may react by consciously denying what the other person is saying. In this situation, according to Litman, 'conscious recognition of its significance is avoided, denied, and repressed' (1970b: 442), a denial well described by one of the characters in Susanna Mitchell's novel, *The Token*:

> She closed her eyes to face the old self-deception. It was clear to her now, subconsciously she had always known that Julia's suicide had been no sudden brainstorm. All the signals had been there if she had been prepared to read them.... She had considered Julia better because she wanted her better. She had assumed her pathetic facade of recovery to be real because it suited her to do so; she had refused to admit that her friend was still tormented and bewildered, edging towards the point where self-destruction seemed the only answer. (1985: 57)

Even when the survivor knows what is likely to happen, they may find they are ignoring their instincts, as Colin found:

> I regret I didn't follow what had been my instinct at the time

[which] was to go round and talk to her ... I knew what her situation was and what moved her to do things, but I don't suppose I was really conscious of ... what was going to happen. (Colin)

Writing of his friendship with the poet Sylvia Plath, Alvarez describes this sort of mental gymnastics which survivors can perform: 'In common with her other friends of that period I chose to believe in this cheerfulness ... or rather *I believed in it and did not believe* ... but what could one do?' (1974: 42) (my italics).

Alvarez's question 'but what could one do?' illustrates the sense of helplessness which survivors can feel when they know someone is likely to commit suicide, a reaction which Litman has aptly described as the 'immobilisation response' (1970b: 441). Survivors may feel unable even to raise the subject with the other person. Janice had been told by her sister that their mother had several times talked of feeling 'near to suicide', and she knew that her mother had phoned the Samaritans, but she found herself quite unable to discuss any of this with her mother. 'It was', she admits, 'just much too threatening.'

When Pam and Harry received a phone call from the hospital where their daughter nursed, telling them to come immediately as Frances was seriously ill and unconscious, both in their different ways realised that suicide was a possibility. It was as if once it had actually happened, the conscious mind could admit what had hitherto been repressed: 'My mind turned immediately that she'd done something to herself – I suppose it must have been at the back of my mind' (John); 'I had my own suspicions that this might happen [but] you just think oh no, I must be going mad, I must be imagining it, but the suspicion was there all right' (Pam). Marie, whose husband committed suicide, acknowledges now that 'all the warning signs were there' but she ignored them, despite her professional training and experience as a psychiatric social worker. Yet like some other survivors, she knew that, despite a superficial normality, something was very wrong: 'something awful was happening', she recalls, 'and I couldn't do anything about it'. But then, she realised afterwards, neither could he: 'We'd say "How did he keep that to himself?" But at the same time it's so awful, how do you tell anyone?'

Occasionally, the survivor's fears about possible suicide seem to force themselves abruptly into consciousness. Several people mentioned sudden and inexplicable feelings of acute distress before the suicide, as though in some way they knew what was about to happen. Eileen remembers the day she was having dinner with the man she was later to marry. It was Valentine's Day, and as she says, it should have been a perfect evening; she had no idea that one of her twin daughters was about to commit suicide:

> We sat and had dinner and we reached the cheese stage and I just burst into tears, and I said: 'I feel so unhappy and I've no reason to feel unhappy'... and I couldn't stop weeping ... and then next morning, of course I had the news that Donna had died and it must have been about the time that she killed herself that I had started to cry.

Point of no return

How the bereaved person copes with the loss will depend to some extent on their relationship with the suicide victim immediately prior to the death (Bowlby 1985). Kast suggests that guilt feelings will be 'substantially less if the communication between those remaining behind and the dead had been good, if there had been a genuine leave-taking, and if problems could still be discussed with one another' (1988: 56).

But far from being close to the suicidal person, the experience of survivors of suicide is often quite the opposite. They have found themselves living with someone who grew more and more distant from them, a situation described (from the suicidal person's perspective) by Alvarez, writing about the time leading up to his attempted suicide. He describes 'the closed world of suicide' and talks of how his life was being lived for him 'by forces I could not control' (1974: 293). The suicide victim, he writes, experiences an 'imperviousness to everything outside the closed world of self-destruction' (p. 144).

In the last weeks of her husband's life, Marie felt that same sense of distance developing between them:

> I just could not get through to him; he looked so lost ... as though he was drawing away; and the last evening I saw him sitting in the chair and [it] was just as though he wasn't there – and that was frightening.

Marie had realised something was very wrong with Oliver but in Nancy's case she only saw with hindsight how Clare had shut herself off so completely that no one in the family realised how desperate she must have been. Now, with hindsight, she feels that 'when a person knows that they're going to do that, they shut off completely. They cover up, and they make up their minds they're not going to consult anybody.'

Trying to understand what her daughter had been going through before she died, Phyllis felt that 'it must have been like being in a tunnel'. This image of the tunnel echoes a description by the American suicidologist, Edwin Shneidman:

> The person ... suffers from a kind of 'tunnel vision'. One's ordinary thoughts, and loves and responsibilities are suddenly unavailable to the conscious mind.... The suicidal person turns his back on his own past and permits his memories to become unreal; thus they cannot serve to save him ... the world is divided into two (and only two) parts ... a desired life or a 'necessary' death. (1982: 12)

This sense of a black and white world, of the victim living in an 'either/or' situation, was mentioned by numerous survivors. It seems to be something which victims may carry around for much of their lives – a striving for perfection which says 'only the best will do, and if that's not possible then nothing else will do' (see pp. 72–3).

Looking back to the time leading up to the suicide, it felt to some survivors as though death had become a magnet for the suicidal person. For Isabel this was borne out by an article which Eric had written after his first suicide attempt; entitled: 'Half in love with easeful death', while it did not explicitly mention his own recent attempt, he talked of how:

> the boat he is embarked on has room for one passenger only and with no pilot to steer him he must take the wheel himself ... self-destruction is seeking him out, drawing him to it like a magnet, and he lacks the strength of the vertigo sufferer to draw back ... the time for weeping is past.

In some cases, though, the survivor's perspective on the matter will be different. Susan questioned whether the suicidal person's choice of death really is inevitable or whether, at some earlier point, the person could have made an alternative choice. 'You do have some control at the beginning', she says, 'before you slip totally into depression', but, she admits, echoing the title of Eric's article 'there is a point where they almost as it were fall in love with death.'

Bereaved people will often return in their minds again and again to the events leading up to the death 'as if, by so doing, they could undo or alter the events that had occurred' (Parkes 1986: 93). For the survivors of suicide this may become part of a continuing, sometimes unending, search for understanding why the suicide occurred, a search which is explored in the next chapter.

Chapter six

Why did it happen? The search for understanding

It's a riddle that goes round and round and round in your mind and drives you absolutely crazy for years and years and suddenly you think – I'm tormenting myself. I shall just never know the exact and precise reason. (Pam)

The search for meaning

When someone dies, it is not uncommon for the bereaved to question why the person died, to try and reach some understanding of the meaning of the event. According to Parkes, the process of grieving involves:

> the need to 'make sense' of what has happened, to explain it, to classify it along with other comparable events, to make it fit into one's expectations of the world ... trying out new solutions, searching for clues to explain 'why did it happen to me' and repeatedly, monotonously, remembering the sequence of events leading up to the death ... these are what make up the process of grief work. (1986: 94)

When the death was suicide, the search for an explanation may be even more necessary. As Suzy, a survivor of her father's suicide, commented:

> I'm sure if someone commits suicide, it's not at all like they died of a heart attack or a stroke ... it isn't straightforward; there's an awful lot of things to be sorted out, about why they did it, what was wrong.

In largely secular Western societies there are comparatively few people today who would claim that death is always 'God's will'; nevertheless, we still tend to cling to a belief that says death is beyond the control of human beings. But that sort of explanation is not readily available to survivors of suicide who are faced with trying to understand a self-inflicted and possibly self-chosen death. Stengel (1973) has suggested that people intending to take their own lives have less need to make sense of death than those who will be bereaved as a result. This is one of the legacies which the victim bequeaths to the survivor.

The survivor may be left with many different questions. When Alan died, Carol remembers asking herself:

Why did it have to happen? Why do I have to go through this?
Why did I have to lose my son who was such a good quiet boy?
Why does [her other son] have to be an only child now?

The list of questions can be endless. Why do people commit suicide? Why did *my* relative commit suicide? Did they really mean to do it? What sort of person were they? Did I really know them? Why did this happen to me? Where did I go wrong? Why did this happen to *my* family? Why am I having to suffer so much? Am I the only one who feels this way? The survivor is both trying to understand the meaning of suicide in general terms, but also seeking to understand why this particular person, someone who was close to them, apparently chose to die (Calhoun *et al.* 1982).

However, although searching of this kind is a common experience among survivors, it would be wrong to assume that every survivor will necessarily get caught up in it. According to Ann, neither she nor the rest of her family ever felt they needed to question why Giles committed suicide

because it seemed to us to be totally logical, exactly
characteristic of him, that if he suddenly felt that he had had
enough, he would [commit suicide]. I never consciously thought
before it happened that he would, but when it happened, it
seemed not unexpected.

The nature of the search

For some survivors the search can be unending; they find it hard to stop asking themselves why. Eighteen months after her son's death,

Heather still worries that she has not found the answers:

> I'll never know. I've accepted I'll never know, but it does seem
> important that I don't know. I *should* know. Why don't I know?
> I'd like to know why. I don't know why I want to know. It
> doesn't change anything.

Particularly in the early stages of the bereavement, searching can become an obsession which dominates the survivor's waking life. Nine months after her son's death Maureen asks herself why, 'every day of the week, all the time'. Cain's description – of the 'driven endless repetitions and reconstructions of different versions of the events preceding the suicide and a groping quest for the "meaning" of the suicide' (1972: 14) – conveys something of the obsessional nature of the search. The answers to this quest, he adds, will often be painful:

> For too many this floundering search to construct a meaning, an
> interpretation of suicide, of *the* suicide, provides too few
> answers not coloured with guilt, with perceived responsibility,
> with despair beyond redefinition or reparation. (1972: 14)

There are probably few people who, having survived the suicide of someone close to them, have not, at some point, felt guilty in the way Cain describes, and who have not felt themselves to be, in some measure at least, responsible for the death.

Sometimes, though, if that guilt becomes unbearable, the survivor may try and deal with it by seeking a reason for the death which will remove any blame from the survivor. In Hauser's words, this 'relentless pursuit of the why ... represents the hope of finding that which will assuage the guilt' (1987: 64).

In some cases survivors will become involved in a lengthy search for evidence of an 'illness' or syndrome which affected the victim, for something which can provide them with the definitive answer as to why the suicide occurred. Searching for an answer has not actually stopped Carol feeling guilty about her son's death but she is determined to try and find out why young people like him commit suicide. Recently she has been collating and analysing information from questionnaires sent to other parent survivors, in which she asked them about the personality, behaviour, and circumstances of the victims. She hopes that, as a result of this exercise, some common factors might emerge which could aid research into suicide prevention.

Since her son's death, Miriam too has been busy searching for the answer to why he committed suicide. Although she had already realised there was something wrong with Ben as a small child, she believes she may now be closer to finding the answer – a relatively unknown psychiatric syndrome. Since Ben's death she has read everything she can find on this syndrome and corresponded with relevant experts. Looking back, though, she wonders whether, in the early stages, this search led her to more or less denying Ben's death:

> The immediate aftermath of his death was a making sense of his life ... and it was almost as if I sort of deferred the recognition that he'd gone for good because I'd made what seemed like a miraculous discovery of something which had been perplexing me since he'd been born ... it was as if I felt that when I had mastered the subject I could then apply it and perhaps set myself the task of making his life tolerable; and in this way, you know, this sort of magical sense of things fitting together, I've kind of postponed in a way the recognition that there were going to be no second chances.

It is by no means uncommon for survivors to search the literature, hoping to find an explanation of the suicide; survivors will often read anything they can lay their hands on, hoping it will help them make sense of the event (Lukas and Seiden 1987). For Carole, the search began after Jon had attempted suicide:

> I went into the newsagents ... staring out from the front of *New Musical Express* newspaper were the words 'Youth suicide'. For the first time the words had a sort of meaning for me. How many times in the future was I to actively seek out that word in the indexes of many books. The answer to the riddle of my son's death was to be found in one of them, I felt sure.... The need to read about suicide became my priority. I scoured libraries and bookshops, hoping to find the key to Jon's death.

Searching for information in books may not only help survivors make sense of the death, it can also lessen their sense of isolation. A survivor may feel as though they are the only person who has ever been through this experience. Jennifer remembers how, in the weeks following her brother's suicide, she would come home from the library day after day with a pile of books:

> I read anything on death, dying, and suicide. I was almost
> obsessional about it. I so wanted to read about other people
> who had lost someone by suicide, what their feelings were, to
> reassure myself that I was not losing my mind.

In most cases, survivors have few opportunities for meeting with
each other and comparing their experiences and feelings, but those
who are able to do so often find it a very helpful experience (see
Chapter 12). Talking even to close friends about the suicide is often
difficult and, when the survivor does find someone who is prepared
to listen to them, they may still feel that the other person cannot
really understand the unique nature of their loss (see Chapter 11).

You cannot ask the victim why

According to Alvarez, 'the real motives which impel a man to take
his own life ... belong to the internal world, devious, contradictory,
labyrinthine, and mostly out of sight' (1974: 13). Somewhat in contrast, though, Lake suggests that the act of suicide involves 'making
a statement about one's life ... a dramatic public statement' (1984: 28,
123). After the event, survivors are left with the task of trying to in-
terpret what was behind that statement. Like Suzy, they may have
reached certain conclusions but even so, she admits:

> I've offered one explanation ... my father didn't want to go
> through his depression again ... but that's not a total
> explanation ... you will never be able to talk to them about what
> happened, you will never be able to ask them why they did it,
> you will never be able to discuss it with them ... it's the complete
> finality of it and I think that is the most difficult thing.

The survivor cannot ask the victim for an explanation, but this may
not prevent the survivor trying to find out what was going through
the victim's mind in the minutes and hours before their death. The
survivor may, Staudacher suggests, 'try and mirror what [the] loved
one was doing or feeling' (1988: 178).

David could recount in some detail the events of the day Paul
died, but after telling his story, the picture remained incomplete. He
was still unable to get inside Paul's mind. What was Paul thinking
and feeling that day, he wondered? How could he have been calmly
watching a video only two hours before he shot himself? What had

happened to him in that last half-hour when he was alone in the house? Did he have a complete brainstorm? What *was* going on?

Some survivors found it had helped at least to unearth more about the actual circumstances surrounding the death; it enabled them to piece some of the story together, even if some of the pieces were still missing. Jane's brother was living abroad when he committed suicide, but when his wife came back to England, Jane remembers how they talked at length: 'and I just couldn't get enough of hearing about the circumstances ... and the more she talked the more plain it became. And I will never know completely – but I feel I do know.'

What sort of person was the victim?

Some of the survivors I met were hoping that this book would offer a definitive explanation of why people commit suicide. In fact there already is a substantial literature on suicide causation; as Alvarez somewhat cynically comments: 'As a research subject, suicide has, as they say, come big' (1974: 100). But whereas researchers will be taking an objective look at the suicidal person, the survivor's quest is of a more personal kind.

When someone commits suicide, survivors can be left feeling unsure as to whether they ever really knew the person. Perhaps they had always thought they understood them well enough; now they may feel less sure. They may wonder whether there were things about the person and their life of which they were unaware; sometimes that will turn out to have been the case. More often, though, it will seem as though the person was acting completely out of character, leading survivors to conclude that when the suicide occurred 'they were not themselves'. Sometimes, though, survivors will casts doubts on whether the death really was self-inflicted. In Pauline's case, although the verdict on her son's death was suicide, the rest of her family are all convinced, she says, that Michael would never have taken his own life, and Pauline herself seemed unsure.

The phrase 'while the balance of mind was disturbed' no longer has any legal significance, but is still appended to some verdicts of suicide. The results of research by Barraclough and Shepherd (1976) suggest that its use can sometimes make acceptance of the suicide easier because survivors see it as an accurate assessment of the situation. The implication that the person committed suicide while their mind was not 'balanced' may strengthen the survivor's belief that the person was acting out of character at the time.

Whatever conclusions survivors reach about what triggered the actual suicide, they may also need to try and understand the rest of the survivor's life and how that may have contributed to the death. In conversation with survivors, two words used to describe the victim seemed to crop up frequently – 'perfectionism' and 'loss'. Neither can provide the complete answer, and they cannot be regarded as definitive causes of suicide, but because they were mentioned so often, they may have some relevance as possible contributory factors.

The previous chapter (p. 64) mentioned how the victim may be the kind of person who constantly strives for perfection, a point echoed by many survivors when trying to describe the victim's personality:

> Susie was impossible about the idea of failure ... [she had] a sort of refined perfectionism about things ... she was an ultimate perfectionist. (Peter)

> Lesley was a perfectionist and I think perhaps that was part of the problem, you know. She always liked things just so. (Joan)

> From the start Patricia was a perfectionist. She had to have As in everything. (Mark)

But as Staudacher points out, there are pitfalls for the perfectionist:

> Many suicidal people have very high expectations for themselves which makes perfectionism even more mandatory than it might be for the average person. The suicidal individual often makes unrealistic demands on himself or herself. The person often wants more than actually exists or is possible to obtain. (1988: 178)

People often set themselves goals, and it is not a particularly abnormal thing to do: they may aim to be a better worker, or a more successful student, or a more considerate spouse, but these are usually seen as ideals, as desirable rather than imminently achievable goals. With suicide victims, though, a different set of rules seems to operate; it is as though they are setting themselves up for failure, for what Keir describes as 'the frustration of desires' (1986: 57).

> She had this sort of desire to do something that everybody else

knew she wouldn't be able to do. It was as though she lived in this strange dream world of desperately wanting to be something she could never be and all she ever did was face herself with failure. (Pat)

Frances was a perfectionist who could never reach the perfection that she tried to achieve. (Pam)

Significant losses of various kinds were a feature of some victims' lives, leading the survivors to question whether the impact of these losses had contributed in some way to the suicide. Different people can react very differently to the same kind of loss, and research into the impact of losses sustained in childhood has frequently produced contradictory results (Bowlby 1985). Nevertheless, many of the survivors felt that losses which the victims had faced as children or young adults had possibly contributed to their deaths. Of the seventeen young people who had taken their own lives, seven had lost a parent through death or divorce, and a further two had experienced the death of a close friend shortly before the suicide occurred. As Caroline remarked, not long before her death: 'Everyone I love dies.'

Other types of loss may contribute to the victim's decision to commit suicide. Wendy's father, for example, took his own life when terminal cancer meant he no longer enjoyed good health or a pain-free existence. Anticipation of loss may also affect some people; after her husband's suicide, Marie wondered whether Oliver had taken his life because he was possibly losing his sight.

Suicide notes

Almost half the survivors who were interviewed had been left some kind of note or letter by the victim, an unusually high proportion compared with the results of various studies carried out in the UK and elsewhere. Stengel (1973) quotes a figure of 15 per cent, while Shneidman (1982) suggests that between 15 and 30 per cent of victims will leave a note. Conley (1987) cites evidence from two studies in which there were notes in about a quarter of reported cases of suicide. Attempts have been made to discover whether those who write notes differ in some way from those who do not, but according to Shneidman (1982), there are no particular features which mark out the note-writers from other victims.

For some survivors, the note will assume great importance in their attempts to understand the suicide. Irene has read and re-read Bill's note, hoping each time that it will yield fresh evidence: 'I've studied it so many times, so many hours, looking for a clue – even [reading] between the names, just anything', but, she admits, 'I can't find any peace in it'. Notes do not always provide the hoped-for answers. Pat and Robert felt that, if anything, Caroline's letter to them made her death even more of a mystery. Although Robert read it constantly for the first two weeks, they have since thrown it away.

Perhaps notes do not provide all the answers because, as Keir suggests, 'the victim tells us only what he wants us to know' (1986: 17), a point echoed by Staudacher who warns survivors against assuming that the note will give them the definitive answer:

> It is important to put the note in perspective. That is, it is one item which reflects your loved's one's thinking along a whole continuum of thought. The note is not necessarily representational of the same mind which conceived the suicide and carried it out. The note only represents your loved one's state of mind when the note was written. It is a mistake to try to extract the essence of the tragedy from this one piece of communication, however lucid it proves to be. (1988: 179)

Nevertheless, even if notes do not yield any answers, they are messages to those left behind. Various attempts have been made to analyse suicide notes and categorise those messages. Osterweis and colleagues (1984) suggest that there are two types of notes: those which are overtly hostile, and those which aim to relieve the survivor of any responsibility for the event. Staudacher (1988) and Keir (1986) suggest that notes may also include statements about: the victim's low self-esteem and sense of failure; the person's inability to continue living; and messages of farewell. According to Shneidman, who has made extensive studies of suicide notes, they dispel the myth that suicidal acts are 'uniformly motivated by a single formula ... they are complicated psychological events' (1982: 543–4).

In one study, quoted by Keir (1986), over half the notes were found to include statements to the effect that the victim felt unable to go on; life was perceived as intolerable. Survivors are often left with these messages about the victim's sense of utter hopelessness. Frances's note is typical: 'Much as I love the world', she wrote, '... I can no longer live with myself.' Any glimmer of hope that the victim might once have had has finally disappeared and suicide is the only possible solution; as Caroline wrote: 'I'm a total failure. I keep thinking things are going to get better, but it just gets worse.'

Messages telling the survivors not to blame themselves for what has happened are a common feature of suicide notes (Osterweis *et al.* 1984). Jon wrote that 'too much had gone too wrong' but he wanted his parents to know they were not to blame for this. Whatever the survivor's own feelings of guilt or responsibility, it can help when the victim at least is saying 'I don't blame you'. Brian found this to be the case when his wife left letters which he described as being 'very kind'.

Graham and Christine were in the middle of an argument when Christine told her husband to leave the house. Graham drove off, and that was the last time Christine saw him alive. They had both been under considerable stress for some time (see p. 58), but when Christine realised what had happened, she blamed herself because she had told him to go. In his note, though, Graham made it plain that she was not to feel responsible for his death, a message she has been able to accept. It confirmed what she had begun to realise anyway: it had not been a spur-of-the-moment decision; Graham had almost certainly been thinking of committing suicide for some time.

However, not all suicide notes are intended to make the survivors feel better; some are clearly intended to hurt those left behind by blaming them in some way for the suicide (Staudacher 1988). Jan, who was thirteen and away at boarding-school when her father shot himself, remembers reading his farewell message a few days later: 'he'd left a very long letter to the three of us girls ... saying that we'd let him down, that we were bad, awful daughters, that we'd all gone away and left him and a lot of very blaming stuff'. In the twenty-five years since his death, Jan has struggled to accept that despite what he wrote, the responsibility for her father's death does not lie with her – it belongs to him.

Melanie's husband left two farewell letters, and although she actually never read them, she was told by her father that one was full of anger towards her, and the other was only slightly less hostile. Although she now regrets the fact that her father destroyed the letters, if she had read them at the time of Ian's death, she knows they would only have reinforced the guilt she felt anyway; as she admits, she felt that by leaving him and asking for a legal separation, she 'as good as killed him'. Nearly four years later, though, she can see things in a somewhat different light:

Now I can see that it was his responsibility and he had a lot more options than killing himself. I don't believe Ian was that depressed. I think he made a decision and it was all anger to get at me ... I found a tape in the house ... and it was addressed to [their daughter] saying how he hoped one day she would forgive me for what I'd done, and he didn't want this to blight her life.

If the survivor suspects (or has actually been told) that the note expresses angry feelings, deciding whether to read it can be difficult. When Nick's mother died she left behind detailed notes about how she felt, but at the time of her suicide he didn't read them; he only knew that they apparently said 'some nasty things'. Five years later he is still undecided as to whether he will read them at some future point.

When a suicide happens unexpectedly, and the survivor has not even seen the body, the death can seem very unreal; but having a note which makes it clear that the victim intended to die can help survivors accept the reality of the death. Clare's suicide was one of those deaths which took everyone by surprise. Nancy and her husband were abroad when she died and they never saw her body afterwards. It must all have seemed very unreal. Although it could not have been easy to read Clare's statement that she had made a complete mess of her life, Nancy is still glad they were left a note. She feels that otherwise she would never have been absolutely certain that it was suicide; she would always have wondered whether someone had in fact murdered Clare by pushing her on to the railway line.

Survivors can find it hard sometimes when the victim leaves them no personal farewell. Although Susan has never doubted that her husband's death was suicide, she still feels hurt that Richard left no note for her or their son, even though he did leave a note (not addressed to anyone in particular) saying, among other things, that 'Susan has been the support of my life'.

Since suicide victims rarely give other people the chance to say goodbye, the note may be important because it represents their only farewell. Although Maureen does not believe that Paul's note gives any answers as to why he committed suicide, she feels that if he had died without leaving the note, it would have made things even worse. This is borne out by the behaviour of some survivors who described how they desperately searched the house, unable to believe that the person could have died without leaving any sort of farewell communication.

Although the suicide note is usually a personal communication, at the time of the death it has to be handed over to the coroner's officer as evidence which may help the coroner reach a verdict. After the inquest, though, it has been known for coroners to withhold the note permanently on the basis that it might cause the relatives pain (Barraclough and Shepherd 1976). Legally, however, the note belongs to the person to whom it was addressed.

When the police discovered her husband Eric's body, they informed Isabel that a note addressed to her and the three children had also been found. According to the policeman who gave her this news, the note said something to the effect that he just could not go on any longer; but, the policeman added, he could not remember what the rest of the note said. She never had the chance to read the note herself because the police subsequently told her they had lost it. As a result, she feels she has been deprived of Eric's last message to her and fifteen years later she still feels frustrated and angry at times because she can only speculate as to what the rest of the note said and whether the note really was lost.

It can be hard enough for survivors to accept that a personal letter addressed to them will be handled and read by complete strangers, but it might be somewhat easier if people at least knew what their rights were in this situation; most do not. In Pat and Robert's case, although they had found and read Caroline's note before it had to be handed over, when the letter was handed back to them, they were told this was not the usual procedure, information which was factually inaccurate. Too often, it is left to relatives to ask for the note to be returned, rather than this being a routine procedure once the inquest has been completed. Meanwhile, pending the inquest, relatives could at least be given photocopies of the original documents (Conley 1987).

Doubts about the victim's intentions

Of the fifty survivors I talked with, most had no doubts that the victim had intended to commit suicide, even in those instances where the coroner had passed a verdict of accidental death or where there had been an 'open' verdict (see pp. 89–90). Since they had volunteered to talk about their experiences as survivors of suicide this was not entirely unexpected. But there were still occasional instances where survivors seemed less sure. After Julie was found dead, the verdict was accidental death, and Phyllis referred to her daughter's death as an 'accidental suicide':

> I thought that she contemplated suicide; in fact I mean really it wasn't ... well, she did take her own life, but it was an accidental suicide ... in the back of my mind I can see the reason but in another way I know for certain that it wasn't deliberate because she didn't leave a note.... I don't think [people who commit suicide] know what they're doing.

Even for someone like Suzy, who talks about her father's death as suicide, there can still be doubts about what happened at the end; she still sometimes wonders whether he really intended to take his own life on the night he died:

> Someone once said to me that after he'd been sick on the landing he might have felt that perhaps ... he wasn't going to die after all and I have found that awfully hard to cope with, that he might perhaps have died when he didn't really mean to after all; and that gave me an awful shock ... I've got absolutely no way of proving that.

Survivors, as she says, have absolutely no way of proving conclusively what the victim's intentions were. They can only make guesses. Do people really intend to take their own lives? Are they perhaps hoping to be rescued in time? Do they see it as a gamble with death? Or, as Phyllis suggested, is it the case that people committing suicide simply do not know what they are doing?

Wisdom with hindsight

As the following comments illustrate, for many survivors, going back over the events leading up to the suicide is often about the 'if onlys', a case of 'if only I knew then what I now know':

> What suicide does is to curiously give you sight, but it is hindsight. (Mark)

> It's very easy I think to look back retrospectively and understand things that you don't actually understand at the time. (Peter)

> It was completely out of the blue, but since [then] we've had so

many clues. I mean, hindsight has told us we had a lot of
warning but [suicide] never came into our thoughts. (Nancy)

Apart from overt threats of suicide there are other warning signs,
unspoken clues that a person may give when they are intending to
commit suicide (Shneidman 1982; Keir 1986). Many survivors, however, unaware of these warning signs, only understand the significance of certain behaviours after the event. This is the wisdom survivors achieve with hindsight; survivors tend to become experts on
suicide when it is too late.

A common warning sign is when someone who has been very depressed or very disturbed appears to be in a calmer and more positive
frame of mind (Keir 1986). Sudden upswings in mood can be decept-
ive. Miriam's son had given plenty of explicit warnings of his intention to commit suicide (see p. 54), but when, shortly before his death,
he seemed very composed, she thought that things were looking up.
Only now does she realise that he was, as she says, 'laying false trails'.

Some victims will destroy their personal possessions or give
things away to other people shortly before their death. It was only
after Alan died that Carol discovered he had destroyed all his certi-
ficates, together with his college notes, and all the photographs he
had taken. That was not the only clue: early in December he told his
mother not to buy him any Christmas presents – he died ten days
before Christmas. Liz, who was living abroad at the time of her
brother's suicide, found out subsequently that there had been at least
two classic warning signs: not only had Tony stopped wearing his
jewellery, but shortly before he disappeared, everyone had noticed
how much more cheerful he seemed to be.

Living without all the answers

However many clues they may find, and however much of the story
they piece together, ultimately survivors will invariably have to live
with something which they can only understand in part. One stressful
event may be the trigger (Keir 1986), the factor which tips the balance, but it will seldom be the sole reason why someone commits
suicide.

According to some survivors, the victims had often been faced
with a whole series of problems and setbacks; it seemed as though
they had reached a point when 'enough was enough': bereavements,

the ending of relationships, exam failures, physical ill-health, and re-
dundancy or problems at work were common events in their lives,
but despite this, many survivors, like John, were still left without the
full story:

> It would be much easier to be able to say to myself that this is
> exactly what happened. But even if somebody told me that, I
> couldn't accept it, because I know from my own experience that
> life is far too complicated. There are no simple answers.

For others like Christine it is a matter of finding answers that they
can live with: 'I still think about it', she admits, 'but I don't really ask
why. I mean I'm fairly satisfied that I know why he did it. I may not
be right, but it seems right to me.'

This need to search for clues, to try and understand what led the
person to commit suicide, is one of the most difficult legacies which
the survivor will inherit. In the end they may, like John, decide there
is no single answer, or like Christine, they may find answers they can
live with. Whichever of these paths they choose to go down, what
does seem important is that survivors are able at some point to give
up what can otherwise become 'a frustrating, fruitless quest' (Lukas
and Seiden 1987: 93).

Chapter seven

The inquest

I just wanted to be part of it. I didn't want it to be something done by strangers – the last thing that would happen to Patricia, where, in a sense, there was some sort of decision to be made. There were certain possibilities, certain choices to be made, and I suppose I just wanted to have something to do with it. I just wanted to say my bit. (Francesca)

In England and Wales, all unnatural deaths are subject to legal investigation, including those where suicide is suspected (Office of Health Economics 1981). Enquiries begin immediately after the death has been discovered, when the police will take statements from relevant people such as members of the victim's immediate family, the person who discovered the body, and any other witnesses; other evidence will include farewell notes or letters, and the pathologist's post-mortem report. The coroner's officer (see below), who acts as the coroner's agent, is responsible for ensuring that the necessary evidence is available to the coroner before the main inquest takes place.

In accordance with the Coroners Rules (HMSO 1984), the inquest must ascertain the identity of the deceased and how, when, and where the person died. It will usually be opened formally by the coroner within a day or two of the death, and this is normally a brief hearing; formal identification of the person is made, after which the body can be released for burial or cremation. The inquest is then adjourned. In the ensuing weeks, the gathering of evidence will continue, and the full inquest will take place at a later date when statements are read out in court, witnesses may be cross-examined, and the coroner's verdict will be given.

Does the inquest represent a medical or a legal investigation?

Barraclough and Shepherd, who carried out research into the inquest system in the 1970s, have described it as 'a formal court of inquiry, conducted in public' (1976: 110), the word 'court' implying that this is a judicial exercise. They suggested, however, that under the current system, the inquest is no more than 'a survival of a medieval trial for self-murder which results in a verdict' (1978: 795).

The fact that coroners can be either medically or legally qualified is a reflection of this prevailing confusion – though, in practice, the majority of coroners currently hold a legal qualification (and a minority are both medically and legally qualified). The local authorities are responsible for the appointment of coroners and for meeting the cost of running the courts; the coroner's officers who staff the courts are former members of the police force, although a government-sponsored committee of inquiry proposed that they could be replaced by specially trained civilians (HMSO 1971); the whole process still has a strongly legal flavour, with the paraphernalia of statements, evidence, summonsing and cross-examination of witnesses, verdicts, and, in certain cases, the presence of a jury. It is hardly surprising that to some survivors the inquest feels like a trial where both they and the person who died are under judgment.

For most bereaved people, the funeral is the sole occasion when their otherwise private grief is made more public, but for survivors of suicide, the inquest necessitates further public exposure. Not only are very personal aspects of the victim's life likely to be investigated and discussed in court, but their own actions, and the nature of their relationship with the dead person can also be called to account. Maureen remembers how shocked she felt at her son's inquest when she had to answer questions such as 'did you row?' For Frank, the very worst part of the whole experience was this contact with 'officialdom', at the very time when he was struggling with his worst feelings of grief.

The circumstances surrounding the suicide are not only open to scrutiny by public officials such as the police; the general public, including representatives of the Press (see pp. 90–93), are also permitted to attend the inquest – although until 1953, coroners could exercise discretion as to whether or not to admit the public (Barraclough and Shepherd 1978).

Waiting for the inquest

It is not uncommon for the full inquest to be held up to two months after the death has occurred. The coroner's officer will usually need several weeks to obtain all the relevant evidence and ensure that the relevant witnesses are able to attend on the day. Sometimes, though, survivors may have to wait even longer. Several people had waited at least three months, and Frank and Ursula, who had originally been told they could expect to wait about two months, in the end had to wait six months for Josie's inquest. Ursula knew that though the inquest would be an important event, it would also be a stressful occasion, and she found the long wait very distressing: 'You felt that you were in limbo. You knew this had got to happen and you'd got to steel yourself to deal with it.' Faced with this situation, survivors may feel that their grieving somehow has to be suspended until the inquest is over.

The sheer anticipation of the inquest can leave survivors feeling extremely apprehensive, particularly if they have been called as witnesses; postponement only adds to the stress, particularly when the survivor is only told about the delay at short notice. In Christine's case, the date of her husband's inquest was changed several times, and each time, having steeled herself to go to court, she was only phoned with news of the cancellation the evening before.

There were a number of reasons why these postponements occurred; often it was because evidence such as a psychiatric report had not been prepared in time or there were problems with assembling the witnesses on a particular date. However, survivors were not always kept informed of the reasons for the delay, and this could create additional pressures in an already stressful situation, as Heather found when they ended up waiting a week for the inquest into her son's death to be opened:

> He died in the early hours of Wednesday and it must have been all over the weekend that we didn't know what was happening. We rang the police and they didn't know. We rang the coroner and he didn't know. Nobody seemed to know what was going on.... It was an extra pressure on us because I kept worrying about what else they might have found [at the post-mortem]. In fact they found nothing. He hadn't even been drinking.

Because both the police and the coroner's officer are involved, families are not always sure who is responsible for liaising with them. Clearer systems of communication are needed so that relatives are kept properly informed about what is happening (see Chapter 15).

The survivors' reactions to the inquest

For the vast majority of survivors, this is likely to be their first experience of attending a coroner's court; it may be the first time they have even been inside a court building. As a result, they may have little idea of how the inquest will be conducted, what sort of evidence they are likely to hear or see, or what will be expected of them if they have been called as witnesses. At a time when they are likely to be under considerable stress, survivors will not always feel that they can ask about these things. Audrey Walsh, whose experiences were described in a newspaper article on teenage suicide, knows that she would have found her daughter's inquest far less upsetting if she had been given some idea of what to expect. As it was, she found the medical evidence relating to Jill's injuries so horrific that she had to leave the court (Lyall 1987). Liz's experience was not dissimilar; unaware of what might be said about the post-mortem on her brother, she sat in court and choked when she heard details about the state of his body – which had only been discovered seven weeks after his death. No one had warned her what to expect.

In fact, relatives can choose to leave the courtroom if they know that some part of the evidence is likely to cause them distress. When one of Eileen's twin daughters committed suicide on a railway line, it was suggested that she might prefer to remain outside the courtroom while evidence about Sheila's body was being read out. Carol, on the other hand, had no idea whether or not she and her son had to remain in court:

> I was terrified ... very hyped up about it ... terrified about
> whether or not they would be showing [her son] photographs
> which I didn't want him to see.... I wish somebody had told me
> that you didn't have to see the photographs at the inquest and
> things like that.

It is a relatively simple matter for the coroner's officer to explain to survivors attending the inquest what is likely to happen in court. Brian found this very helpful, partly because he has some hearing difficulties, but also because the preliminary inquest and the full inquest were heard in two different places and the latter was a jury inquest. Being able to look round the courtrooms beforehand and find out what was going to happen made both events less stressful for him than they might otherwise have been.

However, despite the fact that the inquest can be distressing and difficult, survivors may also find it a positive and important event. They may see it as an opportunity to put forward their own version of events or, by hearing other people's evidence, they may hope to find out more about what actually happened at the time of the suicide. Jennifer went to her brother's inquest knowing very little about the circumstances of Tim's death. Her only sources of information had been reports in the local Press and on local radio; she hoped that the evidence would tell her more about the actual circumstances of Tim's death. As Hauser (1987) points out, obtaining accurate information – for example, about the actual circumstances of the death – can be an important means of making the whole event feel more real. For survivors who have not seen the body, this can be particularly important.

As with viewing the body (see pp. 46–50), the actual inquest proceedings can turn out to be less daunting than the survivor's fantasies, as Nancy discovered when she attended her daughter's inquest: 'I got the idea that it was going to be something terrible, and in some ways it was just like being in an office.... It wasn't so terrible as I'd been led to imagine.' Unlike most other courts in England and Wales, coroner's courts vary considerably in the way they conduct their business (Barraclough and Shepherd 1976). Individual coroners have considerable discretion in deciding how the court will operate – for example, whether or not they use a witness-box, and whether witnesses sit or stand, or how much of the post-mortem report is read out. On the whole, though, the proceedings are more informal than in other courts of law (Atkinson 1978).

However, although proceedings are generally conducted in a less rigid manner, the inquest is a public inquiry with the degree of formality that that implies. Some people may find this somewhat formal, unemotional approach less upsetting but, in other cases, survivors can feel that the inquest is too impersonal and that it has little or no relevance to their personal tragedy. To Lois, her son's inquest seemed pointless; she felt that it had little to do with Simon, and she only attended because she had been summonsed to appear as a witness:

> The inquest was horrendous ... to have it all read out ... the deadpan way they read these things ... you know it's your son they're talking about; they're talking about a body [but] it isn't just a body, it's a person.... I think for me the inquest was the worst ordeal of the whole lot.

Survivors may arrive at the inquest in a bruised and highly vulnerable state, so the coroner's general bearing and attitude towards them can be very important. Kindness and a compassionate manner are appreciated, and survivors who felt the coroner treated them otherwise tended not to forget that (Barraclough and Shepherd 1976). Fifteen years after her husband's death, Susan still has vivid memories of the coroner's behaviour at Richard's inquest:

> Each time the coroner just gabbled and I was asked to identify the handwriting of this note he'd left in his pocket ... and his age and who he was, and so on. But that's all, and the whole thing was over in about three minutes. I couldn't decide whether he was doing that because he was totally uninterested or because he was trying to spare me. I can actually remember standing and wondering why the coroner was behaving in such an offhand manner.

The evidence

As Francesca said at the beginning of this chapter, the inquest was concerned with her daughter, and she very much wanted to be part of the proceedings. Like Francesca, Janice felt that when such very personal matters were at stake, they should not be dealt with solely by strangers. In her case, she also wanted to find out more about the circumstances of the death which had happened at some distance from where she lived (see p. 41):

> I felt it was really important that either I was there or my sister ... because they would be discussing *my* mother, and discussing what they'd found in *her* stomach and I felt that it would be wrong ... not to be there. I wanted to see the policeman [who found the body] and hear his story.

Not all survivors will want to hear these sort of details about the suicide, especially when the death was violent and the body was severely mutilated. For some survivors, though, hearing this evidence gave them the chance to piece together more of the story. For Brian, who never saw his wife's remains after she died on a railway line, hearing about the last few moments of her life from the train driver meant being able 'to complete the bit I didn't know'.

For some survivors, the inquest is seen as an opportunity publicly to state their version of events, to tell the story as *they* see it. However, they may not always be given the chance to do so, as John discovered. His wife's inquest was scheduled as the last of four cases that day and when their turn came it was already past the time when the court normally adjourned. However, the coroner said he would proceed and John was eventually called as a witness, but his attempts to talk about Averil's problems, to explain about how she had gone downhill after her son's life sentence for murder, were all forestalled. The coroner did not seem to think that any of it was relevant, and appeared just to want to finish the inquest as quickly as possible. As a result, John felt the whole thing was very incomplete.

> I wondered why the devil we'd gone there. And I felt offended, bruised inside.... All he was concerned about was did she use the word 'suicide' ... and I was waiting to get up and tell him about Averil, about what had happened and about how she felt ... even to tell him I'd failed. I was ready to say all this and when my turn came – no ... and I came out feeling that the inquest wasn't over.

John went to the inquest wanting to tell the coroner how he felt responsible for Averil's death; he wanted to make a statement about his guilt. But by no means everyone will want to do this, and survivors can find it upsetting if, intentionally or otherwise, they are made to feel that they are on trial. Jean was on holiday when her daughter committed suicide. It was a much-needed break (see p. 39), but she still found it hard when the coroner asked when she had last seen Anna: 'and I had to say two weeks, and I felt dreadful. I thought, what kind of a mother am I?'

Heather had not actually been called as a witness at her son's inquest, and was waiting outside the court when the coroner decided he wanted to question her about a remark Alastair had made (see p. 55), and which was mentioned in her husband's evidence. It was a remark which, at the time, she had not understood as a suicide threat. Indeed, she had no idea at all that her son was even feeling suicidal. She remembers being called in completely unexpectedly, and feeling so petrified she could hardly stand up. Although she explained that she had not understood the significance of the remark, the coroner's comment that he found that 'a little strange' made her feel as though she was on trial for Alastair's death.

Where survivors feel that other people were in some way to blame for the suicide, the inquest may be seen as an opportunity to set the record straight. They may hope that those they feel were responsible will be publicly identified, and perhaps even reprimanded. If, for example, the person had been receiving psychiatric treatment, survivors may feel that the mental health services failed them, and that they should be prepared to accept a measure of responsibility for the suicide. When her sister committed suicide, Bridget felt that although Catherine's psychiatrist could not be held directly responsible for what happened, he had, at the very least, been negligent in not arranging for her readmission to hospital when it was obvious to everyone around her that she was in a highly vulnerable state. The situation had been somewhat complicated by the fact that staff at the hospital in question were taking industrial action at the time. When it came to the inquest, though, only the industrial action was mentioned and nothing was said about the psychiatrist's role. As a result, it was left to Bridget and one of her brothers to pursue the matter directly with the health authority.

There may be other reasons why the inquest can become somewhat adversarial. In some cases, survivors felt that unreasonable levels of stress at the person's place of work had contributed to the suicide, and they hoped that this would emerge during the course of the inquest. Before her husband's suicide, Christine had warned Graham's employers that problems at work (which, she felt, were not of his making) were placing him under severe stress, but apparently no one had thought it necessary to act on her warning. When it came to the inquest, she was not given the opportunity to raise the matter either. Graham's former employers, having been wrongly informed by the police that Christine was planning to take legal action against them, appeared in court with their solicitors. As in Bridget's case, Christine was left to pursue the matter herself, and as a result, Graham's employers did hold an internal inquiry. Christine felt sufficiently strongly about the issue to want to pursue it herself, but it was an additional strain at an already difficult time.

Having what they consider to be the 'right' verdict matters a great deal to some survivors (see below), but they may be equally concerned that the evidence given at the inquest is accurate and can be fully substantiated – that is, that the true facts are told. In Ursula's case, although she agreed with the verdict of suicide, she was annoyed by the pathologist's report which implied that Josie had been injecting herself with drugs; she believes they could equally well have been marks from injections Josie had been given while in hospital, and the pathologist offered no evidence to substantiate his claim. There were other instances where survivors were angry because the victim had been given a diagnosis or label such as 'schizophrenic' or 'manic depressive' which they considered to be inaccurate. These may seem relatively minor issues, but as Barraclough and Shepherd (1976, 1977) discovered when interviewing a group of survivors some years after the suicide, in some cases these memories of the inquest were still extremely vivid.

The verdict

In cases of apparently self-inflicted death, a number of possible verdicts are available to the coroner including suicide, accidental death, death by misadventure, or an open verdict. For a verdict of suicide to be reached, however, there must be clear evidence that the person intended to take his or her own life, perhaps expressed in a note, perhaps verbally communicated to other people. Probable intent is insufficient, and the presumption will always be against suicide (Chambers 1989).

In a sense, a verdict represents the official pronouncement on the death, and to survivors, what the coroner – a figure in authority – decides about the nature of the death may assume great importance, precisely because it is seen to be an official, authoritative statement. Many people find it hard to challenge authority, so having what the survivor believes to be the correct verdict is also very important. Ursula, for example, was relieved when the verdict on Josie's death was suicide because, as she said, 'any other verdict wouldn't have been right'.

It is frequently assumed that the coroner will try and avoid bringing in a verdict of suicide in order to protect the family from possible stigma (see, for example, Keir 1986; Staudacher 1988). But this assumption may be false says Audrey Walsh, herself a survivor:

Coroners think they are being sensitive to relatives by bringing in an open verdict, but they are doing everyone a disservice. Parents know how their child died, and have to face up to what happened. By avoiding the word 'suicide' coroners are merely increasing the stigma and disguising the size of the problem. (Quoted in Lyall 1987)

However painful the idea of suicide may be, the truth can be preferable to what is seen as a wrong decision. Liz found the open verdict on her brother Tony's death totally unacceptable. As she says: 'I think all the family and friends believed he'd done it himself.' Nevertheless, when, as was her right, she wrote to the coroner asking to have the inquest reopened, he replied: 'I'm very surprised that you even want to ... bring out the fact that your brother perhaps did commit suicide.' (Audrey Walsh is right; coroners certainly can increase the stigma surrounding suicide!) In fact, most survivors are not even aware that they have this right to appeal against the verdict, so it is hardly surprising that few people exercise the right, even though by no means all survivors are satisfied that the verdict was correct (Barraclough and Shepherd 1976).

Like Liz, Christine was also convinced that her husband's death was suicide, and she felt that by choosing suicide, Graham was also wanting to make a public statement. So when the coroner passed an open verdict, she asked if he would change it to one of suicide – which he refused to do, on the grounds that there was insufficient proof of intent. Despite the verdict, she remains convinced that Graham's suicide was a conscious and intentional act.

Not all survivors, though, will question the verdict. Joan is still unsure whether her sister really did intend to take her own life and as a result feels she can accept the verdict of accidental death: 'I don't think you'll ever know. I mean, she never ever suggested it at all ... she'd never said about taking her own life.'

John describes the open verdict on his wife as 'an albatross around my neck', but with no firm evidence that Averil intended to take her own life, that was the only possible verdict. At the time he found that hard because he felt that it laid him open to suspicion. Four years later the verdict remains a problem for John; he finds it hard to mourn her death properly; he has found it virtually impossible to visit her grave, and he feels the verdict has left him with a sense of incompleteness. Unlike a verdict of suicide, an open verdict can leave the survivors unsure as to what sort of death it is they are really mourning.

The role of the Press

While very few members of the public exercise their right to attend inquests, local reporters are frequently present and reporting of suicides in local newspapers is common practice. In fact the story is often covered twice: a brief mention immediately after the suicide, and a longer report after the full inquest. In a small number of cases, there will also be coverage in the national Press.

There has been a long-standing debate on whether the Press should continue to have the right to attend inquests, and the Broderick Committee on Death Certification and Coroners (HMSO 1971) recommended that there should be no restriction on Press reporting of suicide, a view with which others, including Barraclough and Shepherd (1976) who have researched the issue, disagree; their research found that the presence of the Press and the subsequent reporting often caused unnecessary distress to survivors. At present, however, the coroner is only entitled to exclude the Press if issues relating to national security are being discussed (HMSO 1984).

For some survivors, knowing that details of the suicide are there in black and white for everybody in the local community to read is felt to be a major invasion of privacy. When Heather's son committed suicide, his death was reported not only in the local Press but in several national dailies as well, all of which she found very distressing. She felt Alastair's death was something 'very, very private indeed', and the intrusion on her privacy was made worse by finding that reporters from two national tabloid dailies were not only on her own doorstep, but had been approaching her neighbours as well.

Where the suicide is not really talked about within the family, survivors can find it painful to see the death freely discussed in the Press. When Suzy's father committed suicide, she felt that because she believed in Press freedom, she had to accept the reports in the local newspapers. Her mother, on the other hand, had been devastated to read the headline 'Principal Died From Taking Aspirin'. As Suzy said: 'Things weren't discussed in the family, so you certainly don't have it in the newspaper ... [because] the whole of [the city] would see that he actually killed himself.'

Survivors often find it hard to tell other people about the suicide (see Chapter 11), but they may still prefer to have the choice rather than discovering that not only do other people already know, but that they have a version of events gleaned from newspaper reports. As Francesca said after her daughter's suicide: 'I didn't want anyone to know if I had not told them.... I wanted to be responsible for telling people. I didn't want it to be a general statement.'

91

Inaccurate reporting of cases of suicide is not uncommon and can be a particular cause of distress to survivors (Barraclough and Shepherd 1976, 1977; Dunne-Maxim 1987). It can be hard enough to have to read about the suicide in the Press but even seemingly unimportant inaccuracies can add to the distress. Pam and Harry remember how, on the day of the inquest, headlines on the front page of the local newspaper referred to their daughter as 'Nurse Susan', when although that was her first name, everyone had always called her Frances. In Heather's case, it was the local paper getting its facts wrong about where her son's body had been discovered which made her particularly cross. In contrast, though, reports that are factually accurate and non-sensational can make it easier for survivors to cope with the involvement of the Press; Ursula thought they would probably 'twist a few words and totally misrepresent something' and although she had been terrified of reading the newspaper report, she was glad when it turned out to be an accurate description of the inquest proceedings.

Reporting on suicides can vary widely from a brief factual paragraph on an inside page to front page banner headlines, but inquests on younger people and suicides where the death was violent are reported more often, are given more column inches, and have more eye-catching headlines than other suicides (Shepherd and Barraclough 1978). When Bridget's sister committed suicide her death fulfilled both of those criteria; the headline in the local paper was 'Blast girl once took overdose' with a report which Bridget described as being 'completely useless'. Bridget (who is a journalist herself) argues that the paper could have written a much more constructive story about some of the issues surrounding her sister's death (see p. 88 above). Instead, as she recalls, 'they just chose this sort of horrible, sensationalised [reporting]'. What this approach also does, as Peter pointed out, is simplify and trivialise an issue which is far from simple. Several survivors mentioned how they felt that a more considered and informed approach might have helped to educate the public about suicide and suicide prevention, a point also made by Dunne-Maxim (1987).

A considerable amount has been written about whether publicising suicides in a sensational manner encourages other people to follow suit. There does seem to be a measure of agreement among those who have studied this issue that, at the very least, media coverage highlights successful methods of committing suicide and so may act as a spur to people who are already contemplating taking their own lives but may not have found a way of doing so (Shepherd and Barraclough 1978; Office of Health Economics 1981; Lukas and Seiden 1987). Robert believes that this is what happened in his daughter's case. Although he realises other people may not share this view, Robert is convinced that Caroline's suicide was triggered by a newspaper picture of a woman jumping off the cliffs at Beachy Head. (This picture, which was the subject of complaints to the Press Council, is further discussed in Chapter 15.) Whether or not he is right, on the same day that the photograph was published, Caroline jumped to her death from the top of a multi-storey car park.

Despite this, Robert's dealings with the local Press were quite positive. A reporter from their local paper appeared on the doorstep shortly after Caroline's death. The family decided that they would talk to him, and they gave him a photograph of their daughter. Caroline's former nursing colleagues were also interviewed, and the result was a story which not only discussed her death, but talked about how Caroline had been a hard-working nurse and how fond of her the patients had been. As a result, Robert and Pat feel that despite the banner headlines and newspaper placards, the Press coverage was something with which they were able to cope. Stories which include positive comments about the person who died can not only help survivors (Dunne-Maxim 1987), they can also educate readers about suicide victims. As Carol pointed out, if there was more positive coverage maybe 'suicide would not be looked upon as a thing done by baddies'.

Several survivors mentioned that while the publicity was not particularly welcome, it was inevitable because the Press attended inquests, and therefore something they just had to accept. As Marie said: 'It has to be reported, something has to be written up, and I think it's difficult, to put it mildly, to see it there in black and white, but you know that it's happened.' Pam and Harry found the banner headlines about their daughter's suicide not only unexpected but rather hurtful; but at the same time they felt that complaining would not have served any particularly useful purpose; as Harry said: 'it wouldn't have brought her back; it wouldn't have done any good'.

Press reporting may be inevitable – suicide tends to be considered newsworthy – but insensitive approaches to families and inaccurate or sensational coverage could be avoided if the media were to adopt a more sensitive approach (see Chapter 15).

Chapter eight

Funerals

I was very worried about the suicide aspect of it, and thinking what if there is a God in heaven? What on earth is happening to Alastair now? (Heather)

I just wanted to be surrounded by people. I felt very strongly about that. All the flowers and all the people ... it was a beautiful funeral.... I thought it was as good as it could be. (Francesca)

Although suicide victims are no longer denied a proper funeral service and burial, suicide and religion often remain uneasy bedfellows. The Christian position, for example, can be equivocal (e.g. Rubey and Clark 1987, see also Chapter 1), and survivors can still be left feeling that by committing suicide their relative has committed a sin. As Paul, the victim's son in Bel Mooney's novel *The Anderson Question* says: 'Suicide's as much a sin now as it ever was. All your psychology, all your modern ideas about death and about mental illness too, and it all goes out of the window' (1985: 150).

Deep-seated, often pre-Christian, beliefs about suicide which have held sway over many centuries are not easily shaken off. Regardless of whether they hold any formal religious beliefs, survivors can still be worried that the act of suicide has condemned their relative to some sort of eternal punishment. For Pam and Harry, there was a very practical concern; they wanted to bury their daughter's ashes in her grandmother's grave, but thought that because Frances had committed suicide, perhaps this would not be permitted (though fortunately their fears were unfounded). Heather, although she described herself as a non-believer, was still worried as to whether her son was being made to suffer for taking his own life, until she was reassured by her local vicar:

> [He] was really good, he said all the right things.... He put my
> mind completely at rest, and said that God wasn't vicious like
> that, and Alastair would be looked after, and he'd be alright;
> [and] although I didn't believe, I thought, well just in case it's
> true, I can rest in that.

In most cases, though, survivors are not really asking for definitive
theological pronouncements on suicide; rather they are seeking reassurance that the person they knew is not being punished; they want
to know that, in contrast to what may have gone on before, the person's suffering is over, and that they are at peace.

Members of the clergy are likely to be in contact with families
more or less immediately after the death, if only to make the funeral
arrangements, and what they say, and the way they are seen by survivors to react to the situation, will be significant. Individual members of the clergy will have their own particular attitudes towards
suicide and their own feelings about the situation. But although
trained to minister to the bereaved, not all clergy are able to cope
with suicide, as Jane and her family found when the local curate –
obviously unaware of how Christopher had died – came round to
discuss the funeral service:

> He did his stuff and then eventually he said ... 'How long was
> your husband ill?' and [Jane's sister-in-law] said – because she'd
> said it so many times before it just came out – 'Oh, he wasn't ill,
> he wasn't ill at all, no. He committed suicide, he shot himself',
> and the teacup began to rattle ... and the curate was out of the
> house in five minutes. I've never seen anybody move so fast.

Like anyone confronted with suicide, members of the clergy may be
uncomfortable when talking to survivors, but if they can learn to
work with families in a sensitive and non-judgemental manner, they
can be an important source of support, particularly in the days immediately following the suicide (see Chapter 15). Heather and her family found their local vicar extremely supportive; she remembers how
'he sort of took over and steered us through; he was wonderful'. He
acknowledged and respected the different beliefs of individual family
members, encouraged them to plan a service which would be a celebration of Alastair's eighteen years, and suggested that they might
like to include some of their son's own music in the service.

Friends and neighbours may find it hard not to avoid the survivor, but the clergy have at least been trained to work with bereaved people as a significant part of their ministry. However, even clergy may sometimes avoid survivors completely, as Eileen discovered. Being the headmistress of a Church of England primary school she knew the vicar well, and was an active member of his congregation. Yes despite the fact that she was twice bereaved by suicide, on neither occasion did he say anything at all to her about the deaths.

Conley has pointed out how a well-planned funeral which takes account of individual needs can actually help survivors to embark on a healthy pattern of grieving: 'Careful arrangement and co-ordination of the actual funeral service and sensitive attention to individual and private needs of survivors facilitate initial grief reactions' (1987: 172).

The funeral is an important ritual for the bereaved which brings together family and friends to share their loss, to say farewell to the person who died, and to offer one another support. But when someone has committed suicide, the surviving family may decide to have a small, private funeral, attended only by immediate members of the family (Lukas and Seiden 1987). They may feel too ashamed or embarrassed about what has happened to have other people present. Guilt may lead them to conclude that they do not deserve the support of others. In fact, very few of the survivors I met had reacted in this way, and for many the funeral, though painful, had been a very positive experience, and one which had left them with good memories:

> It was really good. We had some very popular hymns that everyone sang very loudly ... lots of friends, lots of people. (Marie)

> It was a good memorial service.... Her friends read poetry that she had loved.... It was important to us at the time and to her friends. (Pam)

The funeral is usually the last act which the bereaved can perform for the dead person (Parkes 1986), and for some survivors, planning an appropriate and personally meaningful ceremony is an important part of the experience. The very fact of being able to do something for the other person can help to counterbalance the sense of helplessness which the survivor may have felt when the person was alive.

It can also be the chance to plan a proper farewell where no other goodbyes have been said. In the weeks following her husband's death, Christine found everyone was urging her to 'get the funeral over with' but she knew that this was not what she wanted to do. Because it was the summer holidays and people were away, she wanted time to contact as many of Graham's friends as possible to enable them to be at the service; and she wanted time to plan a funeral that would be meaningful to her; so she and her son wrote the service together, chose suitable poetry to read, and were able to include some of Graham's favourite music. They also found a clergyman who was willing to help them with these arrangements.

Christine also had a particularly helpful undertaker who did not mind when she rang him at two o'clock in the morning to discuss details of the funeral! Like members of the clergy, the way that staff at the undertakers react towards survivors will be important. Their contact with families may be quite considerable since they will be responsible for arranging the viewing of the body (see Chapter 4) as well as helping to make the funeral arrangements. Writing from an American perspective, Conley's description of undertakers as 'agents of consolation and recognised authorities of grieving' (1987: 171) may strike an alien note with British readers, but his suggestion that undertakers should play a more supportive role in relation to survivors of suicide has universal relevance. At the very least they need to be fully informed about the situation, otherwise survivors can end up having to deal with the sort of question which Susan was asked after her husband's funeral: 'I'm very sorry my dear – and what did he die of?'

Suicide can seem very meaningless to the survivors, and being able to plan ceremonies and rituals which inject some meaning into the event may be even more important than with other deaths (Lukas and Seiden 1987). Suicide is also a violent, often ugly act and a funeral which is made beautiful – whether by flowers, music, the support of friends, words that are spoken, or all of these – can help to counteract the survivor's more disturbing memories. Jean has some very positive memories of her daughter's funeral:

> I certainly like things [to be] beautiful and Anna would have
> wanted a beautiful ceremony and I'm sure a lot of people would
> tell you that it was extremely beautiful ... it's a good memory. I
> was absolutely shattered with the people who came ... so many

people when someone dies young ... and the flowers were fantastic. The house was filled with flowers, the crematorium was filled with flowers which Anna would have loved, and we planned a very beautiful ceremony ... only half an hour but we made it as beautiful as we possibly could.... So it was good, yes ... and her school friends sang beautifully.... It was just amazing ... I think about it a lot.

Idealising the dead person is not uncommon, particularly in the early stages of bereavement (Raphael 1985), and funeral addresses will usually refer to the person's more positive qualities while refraining from any mention of their less endearing characteristics. But what will be said at the funeral of someone who has committed suicide? Will the manner of death even be mentioned? Reference is sometimes made to the suicide during the funeral service, and when there is no attempt to mete out criticism or blame for the death, this open acknowledgement of what has happened can be helpful to the mourners. At Patricia's funeral, both her life and her death were mentioned; the person who conducted the funeral spoke of the mental pain she had suffered, but also of how her life had been complete in itself; her right to choose suicide was acknowledged, and those present were asked to respect that choice. Other survivors could remember how they had been urged not to blame themselves for what had happened, and while this may not have totally relieved them of their guilt, statements of this kind, made within the context of a public ritual, could help to place their guilt in a more realistic perspective.

To many people, suicide can seem a negative and destructive act, and it can easily be forgotten that the suicide was only one final act in a person's whole life. Honouring the person's life may be as important as marking their death. As one survivor explained:

it became more and more important to me that we plan a memorial service for my mother.... I wanted to honour my mother in a formal public setting. I had become her defender and advocate since her death and ... I did not want her suicide veiled. (Alexander 1987)

People who commit suicide often do so believing that they are of no value either to themselves or to others, but the fact that other people choose to come and pay their respects to the dead person can be a positive experience for the bereaved. For Janice, the fact that her mother's friends came to the funeral was an affirmation that, despite her mother's often difficult behaviour, there were people who had cared about her: 'a lot of them had probably been at the raw end of her accusations maybe a few times, so I felt they obviously appreciated the other side of my mother as well, so that was good'. The presence of the victim's friends can be a support to the family, as Pam found when many of Frances's friends came to the funeral 'as a tribute to [her] and to help us on our way'. Funerals to which everyone is invited can allow other survivors to support those most directly affected (Raphael 1985; Conley 1987).

The funeral can also provide other people outside the immediate family circle with the opportunity to say their own farewells, and, where necessary, to deal with their own unfinished business with the person who died (Johnson 1982). Inviting non-family members to view the body at the undertakers can also be helpful. After their son took his own life, David and Maureen were amazed at how many young people came to see Paul's body and to leave gifts and letters in his coffin. Although a suicide may have the greatest impact on surviving family members, other people will almost certainly be affected too (see Chapter 2), so it may be important for them to be able to attend the funeral and perhaps to visit the undertakers.

The funeral is usually an emotionally stressful affair, but the social gathering afterwards can provide for a release of tension and a chance for people to share, talk, and reminisce about the dead person. It can also be another good memory for the immediate survivors; Heather recalled the gathering held after her son's funeral: 'We had a nice party here because the youngsters came; we had drink, plenty to eat, there was plenty of laughter. It made a real party afterwards. It was a lovely day.' Though painful at times, many parents appreciated having their son's or daughter's young friends around them at this time.

Occasionally, however, people will be left with less positive memories of the funeral. The funeral may become a focus for feelings of ill-will. Where particular survivors are being blamed for the death (often by other family members – see pp. 110–12), and everyone gathers together for the funeral, the result can be a fraught experience, as Nick found when his mother committed suicide:

My father reported that her side of the family had been

threatening him, and so I attended [the funeral] and [took] the biggest, strongest friend with me ... sort of as a bodyguard.... I didn't look up in the church, I just sort of went into the funeral and was aware of her side of the family ... but I didn't look at them.

Alternatively, some family members may refuse to attend the funeral because of ill feelings towards one or more of the survivors; in Melanie's case, she was blamed for her husband's suicide by her mother-in-law, who refused to attend her son's funeral.

Sometimes, though, relatives are not even given the opportunity to attend, as Carol found when her son died; her sister's children, who were aged between seventeen and twenty-three at the time, were not even told of Alan's death immediately, and were not therefore given the choice as to whether to attend their cousin's funeral, something which Carol found hurtful.

The funeral is an important marker in the process of grieving; it confronts the bereaved with the reality of their loss and the finality of death. But it can also be a point where, if sensitively handled, healing can begin to take place, as some of the experiences described here demonstrate.

Chapter nine

Facing suicide as a family

I was ignorant of suicide. I didn't think it could happen to me, an ordinary, decent, well-set-up, middle-class family with everything going my way.... I would never have believed it could happen to my family. (Carol)

Any death can disrupt family life and relationships, but when someone commits suicide, the effects may be particularly severe. Grollman writes of how, for the victim, 'life is over. For the family, tragedy is just beginning' (1984: 209). But what is the nature of that tragedy? What are these families likely to face? In the introduction to his book on survivors, Cain described how:

> Psychological processes ... are often shaped by and amidst family interactions contorted by individuals too deeply preoccupied with their own grief to be helpful to each other, brimming with needs to blame and externalise, contending with newly erupted affects and problem behavior in themselves and each other, abruptly forced into restructuring delicately intertwined family roles and skills, caught between divergent, if not conflicting, patterns or pace of grief among family members, urgently pressed to replace previously highly cathected modes of interpersonal relationship and sources of need-gratification, buffeted as well by major practical problems which weigh towards further dissolution of the already harshly rent family structure. (1972: 15)

In those few lines, Cain, in somewhat dramatic fashion, encapsulates a number of different struggles. This chapter is about how some particular families struggled with the impact of suicide in their midst:

their altered perception of themselves as a family; the difficulties some individuals experienced in their attempts to talk to one another; how some family members struggled to support each other in the face of their own grief; the difficulties in allowing individual family members to grieve in their own way; how some families could rewrite history and thus deny the fact of suicide; the temptation to blame one another for what happened; and the fear that suicide 'runs in the family', and that other relatives will now take their own lives.

This chapter focuses on the family as a group or single unit, but though most survivors are part of a family, they are also individuals who will have had a particular relationship with the dead person. The relationship will have been different for each survivor; it may have been warm and intimate, or distant and hostile; it may have been an intimate but hostile encounter. So for each survivor the loss will mean something different. Survivors also have family relationships; they may have lost a brother or sister, son or daughter, mother or father, husband or wife. Not all siblings, for example, will feel the same; nevertheless, certain reactions are more likely to occur with some groups than with others (McIntosh 1987b). The following chapter looks at particular issues facing four such groups of survivors: parents, spouses, siblings, and children.

How the family sees itself

Suicide happens in all sorts of homes, and the only thing that those bereaved by suicide share in common is the fact that they are survivors of suicide. But this was also what often made them feel so different from other families they knew. Sometimes they not only felt different, they thought they must be bad, even wicked, families; after her son's suicide, it seemed to Heather as if 'we must be an absolutely horrendous family to have had a child who could be so unhappy'. So when survivors encounter negative reactions from friends and neighbours (see Chapter 11), this may only serve to reinforce and confirm their own sense of shame.

Studies of community attitudes towards families of suicide victims have revealed that other people frequently not only see them as different, but as blameworthy and generally less likeable (see Chapter 11). Even the textbooks can present a negative image. Worden, for example, in his otherwise excellent book on grief counselling, claims that 'suicide victims often come from families in which there are difficult social problems such as alcoholism or child abuse' (1983: 82), although he offers no particular evidence to substantiate his views.

Suicide will leave some survivors feeling as though they have undergone an amputation, and that a part of them is missing. 'There's a hole in our family' is how Pat described it. Spouses sometimes compared the suicide to loss of a limb (Chapter 10). Like any death, suicide leaves a gap in the family, and the effect may be far-reaching. Within the group which constitutes the family, individuals will usually have particular roles and functions (Cain 1972; Parkes 1986). For example, the dead person may have been the main or even the sole breadwinner in the family; they may also have played less obvious roles – as the family member who did most of the worrying, or the one who made all the major decisions; on the other hand, they may have been the person who was always seen as 'difficult' by the rest of the family, the one who relied heavily on others, and was unable to cope with everyday life. When that person is no longer around, it is as though one of the actors in the drama of family life is missing; to get round this (to enable the play to continue?), other family members may take over the dead person's roles. The survivor who has always been independent may suddenly become the person who relies on others.

Sometimes these changes can be quite positive. While Irene's husband was alive, she had been the dependent, non-coping partner in their marriage. When Irene was going through periodic bouts of depression it was always Bill who took care of things, who kept things going at home. Indeed, this was what seemed to be happening at the time of Bill's death; Irene was in a psychiatric hospital being given ECT in an attempt to relieve her depression. Although she still needed further help, four years after Bill's death, and after many struggles, Irene is aware of how much she has changed. She has discovered she is more capable than she ever dreamt was possible, and she feels in control of her own life for the first time; she has recently attended a counselling course and has started up a local support network for other survivors.

Communication in the family

Suicide is a traumatic event, and feelings of horror can make it hard to talk about the death, even within the family. Survivors may have no option, though, if faced with the unwelcome task of breaking the news to other family members. Jennifer was told by the police that Tim had been killed on the railway line, but although she soon realised that it was almost certainly suicide, her mother had not guessed the truth, and Jennifer felt she would have to tell her, but: 'I was frightened of saying, and I was worried [about] what to say because I wanted her to realise for herself or I wanted the police to have told her so that I wouldn't have to tell her.'

Any discussion of the actual suicide can be a taboo subject between family members. One person may want to talk about what happened, but others may find they cannot face hearing about it. When their son died, Carol was away from home, and it was her ex-husband who discovered that Alan had hanged himself. Although she knows that the memory of what he saw that morning stayed with him, and that perhaps he needs to talk about it, she has so far been unable to let him do so. They will talk about other things to do with Alan, but not that.

Survivors submerged in their own grief may even find it hard to be with other family members; the idea of having to support someone else can seem to be an impossible demand. After Ben's suicide, both Miriam and her daughter, Ruth, felt they were a blight on each other:

> my daughter ... would hear me saying to friends on the phone, 'I shall just have to go and see Ruth as often as I can', and her heart would sink with that and ... in the first few weeks we were simply a torment to each other.... I went to see her a couple of times and she found me absolutely unbearable.... She would say, 'you're so weak', because she, in fact, couldn't bring herself to tell her contemporaries how he died.... She said he'd been killed in a car crash.... What was completely unfamiliar and unexpected for me was that my passionate desire to see Ruth survive and my desperate need to see her didn't mean that I wasn't compounding her pain.

Fortunately for Miriam and Ruth this state of affairs lasted only a few weeks, but the period immediately after the death – the time when family members may most need one another – can also be the time when they are most vulnerable, and least able to care for each other. When Stephen committed suicide, Anne Downey found that although she was left with five other sons, it was about six months before she could even begin to think about the needs of the rest of the family (Downey 1987).

Pam and Harry acknowledge that they were fortunate in being able to talk together and share their feelings about their daughter's suicide – although this was not always so in the early days, when Harry was going off to work every day, and Pam was at home on her own. But sometimes a survivor will decide that the only way to cope is by shutting off all communication, and refusing to discuss the suicide with anyone else. Feeling lonely and desperate after her husband's suicide, Irene rang one of her sons only to be told: 'Don't phone me, I can't handle it.' An attempt to talk with her brother produced a similar response: 'Irene, I don't know what to say to you, I can't handle it. I can't even come and see you – just leave it.' If survivors cannot handle their own feelings, the thought of facing other people's pain may be too threatening. As Marie said: 'I think there's only a certain amount you can put on your family really.' This may be the point when survivors will look for help outside the family (see Chapter 12).

Survivors may need encouragement from others to mention the dead person; family members may sometimes have to give each other permission to talk. When her daughter committed suicide, Jean found that her son would not talk to her at all about Anna; after several months, though, when Jean decided to broach the subject with him, Richard's response was 'it's for you to make the first move'. As a result, although Jean will not force the issue, now they can at least talk about Anna sometimes.

Where family members refuse point blank to discuss the suicide, family relationships can be severed completely. When John's wife died, he had virtually no immediate family to whom he could turn (see p. 58). He did, however, look to his mother for support:

> After the funeral I went to my mother's house and she said: 'Now you mustn't bring your grief here or it will kill me'.... Well, my reaction was that of sheer, utter bitterness and anger, sheer unadulterated anger, and my answer was, 'Well, if you won't let me bring it here in these circumstances, I'll never come here again', and out I walked. I didn't go near them for two and a half years, and that's what I call my two years of wilderness. It was totally a wilderness.

In some families, though, the opposite will happen; the loss of one person in the family will draw remaining members closer together. Since Judy's death, Brian and his two sons have become much closer;

although Chris and Rob were both in their twenties when their mother died and were no longer living at home, Brian feels that as a family they have learned to share much more with each other, and they have been able to talk together about her death. Family relationships often change and regroup themselves after a death, and for Dick it was the realisation after his sister's death that 'there were only the two of us left' which he feels has resulted in a much closer relationship with his brother.

Even when immediate family members are able to talk to one another, survivors can find it painful when more distant relatives no longer mention the person who died. After her daughter's death, Phyllis felt very hurt when everyone outside the immediate family simply stopped mentioning Julie: as she says, when they did this, 'it felt as though she was never there'.

Talking with children

Part of the following chapter describes the experiences of some adults who lost a parent during childhood as the result of suicide. But how do adults cope with talking to children? As we have seen, discussing the suicide with other adults can be hard enough, but what – if anything – do adults tell children? When Richard died, Susan found having to break the news to their twelve-year-old son one of the hardest things she had to face at that time. As she says, 'How do you break the news to someone who has never known of his father's depressions ... who only knew of him as a jolly dad who played rugger with him?... That was terrible.'

Among the research and individual case studies, there are numerous examples of children not being told how the person died (e.g. Cain and Fast 1972a; Shepherd and Barraclough 1976; Bowlby 1985; McIntosh 1987b). But concealing the truth can brings its own complications; children may reach their own inaccurate, and sometimes harmful, conclusions: 'He must have died because I did something naughty that day' or 'She can't really have loved me, otherwise why would she have gone away?'; they may discover unintentionally what really happened – perhaps by overhearing adult conversations; as a result of not being told what really happened, children may decide that adults can never be trusted to tell the truth about anything (Lukas and Seiden 1987).

Sometimes, of course, the child will be too young to understand the meaning of death, let alone suicide. Hannah, for example, was only about two when her father committed suicide; Melanie has since told her daughter that he died in a car accident (in fact, he died in his car – of carbon monoxide poisoning), but she is not altogether happy with that version of events, even though Hannah has accepted it. She wants to tell her daughter the truth, and though so far Hannah (who is still only six) has not asked any more questions, Melanie hopes that one day she will be able to tell her what really happened.

Nick's baby daughter was born some years after her grandmother's suicide, but Nick has already been thinking about what he should tell her. Although he worries about 'getting it right', he feels very strongly that she should eventually be told the truth: 'I feel it would do her an injustice ... for that to be a secret. I feel secrets like that are very bad ... they can dog people's lives.' Suicide can easily lead to the creation of family myths and harmful secrets (see below).

Parents are usually thought to be the best people to tell their children; however, if parents have decided not to tell their children about the suicide, this can create dilemmas for other relatives faced with children's questions, but unable to give all the answers. At the time of her husband's suicide, Irene's grandsons were seven, eight, and nine; although they were told the next day that their grandad was dead, four years later they still have no idea that he took his own life, although Martin, who was closest of the three to Bill, has sometimes asked Irene about his grandfather's death; 'someone's going to have to tell these boys', she knows, but she feels that their parents are the ones who should do that.

The concept of death can be very different for children, according to what stage of development they have reached (Raphael 1985), but even fairly young children seem capable of some understanding of suicide, if they are told in clear, simple terms. When Suzy's father committed suicide, she and her husband decided that they would tell the whole story to their two older daughters, who were then aged six and nine: 'We both explained that ... he got depressed, that he felt it was too much for him to cope with being like that, it was sad, and that he had killed himself taking aspirins.' Suzy is unsure quite how they saw this, but thinks they probably did understand.

Even though older adolescents' understanding of death is likely to be more or less the same as adults' (Raphael 1985), talking about the suicide may not be any easier, as Lois discovered after her oldest son took his own life. Simon had two brothers, both of whom were in their late teens when he died. Lois finds it hard that they don't talk about Simon with her; to her, if no one in the family mentions Simon, then 'there will have been no point in him being alive', and partly to try and counter this, she has been compiling some of his poems and other writings to share with family and friends, but his brothers have not taken any part in this exercise and she wonders whether perhaps this is something they cannot face. It may also reflect Raphael's comment that the bereaved adolescent 'may wish to carry on as though nothing had happened' (1985: 151).

Same family, different reactions

Reactions to bereavement are highly personal, they are shaped by many different factors, and there is no single right way to grieve. Nevertheless, when individual family members react very differently to the same event, this can cause problems, as Caroline's family discovered. Pat went through a phase when she resented both Nicola (her surviving daughter) and Robert (her husband): 'because they weren't grieving the same way as I was ... I thought they weren't grieving, you see. I thought "Look at them, they've got over it."' When Nicola did not visit Caroline's grave as often as her mother, Pat found it hard to come to terms with that too:

> I didn't like to say anything.... I knew she hadn't forgotten
> [Caroline].... It just appeared that Robert and Nicola were able
> to adjust better than I was, and get on with their lives quicker
> and better than I was, and I resented it.

As a family, Pat, Robert, and Nicola found there were other differences, apart from the time scales of their grieving. In the early days, at least, Robert felt driven to discover why Caroline had taken her own life, something which the other two have never felt they needed to do. Nicola believes her sister's suicide was a 'spur of the moment thing', and she prefers not to think about what actually happened on that day. Their initial physical reactions were very different too: while Pat was rushing around being constantly active, all Robert wanted to do was curl up and sleep. It was only when Pat had the chance to talk to other survivors that she was able to accept that she and Nicola and Robert were all different, and 'their way of grieving wasn't mine, and they had to be left to get on with it in their way'. Now, talking together, they can recognise and accept these differences.

Where one person feels that others in the family are not grieving properly, this can be an additional strain. Someone who weeps more often than other family members, and who generally displays their grief more openly, may conclude that other people did not really care that much about the person who died. At one stage after their daughter's suicide, Frank began to feel that he and Ursula were not as close as they might have been because they were grieving differently. Ursula felt that Frank didn't care as much as she did. 'I don't feel that now', she admits, 'and when I thought of it logically I didn't ... I realised that different people deal with things differently and at different speeds.'

Individual reactions to the death and styles of coping will be partly determined by the survivor's relationship to the dead person, as Peter realised after his sister's suicide:

> I think each of us in the family views all the events differently. I mean for each of us it's a different investment, and a different relationship, and inevitably each of us will account for everything in a different way ... [will] understand things differently.

After Susie's death, Peter went back to New Zealand to spend time with his family, and although he found he could talk about her with some members of the family, this was not always the case, and it was something he had to learn to accept:

> One has to accept people's reactions and my father can't talk about it, and you simply have to understand that. He was the person who found her; he was devastated, and he never fully understood what was happening in Susie's life ... and I can't ever put myself in his shoes.... He's eighty-four ... and I simply can't imagine what it's like at that point in life to find your youngest daughter [dead].

There is a further issue relating to individual patterns of grieving: are there measurable differences in the way men and women cope with bereavement? Research in this area is limited, and the work that has been done has focused mainly on widows and widowers, and on non-suicide bereavements. From their encounters with a self-selected group of survivors, Lukas and Seiden (1987) concluded that men were generally reluctant to express emotions and tended to say they did not need to talk. This is borne out by the fact that of those who volunteered to be interviewed for this book, women heavily outnumbered men (see Chapter 3). Many contacts came through bereavement organisations (see Chapter 12), which again concurs with Lukas and Seiden (1987) who found that few of the male survivors they came across had joined self-help groups and those that did tended to listen rather than participate more actively. It is important to recognise, however, that this does not necessarily mean that men experience less pain and grief than women; they may have other ways of dealing with their feelings. Many men are bound by cultural stereotypes which demand that they behave in certain ways; as Brian said, talking of how he grieved alone in the days after his wife's suicide: 'Men don't cry – do they?'

Blame within the family

Anger is a common reaction to bereavement; it is a response to loss which may be directed at the dead person, at other people, or at oneself (Bowlby 1985). It can be turned inwards, causing feelings of guilt and self-reproach, or directed towards other people who will be blamed in some way for the loss. When someone commits suicide, blame will often be directed towards self and others simultaneously. How could he have done this to me? How could I have been so stupid not to have stopped him? Why didn't that doctor who was treating him realise he was suicidal? Potential targets for blame are numerous:

> On the one hand, the dead person can be blamed for having deliberately deserted the bereaved; on the other, one or other of the relatives can be held responsible for having provoked this action. Very often blame is laid on close kin, especially the surviving spouse. Others to be implicated are parents, particularly in the case of suicide by a child or adolescent; sometimes also a child is blamed by one parent for the suicide of the other. Those who mete out such blame are likely to include both relatives and neighbours; and not infrequently the surviving spouse blames him or herself, perhaps for not having done enough to prevent the suicide or even having encouraged it. (Bowlby 1985: 184)

At a time when survivors are looking for comfort in their grief, the eruption of these feelings can be particularly distressing and painful.

When Alastair committed suicide, Heather remembers how she and her husband started arguing with each other about their son's death:

> We also did accuse each other which was horrendous. I was expecting that to happen.... I'm not sure who started it, but I was very aware that we shouldn't do that and yet we just did. We just ended up shouting 'It's your fault!' 'It's your fault!'

Parents may blame each other for the death of a child, but they may also be accused of causing the death by surviving brothers and sisters. Betty can still remember how, after her son's suicide, one of Jonathan's sisters when she was feeling particularly distressed, angrily accused her mother of killing him.

Spouses are sometimes considered to be responsible for the well-being of their partner, so that when something goes wrong, then the surviving spouse will often be a target for blame (Bowlby 1985). When Melanie's husband committed suicide, members of his family made it plain that they thought she was to blame. In the four years since Ian died, his mother has never spoken to her, because apparently she holds Melanie totally responsible for what happened to her son.

Accusations of this kind can result in family relationships being permanently severed. When Nick's mother committed suicide, both he and his father were blamed by his mother's family (and, as if that were not enough, by some of his father's family too). Looking back, Nick thinks that his mother's relatives probably blamed them as a means of avoiding their own sense of guilt, but the hostile phone calls and the way his father was generally hounded has left both of them with unpleasant memories. As a result of all this, Nick is now completely cut off from one half of his family and does not expect he will ever see them again.

Blame can drive a wedge between survivors even at times like funerals when people are generally expected to be mutually supportive. What is often a highly emotional experience can become even more fraught when feelings of blame are in the air. When Liz's brother died, she felt that though Tony and his wife had separated, his wife was at least partly to blame for his death. Despite the separation, his wife came to the funeral with her parents, and although Liz never spoke to them and made sure they did not sit together at the crematorium, she remembers how 'it was kind of them and us ... it was horrible'.

Sometimes the only way survivors can cope with feelings of blame or guilt, whether directed at themselves or at others, is to remain silent:

family members don't want to expose the guilt and blame they feel; the blame they feel towards other family members, the guilt they feel about themselves.... The silence is an attempt to keep the cap on terrible accusations ... towards others and towards oneself. (Lukas and Seiden 1987: 111–12).

Not talking about the suicide can be a way of not having to face the truth of what happened. The result may be the creation of family secrets.

Secrets in the family

'You must not tell anyone', my mother said, 'what I am about to tell you. In China your father had a sister who killed herself. She jumped into the family well. We say that your father has all brothers because it is as if she had never been born.' (Kingston 1981: 11)

Maxine Hong Kingston is writing here of avoidance taken to considerable lengths; as far as her family is concerned, the victim never even existed. By no means all families will react in quite such an extreme fashion, but many people are the inheritors of family secrets about suicide. When I asked survivors whether this was the first suicide in the family or whether, in the past, other family members had committed suicide, they were often unsure. They *thought* perhaps there had been an uncle, a great-grandparent, or some other relative. As children they had perhaps overheard the whispered conversations of adults, but it was something never really talked about in the family.

But this kind of secrecy does not just belong to the past; family members may still decide that the suicide is not to be discussed. It is four years since Dick's sister committed suicide, and he still regrets the fact that Sally's death was not talked about more in the family:

We did talk about her to some extent, but I don't think the whole thing was all that talked about. I think that might have helped. My mum tended to deal with things by carrying on regardless almost, and trying not to acknowledge it too much ...

but I used to think sometimes it was a shame; it was almost as though Sally had been wiped off the map practically.

Of course it is possible to prevent the establishment of family secrets. Survivors like Nick and Melanie with very young children (see p. 107) had already made up their minds that at some point their children would be told the truth. Their children, at least, would not become the bearers of family secrets.

Living with the aftermath of suicide can be painful, and rewriting the story can be one way of removing the source of pain; according to Pincus and Dare, 'secrets in the family are often an attempt to avoid guilt and the pain of loss' (1978: 134). If the death was 'an unfortunate accident' or 'due to natural causes', then no one is to blame, and no one need feel guilty.

When Wendy's father committed suicide with an overdose, the fact that he took his own life was not mentioned except by those members of the family who had been in the house at the time. But even they did not mention suicide again once the funeral was over. After a few days Wendy's stepmother started saying that perhaps it had been an accident; 'she had all sorts of explanations', Wendy recalls, except suicide.

Secrets created at the time of the death can subsequently be unravelled, but it is not always straightforward, as Isabel discovered. When she visited her family (who live abroad) shortly after her husband's death, Isabel told them Eric had died of a heart attack. Her family are Roman Catholic, and she felt that if she told them the truth they would see it as a sin. At that time, she wanted to protect her three children from finding out the truth. When, at some later stage, she told her family that Eric had taken an overdose, her assumption that they would consider his suicide a sin was correct, and her brother's response – 'we forgive him' – left Isabel feeling very angry.

Does suicide run in the family?

One of the callers to a radio phone-in on suicide, a man whose brother and sister had both taken their own lives, described how he felt that people were looking at him now and saying, 'two down, one to go'. Had other people actually said that, or was it what he thought they would say? Were they even right to assume that is what might happen? Whatever the answers, many survivors do worry about whether suicide is something that runs in the family.

It is beyond the scope of this book to review the literature on suicide and heredity. Anyway, others have already done so (Cain 1972; McIntosh 1987c), and the evidence remains inconclusive. So survivors trying to find out whether other family members will go on to commit suicide are unlikely to find definitive answers; but it may be just as important for survivors to be able to voice those anxieties, and that can be difficult if they feel that other people may be asking the same question. Nick believes this is one of the reasons why survivors tend not to talk about suicide. As he says, if you do mention it, people think 'Oh gosh, it's in you, sort of thing.'

Survivors who are worried about whether suicide runs in the family may really be asking 'Am *I* going to commit suicide too?' Jan was thirteen when her father, who also had a drink problem, shot himself; later, as a student, she found herself facing that question:

> One of the things that horrified me when I read about suicide and about alcoholism was about how it runs in families – and that felt very alive for me because I could see that that was a very real option for me.... I was certainly afraid that I might become an alcoholic, and afraid that I would find myself, when I was low, thinking, oh well, I'll show them, I'll commit suicide.

After a considerable time in therapy, Jan reached the point where she felt that neither alcoholism nor suicide was a real option for her. She remains reasonably certain about that, but at the same time acknowledges that perhaps this will always remain in the background, something that will surface from time to time.

People like Jan may have to confront fears about their own potential for suicide or other self-destructive behaviours, but other survivors will worry more about whether children or grandchildren will be affected. Ann actually went for genetic counselling when she became engaged to be married. Her brother had committed suicide, and her sister was suffering from chronic mental illness, and she was worried about whether it would be safe to have children. (She now has 'four perfectly normal children, and ten perfectly normal grandchildren'.)

Survivors can sometimes find themselves faced with the real possibility of history repeating itself. Martin, whose mother committed suicide, found that when his teenage daughter was going through a phase of self-destructive, quasi-anorexic behaviour, he was reacting in exactly the same way as he had when his mother was alive. The young boy who had felt he should be looking after his mother reappeared as the grown man who felt he had to persuade his daughter to eat; as he says: 'again I found myself being a caretaker, and making all sorts of arrangements'.

Families where there has been a suicide may be seen by others as having some inherited streak of madness or insanity (see Chapter 11), but this may concern survivors themselves. It may worry them more than the possibility of suicide. Seven years after Bridget's father and sister committed suicide, it is not so much the possibility of suicide that worries her, but what she calls 'madness':

> There's a whole history of it in my father's family and though I figure that if I was going to go mad I would have done it by now ... if I have children, then that's going to be something I have to think about and so that side worries me.

Ultimately, genetic studies and other scientific research may be of little immediate relevance to the survivor. Rational explanations may not relieve anxieties which can have more to do with feelings than rational thought processes. It has been said that when someone commits suicide, 'the unthinkable becomes thinkable', and that can feel very frightening. For survivors, being able to acknowledge those feelings – to themselves and to others – may be more important in the long run than searching in textbooks for answers.

Chapter ten

The impact of suicide on individual family members

The family network plays a central part in some people's lives, while in others, family members may have little to do with one another. Nevertheless, the family is always there, and though we can choose our friends, this is not so with our family. Our place in the family also helps to shape our sense of identity; we are a son or daughter, perhaps also someone's brother or sister; as adults, we may well have established our own family, creating new identities – husband or wife, and father or mother. But whatever our place in the family, when a death occurs in that family, it usually draws everyone together, if only for the funeral. With one exception, the people whose stories are told in this book were either parents, or siblings, children, or spouses of suicide victims. It is the particular issues facing these groups which are the subject of this chapter.

Parents as survivors

> I think there's self-doubt in what you've done ... your role as a father or as a mother ... the thought that you'd done something wrong or didn't play your part right in the bringing up of your daughter. It's that that chisels away at you. (Robert)

> And I am pregnant
> With your death
> I carry you again
> – a dead weight –
> No birth to come.
> J.C. (1987)

The annual suicide rate among young adults in Britain is on the increase, leaving bereaved parents like Robert questioning their role as parents, and wondering where the mistakes occurred. For some parents, the suicide means the loss of an only child – an abrupt and total cessation of their parental identity and role. It would be wrong to assume that the loss of a child will automatically be worse than, say, the loss of a parent or sibling, but there is no doubt that for many parents of suicide victims it was felt to be the most devastating loss they would ever face. Many of them would agree with Gorer's conclusion that this particular loss, especially when it involves a fully grown child, may be 'the most distressing and long-lasting of all griefs' (quoted in Bowlby 1985: 177). The fact that the child may have reached adulthood does not usually make it any easier. For many people, parenthood is seen as a lifelong commitment and responsibility for their children's well-being as continuing into adulthood.

Turning aside for a moment from the issue of parental responsibilities; to many parents, their children offer a sense of continuity; they will grow old and die, but their children will live on after them, and with luck will have children of their own. When a child dies, regardless of whether there are other children, this line – this sense of continuity – will be severed. It felt like that to Francesca after her only daughter committed suicide: 'You see when a daughter dies – when a daughter chooses to die – you've lost the mother–daughter–grandchild ... it's gone.'

Children are commonly seen to represent their parents' future. Parents who, for example, have not had a university education, or who may have had limited success in their career, may look to their children to achieve their own unfulfilled ambitions. When Frances died, although she left behind a brother, her death seemed like the end of Pam's hopes for the future:

You don't expect to lose your children, do you? You expect that you will die and leave them behind ... we just didn't imagine.... I mean we'd always looked to the future, and our future and the children's future all wound together, and suddenly there wasn't much of a future.... We always thought she'd do pretty grand things ... go abroad and nurse and do great things.

Parents do not expect their children to die before them, that is not the natural order of things, a point echoed by Mark whose daughter, it seemed to him, 'went too soon ... went out of order'.

A great deal has been said and written about parental neglect and abandonment of children, but the suicide of a child reverses that situation. When a child seemingly chooses to die, and for whatever reasons, parents can be left with an overwhelming sense of rejection. As Pat said after Caroline's death: 'It's the ultimate rejection of you as a mum if your child cannot face life and cannot face you. There can't be any greater rejection than to obliterate yourself and detach yourself totally from that person.' Invariably this leads parents to question why? What was there about me as a parent that led my child to do this? Where did I go wrong?

In the days and weeks following the suicide of a child, many survivors will place their parenting under a microscope, often going back over many years, searching for clues as to where things might have gone wrong, and wondering if they can pinpoint a particular incident which could have caused the death. Carole was preoccupied with this for some time after her only son died. She recalled how, nearly twenty years before his death, Jon had been separated from her when his sister was born. According to Carole, he returned home traumatised by the separation: 'I had unwittingly and unthinkingly hurt him deeply.... I have suffered deep distress and anguish over this since Jon's death. This has caused me more pain and guilt than any other episode in our life together.'

After her son's suicide, Anne Downey wrote: 'I'm sure every mother, under the circumstances, digs and digs and finds so many areas where she went wrong. We aim at perfection, which is impossible' (1987: 71). The perfect parent almost certainly does not exist, and most people get by as 'good enough' parents, but when the child commits suicide, even 'good enough' parenting can feel like failure.

As with other survivors, though, retracing the past only brings wisdom with hindsight (see Chapter 6). Mark's daughter was twenty-nine when she died and much of her adult life had been punctuated by breakdowns and crises, including attempts at suicide, but he has found it hard to come to terms with the fact that, as her parents, they failed to notice anything seriously wrong during her childhood; for Mark, that was 'the most shattering discovery of all'. There is a kind of double burden: not only have they apparently failed as parents, but they did not even realise that they were failing. As Heather said, after her son died: 'We failed him ... without realising that we had.'

After meeting and talking with parents in the USA, Lukas and Seiden concluded that 'the guilt and depression among parental survivors *does* seem to be more intense and longer lasting than among others.... Their job had been to protect their child – and they had failed' (1987: 139). McIntosh, too, has pointed out how particularly severe feelings of guilt experienced by many parents are linked to feelings about the parental role:

> Parents have the responsibility for the growth and protection of their children. When a child commits suicide, therefore, the competency and credibility of the individuals as parents are called into question.... How could the parents have been so insensitive, so unaware of their child's mental state? ... For some of these parents the self-doubt resulted in a 'parental identity crisis'. (1987b: 74)

This identity crisis can spill over and affect the way parents feel about their relationship with surviving children. If parents believe they have failed one child with such devastating results, they may question what sort of parents they can possibly be to the others. They may ask themselves, hasn't the suicide shown them to be unfit for the role? There may be very real fears too that other children will go on to commit suicide (Lukas and Seiden 1987), or that they will be harmed in some way. As a result, parents can find themselves becoming over-protective. After her only son died, Maureen remembers how she started following her two teenage daughters round the house, always needing to know where they were, and frightened to let them go out on their own. This excessive concern about other family members is not unusual according to Wrobleski (1984–5).

At the same time, though, parents may feel – however irrationally – that because fate has dealt them one blow, this should grant them immunity from any further tragedies. Since her daughter's death nine years ago, Nancy has struggled with anxieties about her two sons:

> I have a sort of angry feeling inside me which is quite illogical ... that it ought to have been one of the rules of life that if you've lost one of your children, that should be insurance against losing any others.

Anyone who has experienced the death of someone close to them, whether or not it is by suicide, can feel very insecure as a result, wondering who will die next – and thus abandon them (see Chapter 13). Parents may find they are caught up in a sense of despair, almost convinced that further family tragedy is now inevitable. Lois has two surviving sons, the youngest of whom is still at school:

> I can't watch over him all the time, and I'm not basically a posses-
> sive person ... but it's hard ... you know it could happen again ...
> that's the sort of pessimism that comes over you; you think, oh
> that'll be the next thing I've got to cope with – a car crash.

Parents' own feelings of guilt, their sense of having failed as a parent,
may be compounded by the belief that other people see them in the
same light. As Lois said: 'You know that suicide is bad in the sense
that there's still this social stigma of failure, and you feel you've
failed as a parent, or mother, or whatever.' Attitudinal research has
shown that the parents of suicide victims are less liked and are
blamed more for the death than parents whose child has died of
other causes (Calhoun *et al.* 1980; Rudestam and Imbroll 1983;
Rudestam 1987). This can make it hard for parents to talk about the
bereavement with other people (see Chapter 11).

For some couples, even sharing their grief with one another, let
alone with outsiders, can be difficult (Chapter 9). One parent may be
trying to protect the other from their pain; or one parent may be
silently blaming the other parent for the death; in some cases, one of
the couple may be refusing to accept that the death was self-inflicted,
making shared grieving over the suicide impossible (McIntosh
1987b). In the end, it may be the victim's siblings who feel they must
reassure and support their parents, but what are their own feelings
as survivors of suicide?

Siblings

> We've had the time for grieving, and although I don't want to
> forget her ... I think I want to go on now. (Nicola)

In families where there has been a suicide, all the attention may be
focused on the grieving parents, leaving the victim's siblings as forgotten mourners; this can occur with siblings of all ages. As Mc-
Intosh (1987b) has pointed out, the impact of suicide on surviving
siblings has been almost totally neglected by researchers, a view
shared by Henley (1984) in her review of the suicide bereavement
literature. Those responsible for developing support services to
survivors have also largely ignored this group (see Chapter 12).

If not exactly forgotten by the family, a sibling can be quite literally an 'absent mourner'. It is over fifty years since Ann's student brother committed suicide, but she still remembers how, on the day Giles died, her parents did not allow her to accompany them to the university; she very much wanted to go, but they assured her they would manage without her. She did not attend Giles's inquest either, and when it came to the funeral her parents again said they would be going alone. Although already an adult (aged twenty-four) Ann felt unable to challenge them; now she thinks they were probably trying to protect her rather than deliberately excluding her.

Discussing adolescent bereavement in general, Raphael (1985) points out how their reactions are likely to be determined to some extent by the kind of relationship they had with the dead sibling, a finding shared by Todd (1981) and Morse (1984) (cited in McIntosh 1987b), both of whom carried out small-scale qualitative studies of sibling survivors of suicide. Although it is often assumed that brothers and sisters drift apart as they grow up, adult survivors can be devastated by the loss of a sibling with whom they had a particularly close relationship. This had been the case with Jennifer and her brother Tim; her memories of childhood were that it was 'never just me ... always me and Tim'. Close to each other in age, as small children they played together constantly; as they grew up they purchased their first car jointly; and they always went together to the local discotheque. For Jennifer, Tim had been a permanent fixture in her life: 'I can't think of any time growing up when he wasn't there.' Now, Tim's death has left its mark on her childhood memories, because her own childhood and Tim's were inseparable.

Jennifer had no other siblings, and Tim's death left her as an only child. But for survivors from larger families, suicide can involve the loss of the favourite brother or sister, the one with whom the survivor had had a special relationship. Although Peter was the eldest of four, it was Susie, the youngest of his three sisters, who had always been closest to him. Even after Peter had left his family's home in New Zealand, and come to live in England, he and Susie remained very important to one another:

> I was always entirely besotted with Susie, right from the beginning .... I mean one shouldn't perhaps, but one inevitably does have favourite siblings and we had lots in common ... there was an indulgent relationship too because she was much younger and I was the eldest.

Writing about the impact of suicide on the family, Rosenfeld and Prupas have pointed out how 'siblings often assume responsibility for taking care of things' (1984: 77). When Francesca's daughter committed suicide, she remembers how her son, then in his late twenties, and suddenly an only child, 'somehow stepped out of being a son and became a parent'. Pam and Harry's experience was similar; they felt as if their twenty-year-old son had literally grown up overnight. The more usual roles of parents and child as carer and cared-for are reversed. This may be more likely to happen where the surviving sibling is now the only child, and as a result may feel they now have the sole responsibility for their parents.

But what about the siblings' own needs? Who is there to support their grieving? As Jean's son complained after his sister died: 'It was my only sister, and I'm all on my own, and no one makes a fuss of me!' Eileen's sole surviving daughter, Marjorie, experienced similar reactions; after Marjorie's twin sisters had committed suicide, it seemed that her own needs were being ignored; everyone kept asking how her mother was coping, but nobody thought to ask how she was feeling. It can be difficult for young adults to know who they can turn to for support. They may feel they need to protect already grieving parents from further distress, and as a result, parents may conclude that the suicide has not really affected them that deeply. Talking to friends of their own age can also be difficult, particularly if the survivor feels embarrassed or ashamed about the suicide.

Like any survivors, siblings will be left with their own particular feelings about the suicide and their own difficulties to resolve. They may feel guilty simply about being the one who survived, or they may worry about whether they will become suicidal too. They may feel, as Nicola did, that simply because of who they are, they created problems for the dead sibling:

> I hate myself sometimes because ... she obviously did think
> 'Nicola does this', and 'Nicola's that', and put herself down and
> [she] always said 'Oh, I wish I was thin like you, and I wish I had
> blonde hair like you', and I sometimes think that if there hadn't
> been such a difference between us or she hadn't looked at me
> and thought I was everything she wanted to be.... She never saw
> any faults, although there are lots, she never saw any, and
> sometimes I find that hard.

Where parents appear to be totally wrapped up in grieving for the dead child, surviving siblings may start to feel unloved and neglected, as happened to Jon's surviving sister. When her mother started crying at Christmas, Gilly's response was: 'I'm here and you've got me, so don't spoil the day.' As Carole realised afterwards: 'I could feel in a way jealousy, you know.... She felt I was thinking about him and I wasn't thinking about her.' Siblings can end up feeling very excluded by parental grief.

Young adult survivors, particularly if they are now an only child (see p. 122), may be torn between feeling, on the one hand, that they should be around supporting their parents, but at the same time wanting to get on with their own lives. After her son's suicide, Carole saw that this might be a problem for her daughter who had just left home for university; as she has realised: 'I don't want to be a burden to her ... she might feel she's got to come home every so often, and she's got to ring me up, and she's got to see how I am.'

Writing about her work with families facing terminal illness and bereavement, Hildebrand stresses the need for young people being able 'to retain their energy, to feel alive, and to have permission to move on' (1989: 26). Eighteen months after her sister's suicide, Nicola felt the time had come for her to look to the future:

> I think that is the difference between Mum and Dad and me. They're always looking back on what was ... and I want to [say] it's happened, and we've had the time for grieving, and although I don't want to forget her and not talk about her and forget things that happened, I think I want to go on now.... I feel that now's the time to, hopefully, when I get married and move into a house; it's going to make a big change for me, a new start.

The fact that young people may have a different perspective on death does not mean that they are immune from grief, but on the threshold of adulthood they need to be able to look to the future as well as mourn the past; it is a normal and healthy reaction at that stage of life. As Carole's daughter told her: 'I've cried for him for a year; I'm going to get on with my life now.'

Children as survivors of parental suicide

> Her death has been buried for so long and there has been a conspiracy, almost to the extent of wiping her away, as though she never existed, and that really makes me very angry. And so

now, if anything, there's a sense of wanting to get back a sense of her, and a value for her. So I don't feel stigma; there's a sense of wanting to honour her. (Kevin)

Bowlby suggests that 'relative to deaths due to other causes, the death of a child's parents by suicide is not altogether uncommon' (1985: 381). On the basis of UK figures, he believes that the proportion of parental death due to suicide 'for children born to parents in their twenties ... may be as high as one father in fifteen and one mother in seventeen who die' (1985: 381). Shepherd and Barraclough (1976) have estimated that in Britain, as many as 2,000 children under sixteen may become survivors of parental suicide annually.

The people whose experiences are described in this chapter are all adults now, but the suicide had occurred during their childhood or adolescence, the youngest being four and the oldest eighteen at the time of the death. Despite the fact that in some instances the suicide had occurred over twenty years ago, their memories of the event were often still very vivid.

Given the difficulties many adults have in talking about suicide with each other, it is hardly surprising that children are often told little or nothing about how their parent died; even when they are told something, the information they receive may not even be an accurate version of events. Non-existent or distorted communication is common in this situation; as Cain and Fast discovered when studying a group of child survivors of parental suicide, many of them had received 'the message ... that they *should not tell* and they *should not know*' (1972a: 103, italics in original). Shepherd and Barraclough's findings (1976) were not dissimilar; in a group of thirty-six child survivors, only half were given any sort of explanation about the suicide; of the remaining eighteen, some of whom would have been too young to have understood about suicide at the time of the death, twelve still knew nothing about the manner of death between five and seven years later.

Kevin's story is worth recounting in some detail at this point because much of what happened to him around the time of his mother's death is typical of the experiences of child survivors. When he was ten, Kevin came downstairs one morning to find his mother lying on the kitchen floor with her head resting in the gas oven. He decided that she had probably fallen over and banged her head; he certainly had no idea that she was dead, let alone that she had taken her own life. He remembers lifting her head from the oven, after which he was sent upstairs to his bedroom; he can recall next looking out of the window and seeing the bright red blanket as the ambulancemen carried her away. All that day, relatives came and went from the house, but Kevin and the other children were told nothing until that evening when their father told them their mother was dead; there was no proper explanation, though, of what had happened, and suicide was not mentioned. Feeling numbed and shocked, Kevin was sent off without his siblings to stay with relatives. No one suggested that he might want to attend the funeral, and he only realised that his mother had gone for ever when, on returning home, he looked in her wardrobe and saw that all her clothes had disappeared. About two months later, playing round at a friend's house, he overheard something which suggested that his mother had committed suicide, but within the family, the manner of her death remained a secret. Within the next year, he had left home to go to boarding school.

Seeing or hearing things but not having them properly explained; being sent away from home, or being looked after by distant relatives or by neighbours; not having the chance to attend the funeral; finding out about the suicide by overhearing adult conversations; going away to school (or moving home); all these are common experiences of child survivors.

Although some victims will have ensured that their children are not around at the time of the suicide, this is not always the case; Kevin's experience is not all that unusual. In their study of families (see above), Shepherd and Barraclough (1976) found that almost half the children had been in the vicinity of the suicide, and even this they consider to be an underestimate since the information was not obtained directly from the children.

Denise was four when she saw her father hanging from the staircase, but despite having had to live with that memory, she does not regret the experience: 'I just think if I hadn't found him, that I wouldn't have been able to fit it into my understanding.... I don't think it would have been explained adequately.' Indeed, for the next twelve years no one did explain to her what had happened and Denise kept quiet, sensing that the subject was taboo in the family. As she reached her teens, she would spend hours alone in her room, crying, and trying to make sense of what she had seen as a small child. It was only finally when she was sixteen that she and her mother were able to talk to one another about what had happened.

Despite these difficulties, in some ways Denise was fortunate because even if the suicide was not discussed, at least it was not denied. This does not always happen; Cain and Fast (1972a) came across families where the child who had witnessed the suicide was either given a version of events which clearly contradicted what had been seen, or they were told that they must have dreamt the whole thing. This can seriously affect the child's entire sense of reality (Dunne-Maxim *et al.* 1987); if a child sees her mother has cut her wrists and is told that death was the result of a drowning accident, what and who is she to believe? What is real and what is make-believe?

Denise was probably right to assume that her father's death was a taboo subject. Suicide is a prime candidate for the establishment of secrets in the family (see Chapter 9). Where children are involved, adults may be so overwhelmed by their own feelings that the only way they can cope is to exclude children and ignore the needs of younger family members (Staudacher 1988). In Martin's case, there were secrets in the family long before his mother's suicide (which happened when he was in his early teens). Looking back to his childhood, he *thinks* his mother was probably having a series of mental breakdowns; he can remember fetching her from hospital on at least one occasion. He *thinks* she may have been addicted to morphine; he can remember coming across phials and syringes around the house. But he is not too sure about any of this, because no one told him what was going on. He is not even sure exactly what month and year it was that his mother died. What he can remember is that one day his mother disappeared, their home was suddenly full of police who practically seemed to live in the house, the story was in the national newspapers, and then she was found dead. With the lack of communication from adults about what was happening to his mother, it is hardly surprising that, as he admits: 'I was the one person who hadn't twigged.' After her death that secrecy was maintained:

> It was sort of in a sense not spoken of, and it was never really discussed afterwards in the family at all ... I can never remember having a conversation with my father about it, ever ... that was the way the family coped.

Now, almost forty years later, he feels that he will probably never be able to piece together the story of his mother's death. He still has dreams in which he is searching for her, and when he finds her, it is always as though she never really died. Perhaps for Martin she never has died.

One of the few things which Martin does recall clearly from that time is hearing his father crying in the night. Realising that the last time he saw his mother alive she had been cross with him about something, he decided that he must have been in some way responsible for her death:

> I did feel that I was to blame and that I'd angered her and upset her in some way ... I really felt that I'd done something.... I think I've spent a lot of my life trying to resolve and make reparation for it.... I remember my last memory of her being angry, very angry, and I now can't remember what it was about and what I had done.

Dorpat (1972) has suggested that in an attempt to avoid feelings of overwhelming helplessness and abandonment, children may decide that they were responsible for what happened; then at least they can feel they are exercising some control over events. But feeling responsible for the suicide can also mean feeling guilty (Cain and Fast 1972a; Staudacher 1988). Like Martin, Jan is another child survivor who for many years has struggled with that legacy of guilt which, in her case, related not only to her father's suicide but to her mother's death three years earlier: 'I spent years trying to be such a good girl so that I couldn't do any more damage.'

Even when children are aware of things going wrong at home before the suicide, because they are not adults they are likely to feel helpless to alter the situation. As Jan found, children tend to have very little power. Although she disliked the publicity surrounding her father's suicide, at least she felt that the secret, which she had been powerless to deal with, was out in the open:

> I hated the [publicity] at the time, I felt it exposed, and at that time I just saw it as a negative thing, that it had exposed what had been a kind of secret all that time [but] I suppose at some level there was relief that it wasn't a secret any more. Prior to the suicide his drinking never led to any sort of intervention and I can remember every time he got picked up [for drinking and driving] thinking now they'll do something about it – but it never happened.

Until her father died, it must have seemed to Jan that even adults were powerless to change things. One of the ways in which the child survivor may try to deal with what has happened is to become the family carer. Kevin talked of how he felt responsible for ensuring that everything was all right; he became, as he says, 'the carer, the coper, someone that the others might look to'. Dunne-Maxim and her colleagues suggest that these children (in common with some sibling survivors – see p. 122) may seek to '"parent" their parents in an apparent effort to bring some order to their disturbed lives and homes' (1987: 238). Assuming the parental role may also be a way of identifying with the dead parent:

> The identification may take the form of noting the many similarities between oneself and the deceased parent, taking on the dead parent's role within the family, or displaying the same behaviour or symptoms as the parent who committed suicide.... A different element of identification focusses on the act of suicide itself. The child may directly repeat the suicidal death of the parent in great detail.... or become resigned that he too will die by suicide. (McIntosh 1987b: 78–9)

Sometimes the survivor will literally take over the dead person's role and functions in the family. Hilary was eighteen, and had just left home to attend secretarial college when her mother committed suicide. She returned home the same day, and, despite being the youngest of three children, it was she who made all the funeral arrangements. She never went back to college, but took over her mother's role and kept house for her father until her marriage some years later. Thirty-five years after her mother's death, Hilary has discovered that 'this is where the scars lie'; her sister, who lives abroad, has recently announced that she does not plan to return home when their elderly father dies. Although Hilary is in many ways a natural carer and coper, she is surprised how bitterly she resents her sister's attitude. Once again, she is going to have to deal with a family funeral on her own; once again she is going to be the one who copes.

Taking over the dead person's functions like Hilary did is one way survivors may identify with the dead parent, but identification can take more subtle forms. Martin's mother had been a doctor, and he spent much of his early adult life unsuccessfully attempting to become medically qualified – despite being advised against this by other people. It was, he subsequently realised, 'a blanket attempt to try and be her almost' – and an attempt perhaps to repossess that which he had lost?

At its most tragic, identification with the dead parent can result in the child survivor committing suicide too (Cain and Fast 1972a; McIntosh 1987b). For Denise, being a survivor has meant facing the question 'Will I do it too?' As she grew up, it became increasingly important for her to feel sure that even if she resembled her father in some ways, unlike him she was not going to take her own life:

> I do remember in my teens my mum used to say, 'oh, you're very highly strung', and that I was just like my father and ... it was terrible.... There was always this fear that if something happened, I might end up taking my own life ... I might not be strong enough [not to]. There was a fear, yes.

Discussing his work with a group of young men who were the child-hood survivors of parental suicide, Worden writes of how 'many [survivors] seem to carry with them a sense of fate or doom' (1983: 81). The legacy of the childhood survivor may involve a confrontation with that sense of fate.

On reaching adulthood, child survivors may feel the need to try and make some sense of the suicide. Some, like Kevin and Jan, go into therapy, wanting to understand better how the suicide has shaped their lives, and hoping that, as a result, they will become better adjusted, more whole individuals (see also Chapter 12). Like adult survivors, they may also embark on a search for the person who died. What sort of person were they and why did they do this?

The evidence can be quite conflicting and confusing as Jan found after her father's death. The man she had grown up with was someone who had a serious drinking problem, whose idea of a joke was to fire his gun and pretend he had shot himself, and who left a note blaming his daughters for his suicide. But to other people in their local community in South Africa, he was a courageous and highly respected lawyer, a man to whom many people had cause to be grateful, and who had even been known to save people from capital punishment. Piecing this sort of picture together can be difficult.

For Kevin, the silence which surrounded his mother's suicide has left him even more determined not to let her disappear into oblivion. With the help of a therapist, he has been trying to get back in touch with some of the 'good parenting' which he believes he had from her as a little boy. On a more practical level, he has acquired a copy of her birth certificate and newspaper reports of her inquest. He has also made contact with family members who knew her, and has been to talk to them about his mother.

For any child, the loss of a parent will be a devastating experience. The feeling of having been hurt and abandoned may be translated into feelings of 'I won't trust anyone again because then I can be sure of not being hurt or rejected again'. To some extent this has been Denise's experience; although she has made some close relationships with men, she is always afraid they will leave her, and aware that her father's suicide makes it hard for her to sustain trust in important relationships, particularly where men are involved.

Anyone who has been bereaved by suicide will carry that experience of survivorship with them for the rest of their life, unwelcome though that may sometimes be. Denise knows that she cannot shed her past: 'I suppose I do feel that I should not be living in terms of it any more, [but] I still feel it's very much part of me.' She is right, but perhaps what matters ultimately is how far people can confront and integrate that experience into the rest of their lives. Some survivors like Jan and Kevin have chosen to confront their childhood experiences very directly by entering therapy. For Kevin, the decision to seek help came when he realised that he did not have to remain frozen as the ten-year-old whose mother committed suicide – indeed, that he could not do so: 'I [could] either continue to live a lie, or actually confront the past.'

Surviving the suicide of a spouse

I felt as though I had been forcibly divorced. I mean, that's the only way I can put it, that I had no say in the matter ... I wasn't ready to give up on him and he gave up on himself. (Susan)

The survivors of suicide perhaps have more in common with the innocent parties of divorce or separation, because there's this feeling of rejection, of inadequacy. (Brian)

On any scale of stressful life events, the death of a spouse usually comes somewhere near the top. Depending on the age and circumstances of the couple, widowhood can bring in its wake a range of potential difficulties: it can mean having to bring children up alone: possible financial difficulties; and, frequently, acute loneliness. When the death is suicide, this brings its own particular problems:

There was the almost inevitable intense reverberation to the suicide's active rejection of his world and those closest to him.

> Suicide regularly represented an implicit statement that the
> suicide's spouse could not or did not help him towards
> happiness or at least out of despair ... the entire history of the
> marital relationship often seemed put on trial as to
> 'responsibility' for the suicide. (Cain and Fast 1972b: 150)

Marriage can be viewed as a contract into which both parties have usually freely entered, but when one party commits suicide, they not only break the contract unilaterally, they reject the very person with whom they chose to share their life. People may not choose their parents or siblings, but they do (with some exceptions) choose who they marry. Whatever the circumstances of the suicide, this is how it can feel to the survivor at least. Any widow or widower may feel abandoned by their partner, but the sense of rejection can be particularly acute for suicide survivors, as Marie discovered after Oliver's death: 'I mean, you go through the "why" business anyway, but why should someone choose to kill themselves rather than live with me?'

Having to cope with a sense of rejection will be hard enough, but being made to feel in some way responsible for the suicide can make things even worse as Susan discovered. Because Richard had been good at covering up his feelings outside their home, some of their friends found his suicide quite inexplicable. As a result, she felt people were somehow implicating her in his death. They wanted to know what her role had been, and although she believes that their marriage was happy, she feels that other people placed a question mark over the relationship.

When the time leading up to the suicide has been particularly stressful, the survivor could be expected to feel some relief when the death occurs, but spouses may still feel totally bereft. Eric had had fifteen years of treatment for mental health problems before he finally took his life; his difficulties had considerably disrupted family life (see below), but despite that, Isabel found that no longer to be one of a pair was one of the most painful aspects of her bereavement: 'just being cut in half, and feeling so alone really, even though he had been so ill.... Just the isolation, because it's not the same [being] with the children.'

Suicide can result in changing roles and functions for surviving family members (see Chapter 9). For surviving spouses, there is the enforced change of status from husband or wife to widower or widow, but the suicide can also deprive the survivor of a caring role

(Wallace 1977; McIntosh 1987b). Freedom from caring can bring a feeling of relief although this, in turn, may leave the survivor feeling guilty. Although Eric's suicide was a devastating loss for Isabel, it also brought an end to fifteen years of being the one who coped with the various crises, including previous suicide attempts:

> It was a form of relief really, when he died, to be honest.... You know I had had to live with this business of the suicide for a long time, so for a while it was like a relief, a sense of peace in a way.

For some survivors, caring for a dependent spouse has to be combined with the care of young children which can cause further stress in the family, particularly when the needs of children and of the suicidal person conflict. Isabel remembers how on one occasion she decided to try and look after Eric herself, rather than have him readmitted to the local psychiatric hospital, but his aggressive outbursts and heavy drinking disturbed the children, and she found herself caught between competing demands: 'it was hard going for all of us.... He was suffering, but we were all suffering as well.'

In Melanie's case, trying to cope with her husband and a small baby meant she was faced with a painful choice. Things had started to go wrong soon after Hannah was born and as things became worse, Ian became more and more demanding; she began to feel that if the three of them stayed together she would be looking after two babies. She increasingly felt that Ian was forcing her to choose between him and Hannah. After his death, Melanie found that, for a time, caring for Hannah 'became no more than going through the motions', and she resented the fact that Ian had left her to be a single parent. Any widowed parent may find single parenting hard work, but the suicide survivor may also feel aggrieved that the other person deliberately forced them into that role.

Susan remembers how she felt about being left to cope with the aftermath of Michael's suicide. In the next four years, Susan's father, an aunt, and a sister all died. As well as her son, she had a widowed mother to look after. Despite the strain, Susan carried on coping – 'I was the coper and I had to keep going' – but subsequently developed a painful physical illness which, she now realises, was probably a delayed reaction to these losses and to not having enough space for her own grieving. Having to cope with other people, whether they are dependent children or elderly parents – or, as in Susan's case, both – can mean having to put your own grief in cold storage.

Looking for someone or something to blame is a common reaction to suicide (see Chapters 5 and 9) and spouses are often easy targets for blame by other people (Bowlby 1985). Lindemann and Greer suggest that even though

> members of the family in which he has married [no longer] demand that his family of birth recompense them for the man and woman hours they have lost and the shame and sorrow they have undergone ... neither, on the other hand, have we worked out very effective means of neutralizing the hostility which may exist in the mourners. (1972: 64)

Surviving spouses are no longer expected to pay financial compensation, but the ill-will and the blame can still arise (see Chapter 9, p. 111).

With these potential legacies of suicide, it is little wonder that spouses can sometimes find it hard to contemplate the idea of remarriage. Irene was only in her fifties when Bill committed suicide, but four years later she still feels unable to consider the idea: 'I don't think I would ever trust again.... I would never marry again, no. I wouldn't dare.' Feeling that she has once been rejected and abandoned, Irene is not prepared to risk history repeating itself. Isabel was even younger than Irene when widowed, but although friends have urged her to remarry, she feels unwilling to risk the possibility of another fifteen years of the sort of difficulties she experienced in her first marriage.

As Susan found, the survivor may be left wondering whether there is something about their personality that attracts suicidal people. Before she married Richard, Susan had had two other serious relationships; one of these men subsequently committed suicide, and the other she described as 'impossibly neurotic'. Although in some ways she would like to marry again, she reluctantly admits that 'on reflection I have realised that I have an apparently calm personality which seems to attract neurotic men'.

However, by no means all surviving spouses will remain widowed (Cain and Fast 1972b; Shepherd and Baraclough 1976), and remarriage can turn out to be a very positive experience. While he was married to Gwen, Andrew always felt that their marriage was not all he felt it could be. After what he describes as 'the sixteen most wonderful years of his second marriage', he knows that he was right: 'Now', he says, 'I know how marriage should be.'

Chapter eleven

Facing the world

Some people can't handle it. I mean, if you say somebody killed themselves, it's a real conversation stopper. (Melanie)

Society somehow expects us to sweep our feelings of horror and guilt and grief away. (Jennifer)

She was so much there. The one thing of any importance to me was my own daughter ... I wasn't going to talk trivialities. (Nancy)

Bereavement and the social network

As Solomon suggests, friends can be an important source of support to bereaved people:

Throughout the normal grieving process, there is usually a great deal of social support. Family and friends discuss the death and its effects. Mutual aid ensures for most people a relatively smooth transition from life with to life without the deceased. The grieving person and his family are usually helped through such feelings as anger, guilt, and helplessness. (1981: 18)

Apart from the family, a survivor's social network may include close friends, more distant friends and acquaintances, neighbours, and people in the workplace. In the days immediately following the death, the bereaved will tend to withdraw from their wider social network into the privacy of their own home and immediate family, perhaps seeing just one or two close friends. But at some point, often after the funeral has taken place, they will gradually re-emerge, go back to work, start seeing friends again, and resume their normal leisure activities.

Solomon paints a somewhat idealistic picture of social support.

Sometimes the bereaved person will find other people reacting to their loss in ways which are not particularly helpful: friends may be embarrassed, they may not know what to say; they may want to help but end up saying completely the wrong thing; or, if really unable to cope with the situation, they may avoid the bereaved person entirely. Nevertheless, as a society we would probably like to think we are becoming a little more comfortable with death and bereavement. But can the same be said about society's response to self-inflicted death? And how do the survivors themselves feel about facing other people?

From studies carried out in the UK and North America, there is some evidence suggesting that the way other people behave towards suicide survivors does differ from other types of bereavement. In the United States, for example, Calhoun and his colleagues attempted to measure how other people behaved towards survivors by asking a group of funeral directors for their observations; more than four-fifths had noticed how members of the community reacted different-ly to suicide deaths: they did not always know what to do, and they had more difficulty expressing their sympathy to the surviving families (cited in Rudestam 1987).

Like anyone who has been bereaved, the survivor of suicide can be comforted by the support of others, and this informal help is precisely what friends and neighbours can offer. When Shepherd and Barra-clough (1979) asked a group of survivors what sort of help they had needed, comfort and support, together with practical help, were the needs most often mentioned – by 81 per cent of the group. However, a third of those who said they wanted comfort and support felt that these needs had not been met.

The normlessness of suicide death and bereavement

Significant events such as births, marriages, and deaths are usually marked by specific rituals. We have baptisms, christening parties, wedding ceremonies, and funerals, and there are generally accepted ways of reacting and behaving on these occasions: we are expected to congratulate the newly married couple or the new baby's parents; we offer sympathy to the widow whose husband died from a heart attack; and hold military funerals for members of the armed services. Where the person had a long illness, people may say how glad they are that the suffering has ended.

Suicide, though, is a normless event. Unlike some of the more primitive societies which have developed certain prescribed behaviours for mourning a suicide victim, we have no universally agreed ways of reacting to self-inflicted death: 'Western societies have generally failed to develop such guidelines, leaving a highly ambiguous situation for survivors and their social networks in the event of a suicide death' (Hauser 1987: 67). Two further studies carried out by Calhoun and colleagues looked at the social rules and behaviours governing suicide (Calhoun *et al.* 1986). From these surveys, which involved questioning members of the community and undergraduate students respectively, they concluded that in the case of suicide, other people can find it hard to talk either about the cause of death, or about any positive aspects of the death. (The studies are described in more detail by Hauser 1987.) There are no conventional phrases for commenting on suicide, as Nick discovered when trying to talk with friends after his mother's death: 'People sort of had grave expressions and nodded ... and there was nothing they could say.'

Given this situation, it is not particularly surprising that survivors may feel it would have been easier if the person had died from some other cause. Carol believes that people would have reacted very differently if her son had died in an accident, but instead: 'it's almost as if you're not allowed to have gone through suicide, or to be a survivor of suicide or the death hasn't happened that way – it's happened some other way'. As Dick commented after his sister's suicide, 'if it had been a painful cancer or something they might have said "at least she's not in pain" or something like that'. Although he felt able to talk about Sally's death with certain people (and particularly with women friends), he soon realised that the fact that she had taken her own life made some of his friends very uncomfortable.

In Bel Mooney's novel *The Anderson Question*, when the highly respected village doctor disappears and his body is found in nearby countryside, everyone assumes he has had a heart attack. When the real cause of death emerges, however, his son finds attitudes in the local community have changed:

> it all sounds as if everybody thought it was perfectly okay for Dad to be dead. Nice normal heart attack ... no problem. But *now*, when we all know it wasn't normal – that he *decided* to die, we all avoid each others' eyes as if something rude had been said. (1985: 116, italics in original)

Breaking the news to other people

The aftermath of suicide can draw everyone into a conspiracy of silence. Survivors sometimes have as much difficulty in talking about the suicide as those around them. In a study of thirty-nine cases of suicide in Ohio, Rudestam (1977, quoted in Rudestam 1987) found that about half the respondents did not want to discuss the suicide with friends and acquaintances, and nearly a third admitted that they sometimes lied to other people about the cause of death. To cope with this, survivors may sometimes resort to ambiguities; Brian found it difficult to talk openly about his wife's suicide; as he said, 'I think all parties involved in suicide try to hide it to some extent, don't they? I mean, I used the expression "Judy was killed". I don't say that she took her own life.'

Some survivors find it particularly hard to face other people in the early days. As Pam recalled: 'at the time you're so vulnerable that everything hurts, everything. You're bruised so easily.' Having to tell other people can feel like rubbing salt into a wound as Peter discovered; although he has never felt any particular sense of stigma about his sister's suicide, for him, telling other people about Susie meant it was impossible to deny what had happened: 'every time I had to say that Susie had died, I had to admit it to myself'.

In Jane's case, she felt that telling other people was something she really needed to do as part of coming to terms with Christopher's death; she also did not want people to hear the news at second hand; so, when she returned to work after her brother's death and found that a colleague had already told people about the suicide, she reacted extremely angrily:

> I felt violated, and also it made me realise that telling people is part of the process of coming to terms with what you're telling them.... I felt the ground had been pulled away from under me, and I resented it bitterly.

Some survivors find telling other people is easier in the early days, when they are still in a state of shock and everything seems somewhat unreal anyway. For the author Peter Handke, talking about his mother's suicide could seem almost dangerously easy: 'I would not be extorting personal sympathy from my listener or reader', he wrote, 'I would merely be telling him a rather fantastic story' (1976: 6). That sense of the suicide becoming a sort of fantasy – something completely unreal – was echoed by Ursula; after her daughter's suicide, she asked her sister to 'phone round and tell people because, as she explained, 'I knew that ... if I had to keep explaining to everybody, and going over it, it would have lost its meaning. It would sort of become banal by repetition.'

Peter Handke's sense of wanting to keep it to himself in order to maintain a sense of reality left him feeling ambivalent about whether he even wanted attention from other people:

> The worst thing right now would be sympathy, expresssed in a word or even a glance. I would turn away or cut the sympathiser short because I need the feeling that what I am going through is incomprehensible and incommunicable; only then does the horror seem meaningful and real. If anyone talks to me about it, the boredom comes back and everything is unreal again. Nevertheless, for no reason at all I sometimes tell people about my mother's suicide but if they dare to mention it to me I am furious. (1976: 4)

Marris suggests that these conflicting emotions are a common reaction to bereavement. 'The behaviour of the bereaved', he says, 'is characteristically ambivalent: they may be lonely but shun company ... they complain if people avoid them, embarrassed how to express their sympathy, yet rebuff that sympathy irritably when it is offered' (1978: 28).

Anne Downey experienced that sense of confusion and ambivalence after her son's suicide:

> I wish the lady in the bank would not be so pleasant. She knows about you taking your life. I blurted it out one day to her friend who must have told her.... Now she looks at me with that face, and I become confused, almost apologetic. I am afraid of suddenly saying 'Yes, I'm the lady whose son killed himself. Please do not treat me differently because you make me feel guilty and he would not like that. He never meant to hurt me. It was just something he did without thinking. If he had been killed in a car crash you would not look at me like that.' (1987: 41)

Should she say something, or should she remain silent? Is that woman really sorry for her, or just curious? Does she want her sympathy anyway? Do they think Stephen deliberately set out to hurt her?

But even a completely open and truthful approach does not always elicit a particularly sympathetic response. Other people can find the unexpected news of the suicide deeply shocking. When Betty's son died from an overdose, she rang the woman she used to work for and told her the news:

I said, 'A dreadful tragedy has happened, I've lost my son', and she was terribly upset, and then, when she found out it was suicide, never a word; she'd gone. It's incredible. How did he die, you know, what did it matter? I'm never going to say he died any other way because it's not true.

Having to cope with other people who are clearly not coping with hearing the news can be an added and unwelcome burden for survivors, but avoiding this situation by not talking about the victim was not always what they needed either; survivors mentioned how there were times when they would go around almost compulsively talking about the suicide – occasionally telling complete strangers. After her son's death, Heather really wanted to talk about what had happened, but she found that just mentioning Alastair's name, let alone his death, made everyone freeze. Even finding an acceptable way to talk about the death can be difficult, as Nancy discovered after her daughter died: 'I learned quite early on not to say "my daughter committed suicide" because that embarrasses people. Then I toned it down a bit to "she took her own life"; but now I say "she died".'

Faced with other people's reluctance to talk about the suicide, some survivors will decide that the only way to deal with the situation is to broach the subject themselves. Being able to talk about her daughter mattered a great deal to Phyllis, and she found that other people were quite willing to talk about Julie provided she mentioned it first; as she says: 'then they know it's all right'. Not that survivors necessarily find it easy to be the instigators. After his sister's suicide, Dick realised that other people were tending to wait for him to mention Sally, and although he recognises now that they were probably only trying to be tactful, he sometimes found it hard having to make the first move.

Other people's reactions

Survivors can find it hard to make any sense of the death themselves (see Chapter 6) and if asked by other people, they may find it difficult to explain why the suicide occurred. Sometimes, however, other people will offer their own explanations, presumably believing that this will be helpful. In fact, it can have the opposite effect. After her son's death, there were well-meaning people who assured Maureen that Paul had obviously committed suicide because he wanted to, implying that this was some freely made decision, rather than – as she sees it – an act of desperation; as she says,

> don't they realise what torment that boy was going through?
> Would they have wanted that for their son? Would they have
> wanted that mental torture or heartache that he must have been
> feeling for weeks and weeks.... They're the remarks I find very
> unkind, and very hurtful, although they're not meant to be
> unkind; they weren't said maliciously.

Maureen's friends may have genuinely believed that Paul wanted to take his own life and that he had the right to do so, but their explanations were of no help to her. Simpson has some useful advice to anyone tempted to air their views in this manner: 'Whatever your personal views on the morality and ethics of suicide, this is no time for offering either condemnation or support for the act. Save your arguments for or against for some suitable formal debate' (1979: 220).

Confronted with the survivor's unhappiness, other people may feel that by offering some sort of explanation they will lessen their distress. When another person is clearly distressed, it is tempting to want to 'make things better', but, as Lukas and Seiden suggest, 'You need to know that as a helper you do not have to fix things up for people.... Survivors need help in working out their answers. Ultimately, it is their answers that are the only ones that are not irrelevant' (1987: 146–7).

The maxim 'never speak ill of the dead' is usually seen as an appropriate response (in public, at least), but when a person commits suicide this is sometimes ignored. Other people may feel free to pass judgement on the person who died, despite the pain this can cause; as Janice discovered, even when the comment is made by a comparative stranger, it can still be hurtful:

> [She] wasn't actually someone that I do know very closely; there
> were a lot of people there, and we were all sort of like-minded
> people getting on well, so I felt quite easy saying to her ... 'Yes,

my mother's just died and she took an overdose and it's been difficult', and she said something like 'wicked woman' – that she thought it was really wrong – and I felt very upset by that because I didn't think it was wrong.

Seeing the survivor's distress, friends may feel it will help to tell them how selfish or wicked the victim must have been to cause them this much suffering. But regardless of the survivor's own feelings about the death, having to listen to criticisms of this kind from other people can be extremely hurtful. Jean was pleased when friends told her how much they had loved and valued Anna; but there were others who criticised her daughter, including one person who told her, 'Anna was such an awful child to you and an awful nuisance; years and years from now, you'll think it's the best thing that ever happened.' Losing her only daughter has never felt like that to Jean, and she certainly never wanted to be told that Anna was an 'awful child'.

I came across survivors who had been on the receiving end of all kinds of negative remarks about their relative, such as 'Why did she do this to you?', 'What a waste of a life', and 'We forgive him'. Survivors found these sort of comments unhelpful, partly because there was often an implied judgement about the victim's worth, and as Suzy said: 'I think you need exactly the same as other [bereaved] people get ... a valuing of the person.'

Avoidance

Although survivors may understandably feel hurt when people who they thought were friends appear to be avoiding them, as Jean discovered, part of coming to terms with the loss can involve acknowledging that other people are not always going to be able to cope with the suicide:

I've lost a number of friends whom I've had to let go. It's no use being angry with these friends that they cannot share my grief ... unless someone has experienced our sort of pain how can they possibly share? Once upon a time we were lucky not to know what it was like either.

The tendency for friends to avoid any discussion of the suicide was noted by Rudestam in a survey carried out in Ohio (see p. 137). From questioning a group of survivors, he concluded that 'The pattern was for friends to listen and be sympathetic ... while at the same time avoiding the topic of death itself' (1987: 32–3). After her brother's suicide, Liz found that although other people knew the circumstances of Tony's death, no one would actually use the word 'suicide' when talking to her. If friends cannot cope with the idea of someone taking their own life, they may even want to try and convince the survivor that the death was not really suicide, as happened to Isabel, some of whose friends told her they were sure Eric had not really taken his own life. It can be hard enough for survivors to face the fact that it was suicide, but when other people try and persuade them that the truth was otherwise, survivors may end up unsure what sort of loss it is they are really grieving.

For some survivors, one of the most difficult aspects of their bereavement is finding that other people will not even mention the person, let alone talk about their death. As Pam discovered after Frances died: 'You're allowed to mention your son who's living, you're allowed to mention *his* childhood, but you're not allowed to mention your daughter's childhood.'

However, even when survivors have initially been able to talk about the suicide, after a time other people may assume that the survivor will have recovered, and that the best thing is not to mention the person any more; the victim is virtually consigned to oblivion. It may also be other people's way of saying that *they* no longer want to have to cope with the survivor's possible distress. A year after her daughter's death, Pat finds this very painful:

> I find now that other people don't mention Caroline, and that hurts me.... Her name never comes into the conversation unless we bring it into the conversation.... Someone might be talking about dieting and I would probably say 'oh, Caroline tried this or tried that', and there's this silence and the subject is changed.... I get angry ... I don't express my anger but I want to say, 'She was here, she was a person, she lived with us and with you for twenty years, and she laughed and she cried, and she did all the things that we do'.... Whether they think it's because it would hurt us, but it hurts far more for people not to talk about her.... I don't honestly think it's because they've forgotten her. They probably don't feel the need to keep her alive as much as I do.

This sort of behaviour, Pincus has suggested, may also be other people's way of avoiding their own painful or disturbing feelings evoked by death:

> the expectation is that the bereaved will be brave ... and not embarrass others with his grief. For unlike the pleasant feelings stirred up by lovers, the loss of a loved one reactivates everybody's most painful nightmares, the most primary infantile fears and panic, the anguish of abandonment and the terror of being left alone, having lost love. (1974: 42)

If this dreadful thing has happened to the person sitting opposite me, who is to say that the same thing might not happen to me? When death was the result of suicide, other people may react even more strongly, and there are no conventional phrases to hand which might camouflage their possible discomfort or distress. Writing of the aftermath of her son's suicide, Diana Davenport had this to say to the people she felt were avoiding her: 'Many still are the stalwarts to whom death is a conversational avenue not to be trodden.... Oh can't they realise that I want to speak of him, want their soft and stumbling words?' (1989: 129)

Another way in which friends may try to deal with their own feelings of unease or distress is by projecting those feelings on to the survivor who, they decide, needs to be diverted – the 'take your mind off it' approach. After his sister's suicide, Peter found some people were trying to jolly him along in an attempt to stop him thinking about Susie. But as he said: 'I didn't want to be taken out of myself. I didn't want not to be thinking about Susie, I didn't want not to be thinking about what was happening at home.'

Talking about the suicide victim

In some cases, survivors will be reluctant to mention the suicide to everyone; some people will consciously choose who they will or will not tell, perhaps deciding not to mention the fact that it was suicide except to close friends or to people with whom they would have some sort of continuing relationship. Susan's approach to coping with questions about Richard's death is typical: 'If I think they're going to remain an acquaintance, I just say he had heart trouble.'

Talking to other people immediately after the death has its own problems, but how do survivors deal with this if the issue arises at some later point? Do they even mention the person who died? Parents whose children had committed suicide often found themselves faced with this dilemma when people asked how many children they had. Brothers and sisters may also be asked about their siblings.

Parents who decide to mention the child that died can find that their honesty is not always well received. After Alan's suicide, Carol decided that if people asked her about the children, she would tell them she had two sons and that one had died. But, she says, if the fact that Alan committed suicide emerges, 'they shut off immediately; they don't ask any more questions ... it's almost as if you've said something [that] upset them'. Just the mention of suicide can shock people; as Lois commented: 'it is hard to say I've got three children, my eldest son committed suicide, hope you have a nice day.... It would have been easier to say my son died of cancer or anything ... anything would have been easier.'

As survivors like Carol and Lois have discovered, coping with other people's reactions can be difficult; at the same time, though, parents sometimes feel very strongly that they do not want to deny the existence of the son or daughter who has died – or, as in Eileen's case, the two daughters she had; since Donna and Sheila died, she has found a way of talking about them which gives other people an opening:

> I usually say, 'I've now got one'. If they pick up the 'now' that's fine; if they don't, that's OK. Because I cannot, I will not, deny the fact.... I won't say 'I have one', because that denies the fact that I had Sheila and Donna, and I did have them, and they were a big part of my life.

Others like Frank will decide they are not going to tell people, and his way of coping has been to say he has two – rather than three – children. His wife, on the other hand, feels she really wants to tell people about Josie 'because it's so much a part of me'. There are no straightforward or comfortable solutions to this dilemma. Individuals will work out what they feel is best for them. For many survivors, though, the situation creates a dilemma; to keep silent can feel like denying that the person ever existed; on the other hand, they know that if they mention the suicide, other people may well retreat into embarrassed silence.

Stigma – where does it come from?

Any bereaved person can feel that their loss sets them apart from other people. After his wife died of cancer, C.S. Lewis wrote: 'I'm aware of being an embarrassment to everyone I meet ... perhaps the bereaved ought to be isolated in special settlements like lepers' (1966: 11). But suicide, with its normlessness, and its potential for guilt and anger, can further accentuate that sense of differentness. After her son took his life, Maureen felt she was no longer normal:

> people on the outside [need] to try and understand how we are feeling, what we are going through ... because [we] can't cope with people on the outside.... So it's important for them to know that it's far from normal for ... the people who are left.... I feel like some sort of sect; we are different. Yes, that's how we feel, different, totally different, not normal any more. We never will be normal.

Several survivors I met referred to other people as 'outsiders', yet it often seemed that it was they who felt they were the outsiders, the ones who had become 'a sort of sect' in Maureen's words. After her husband committed suicide, Irene imagined how, if she were to tell people what had happened, 'they were going to stand in the market square and shout to everyone, "this is the lady, this is the one"'. As Smith points out, survivors may feel publicly insulted by the victim: 'they feel he has made a public declaration that he prefers death to them' (1978: 62). As a result, survivors like Irene may feel branded by the rest of the world, as though the stigma attached to the suicide victim becomes attached to the whole family, or as Harry said, 'you're a bit of a funny family if something like this happens, you know'.

Because suicide still tends to be hushed up, survivors may feel that they are the only family to whom this has happened. But suicide is not that uncommon; after her son's death, Carol discovered that both sets of neighbours had had suicides in their families; yet despite this, she has still found it hard to accept that someone in her family could commit suicide. 'I don't think I should be ashamed of the manner that Alan died', she says, 'I shouldn't feel that people look at my family as I would have done previously.' Meeting other families, though, can help survivors to realise that they are not particularly abnormal (see Chapter 12).

Is it always the case, though, that other people view survivors in such a negative way, or do survivors sometimes assume there is stigma where it does not actually exist? If they feel guilty about the suicide, are they assuming that everyone out there thinks the same and is waiting to punish them? According to Rudestam: 'It is difficult to know whose reluctance to discuss the event is more responsible for the eventual silence – the survivor's or the friends'' (1987: 33). Perhaps both parties, for different reasons, can only face each other with difficulty.

What helped the survivors

Despite these various difficulties, survivors can still, if they are fortunate, find people who will allow them to grieve openly, and who are not going to be overwhelmed by their distress. Access to this sort of support can be a significant factor affecting the way that the bereaved person will deal with their loss. Describing the findings of various studies by Raphael and colleagues, Bowlby writes of how:

> a widow with a good outcome would report how at least one person ... had made it easy for her to cry and to express the intensity of her feelings, and [she] would describe what a relief it had been to be able to talk freely and at length about past days with her husband and the circumstances of his death. (1985: 193)

Similarly, several of the survivors I met mentioned how much they had been helped by one particular person – usually a close friend – who had allowed them to talk at length about what had happened, and who had not been upset by the survivor's distress. As Susan found, one of the things which had helped her most was the friend who was prepared to sit and listen: 'and it was a relief to talk to her at length ... she didn't get upset like family members would, and she helped me a great deal just by listening'. As Lukas and Seiden point out: 'good listening permits good talking' (1987: 147).

For other survivors, it was the person who had not been afraid to show their own feelings who had been particularly helpful, such as Eileen's friend who came round, sat and held her hand, and cried with her. Eileen also recalled how, when she went back to work at the school where she was headmistress, although the staff had not known what to say, some had come up and put their arms round her. As Parkes reminds us, touch can be as healing as words: 'the quiet communication of affectionate understanding ... can be conveyed as well by a squeeze of the hand as by speech' (1986: 182). This may be particularly so with suicide, when conventional words of sympathy are harder to express.

Some newly bereaved survivors had reacted to the shock by being frantically busy; others, however, had found themselves almost totally unable to function on a practical level, and friends and neighbours who came round, took over the day-to-day housekeeping such as cooking meals, and generally assisted with preparations for the funeral had been particularly welcome. Francesca could recall 'a wonderful sense of just being looked after ... because normally it is me who does the looking after'. Apart from the fact that this sort of practical help provides positive support to survivors, it also offers a role to those friends who feel less comfortable with the listening role described above.

As this chapter has already mentioned, other people will sometimes refer to the victim in ways which are hurtful to survivors. As Pam commented, 'outsiders tend not to think too highly of people who have taken their own lives'. Because this does tend to happen, survivors can find it especially helpful to know that other people had loved and valued the person and that they would be missed. Although Maureen had been hurt by some of the comments made after Paul's death (see above), when so many people felt they wanted to come and say goodbye, it was a healing experience:

> When I went [to the undertakers] on the day of the funeral I was
> so overwhelmed ... and so proud of him.... All those friends
> going to visit him and all those people queueing up to go in and
> say their last goodbye, you know, to touch him and kiss him.... I
> was really touched, really proud of him ... and it took the hurt
> away because I felt proud of him. I think that helped.

Survivors of suicide need to feel that they can face other people, and that friends will be there to support their grieving. They need the opportunity to talk about the death and the person who died, to express painful emotions, including possible anger or guilt. As this chapter has shown, though, facing the world is not always easy; survivors have their difficulties – and so do those around them. Both need to be aware of this, and as Kast has suggested: 'We must learn again to find ways to mourn with one another' (1988: 18).

Chapter twelve

Looking for support

I needed some help totally removed from the family ... I felt safe with her [a GP-based counsellor]. (Ursula)

If I could just have talked with somebody else, just to somebody else that it had happened to, just to say how much I blamed myself and they could say, 'Well everybody feels like that, you know. I felt like that, and it's not your fault.' (Jennifer)

Any bereavement can be stressful, but suicides bring added causes of stress – post-mortems, investigations by the police, inquests, and the possible involvement of the media. Survivors may also experience more intense guilt and anger, and a sense of stigma. In this situation, Shepherd and Barraclough suggest, 'The coping mechanisms of the bereaved ... are especially likely to be thrown into disarray' (1979: 67).

Although in some families, people are able to support one another adequately, this is not always the case (Chapter 9); and even where families are apparently coping well, there can be times when, as Ursula says, the survivor will want to talk to someone who is completely uninvolved. Indeed, there may be real benefits in doing so. Reviewing studies of professional and voluntary bereavement support, Parkes (1980) concluded that such services can actually reduce the risk of psychiatric and psychosomatic disorders, particularly where families are not able to offer adequate support to one another.

What type of help are survivors likely to require? Individual survivors will have their own particular needs, but surveys which have attempted to answer this question indicate that they may have certain needs in common (Shepherd and Barraclough 1979; Rogers *et al.* 1982; Battle 1984; Osterweis *et al.* 1984). These included practical help and advice, as well as what Shepherd and Barraclough have described as 'the more intangible forms of help – consolation, emotional support and aid to incorporate the new event into a personal philosophy or set of ... beliefs' (1979: 66). It is mainly these less tangible types of support which are discussed in this chapter.

To date, specialised services for survivors of suicide have been most widely developed in North America, and from the experience gained in those projects, we already have some idea of the sorts of help survivors may be looking for. When the Survivors Support Program was being set up in Toronto, for example, participants were asked what they wanted from the scheme; they came up with the following goals (Rogers *et al.* 1982):

(1) get the suicide in perspective;
(2) deal with family problems caused by the suicide;
(3) feel better about myself;
(4) talk about the suicide;
(5) obtain factual information about suicide and its effects;
(6) have a safe place to express feelings;
(7) understand and deal with other people's reactions to suicide;
(8) get advice on practical/social concerns.

These survivors were not only seeking emotional support; they also wanted to find out more about suicide, and they wanted advice on practical matters. Similar results were obtained from a survey of survivors using the Memphis Crisis Intervention Center (Battle 1984). Again, survivors emphasised their wish to learn more about suicide (as well as looking for emotional support), leading Battle to suggest that 'the teaching aspect should constitute fifty per cent of the effort and time' (1984: 48).

Although advice, counselling, and psychotherapy services are becoming more common in Britain, many people still claim that a good friend can offer the same sort of help as professionals. In fact, survivors can benefit from the involvement of both friends and professionals; their contributions are not mutually exclusive, and they have different things to offer. After her brother's suicide, Jane found that friends could be very supportive, by 'being able to sit and listen and receive it, and not be embarrassed or frightened'. She remembers one evening in particular when she was with two friends: 'I started to cry a lot, and they didn't try to stop me or even make me talk; they quietly got on with things and let me cry, and in the circumstances it was extremely helpful ... it's acceptance really'. Nevertheless, she has also gained a great deal from seeing a psychotherapist (see p. 159).

Marris suggests that while friends can offer practical help and companionship, 'the stranger' can sometimes more easily support the bereaved in working through and resolving their grief:

> A stranger, who understands grief in general and stands in an acknowledged therapeutic role, can probably give more support to the working out of grief itself ... this support is in a sense impersonal, it does not threaten to pre-empt the personal resolution of the crisis ... it offers reassurance that the crisis is natural, that it will find a resolution in time. (1978: 153)

Marris is making an important point: survivors need to find their own solutions, their own way through their grief. Even friends who are good listeners can sometimes be tempted to put forward their own solutions, but as Staudacher says, 'counsellors don't want to "fix" you' (1988: 221).

There are a number of potential sources of support for survivors, and the fifty people featuring in this book had been helped, in varying degrees, by: general practitioners, health visitors, counsellors (voluntary and paid), psychotherapists, psychiatrists, social workers, members of the clergy, other suicide survivors, and people bereaved by non-suicide deaths. Most of these survivors were identified through two bereavement organisations (CRUSE and The Compassionate Friends), and because they had been in touch with these organisations, it could be concluded that their needs were greater than those of survivors in general. Of course, the fact that they had contacted CRUSE or TCF meant that they had been looking for some sort of help, whether it was for information or support; however, this would seem to be a perfectly normal way of coping with a major trauma such as suicide, and the fact that they needed support cannot simply be equated with an inability to cope with the death. It is also worth pointing out that, unlike many of the earlier groups of survivors – such as many of those described in Cain's book (1972) – this was not a clinical group, identified through a hospital or some other treatment setting.

Finding support

Whatever the events leading up to the death, and however much warning survivors may have been given, when the suicide actually happens it will still come as a major shock to those closest to the person who died. The victim's problems are over, but the survivor's are only just beginning, and who will be there to support them? Immediately after the suicide there are likely to be plenty of strangers or outsiders around – police, the coroner's officer, and undertakers – but are they there to support the survivors? Indeed, do survivors even need to be offered support at this point or can it wait until later? A number of writers on the aftermath of suicide have suggested that help could be made available within the first twenty-four hours (Resnik 1972; Battle 1984; Dunne 1987b), to offer what Resnik has described as 'psychological resucitation' (1972) – a crisis-intervention approach.

Apart from people investigating the death, many survivors will be in contact with their general practitioner either that day or shortly afterwards (see pp. 156–7). But even getting this type of emergency help is not always straightforward, as Carol discovered. The morning after her son's suicide, she rang the surgery requesting a home visit, and was told by the receptionist that this was not possible; she must come down to the surgery. Even when she explained the reason for her request, she was still told a home visit was out of the question, and an appointment was made for her to attend the surgery. It was only after she failed to keep the appointment that her doctor finally came round to the house.

Where else may survivors find help without having to wait? There are an increasing number of walk-in centres which offer immediate help for a range of different problems, although they tend to be based in major centres of population. Despite the patchy provision, however, they do offer a potential source of help for survivors. Immediately after her mother's death, Janice (who lives in a large northern city), went to the emergency drop-in service of her local women's counselling and therapy centre. Although they were not able to offer longer-term help at that point, she did see a counsellor at the drop-in service, and this helped her deal with an immediate issue – whether to go and see her mother's body. The undertaker was advising her not to, and her sister told her she thought it pointless; by talking it through with someone who was not involved, and who could look at the situation objectively, Janice was able to make her own decision, rather than going along with what everyone else was telling her to do.

Not every survivor will either want or need this 'psychological first aid' – there is often a great deal of support from friends and relatives in the days following the death – but this can fade away in the ensuing weeks. As the shock begins to wear off, and the survivor's intense feelings of grief start to emerge, this is often the point at which some sort of external support is really needed. Resnik (1972) proposed that a few weeks after the death, another type of support might be needed, which he termed 'psychological rehabilitation'. But support is not always readily available at this point, as Phyllis discovered. She eventually saw the counsellor at her doctor's surgery six months after her daughter's suicide, when a relative realised that Phyllis needed help. She found the sessions helpful, but looking back, knows that she could have done with that sort of help much sooner. It took Brian even longer to find the help he wanted. Although he has benefited considerably from fortnightly sessions with a CRUSE bereavement counsellor, he wishes he had been able to get this sort of help earlier than fifteen months after his wife's death. Getting access to this sort of help at the time when it is needed is not always straightforward.

Obstacles to finding and using support services

The ease with which survivors are able to find the support they need can depend on a number of different factors, including the availability of appropriate services, how well those services are publicised, and whether there is an effective referral system.

As far as actual provision is concerned, most survivors will have access to a general practitioner (see below), but finding other, more specialised help such as counselling or psychotherapy will almost certainly prove more difficult, except in London and some other major centres of population where these kinds of services tend to be clustered. The survivors I met who were receiving therapy (see pp. 157–61) all lived in or near cities. They had the additional advantage that they had usually either known of such services before the suicide occurred, or had been told about them subsequently by friends. In other words, the idea of therapy was not something completely alien to them, and they probably had at least some idea of what it involved.

Carol had been given the local contact for Compassionate Friends by her general practitioner, and her vicar had told her about CRUSE, but most of the survivors who were in touch with CRUSE or The Compassionate Friends had stumbled upon these organisations by chance, either through reading about them in newspapers or magazines, or by hearing them mentioned on radio or television. Finding the information had often been a haphazard process; there was no system whereby survivors routinely received information about organisations which they might want to contact either immediately or at some future point.

After Caroline's suicide, Robert and his wife did eventually manage to get in touch with other parents, but they only discovered the Shadow of Suicide network (see Appendix A) by chance, and they had already given up scouring the telephone directories when their other daughter happened to come across the address at her place of work. Robert and his family found the help they needed in the end because they persisted, but as he says: 'unless you are articulate enough to seek help, then there's no machinery that will follow [you] up'. As he pointed out, though, survivors are in contact with various officials such as coroners and the police who could make this sort of information available (see Chapter 15).

In some instances, survivors will want support specifically from fellow survivors; they may feel that they are the only people who could possibly be of any help to them. After her brother took his own life, Jane really wanted the chance to talk to other people who had been through this particular sort of bereavement; ideally she wanted to meet other sibling survivors. Both her parents had already died, and seeing a bereavement counsellor was not something she felt would be particularly useful; she felt she knew enough about bereavement in general; as she said, 'I'd had lots of it'. She found nothing at that point which could meet her specific needs.

Carol, who had been given contacts in both CRUSE and The Compassionate Friends, initially went to see a general bereavement counsellor, but felt this had its limitations:

> I didn't feel that she had shared the same experiences, and I
> don't think that without shared experience that they can give
> the help that's really needed. They can be a listening ear but not
> the sort of listening ear that understands, and I think that's
> something that you do need in the early stages, [but] whether
> it's just me, I don't know.

There are a number of other reasons why survivors can find it difficult to accept support from people who have not been through the same experience. They may feel they do not deserve to be alongside other bereaved people; after all, as one parent said, 'they would probably think that my child *chose* to die', implying that the survivor's grief is also self-inflicted. Survivors who are blaming themselves for the suicide may feel unworthy of other people's care and support. The sense of being different and set apart from other people may convince survivors that they should remain apart, particularly if they think other people may be blaming them anyway. Finally, if survivors are in a support group with other bereaved people, they may feel inhibited from talking about the more shocking aspects of the suicide.

Although only a minority of survivors will seek help from mental health services, those that do can be understandably reluctant to approach services which they feel have let them down so badly. As Lukas and Seiden comment: 'the mental health profession, to which they have turned for help in the past, seems to have failed them, and to have failed them terribly. It did not keep their loved one alive' (1987: 160). Relatives may feel bitter and disappointed, and these feelings may be focused on those services which seemingly contributed to the victim's death. Although she never sought help for herself from the hospital which had treated her daughter, nine months after Patricia's death Francesca admitted: 'All my anger is towards the hospital, and still is ... I don't think I've plumbed any depths of anger towards Patricia yet ... it's all gone to the hospital.'

Anger apart, survivors may have very real doubts as to whether services which seemingly failed to help their relative can possibly help them either. After her son's suicide, Carole felt unable to cope on her own, and asked her doctor for referral to an NHS psychiatrist. After some delay (during which she saw a private psychotherapist), she had five sessions with a psychiatrist who specialised in bereavement. But despite this, she still feels that, after what happened to Jon, she now has little real faith in psychiatry. She did also go and see her son's psychiatrist once after the suicide, but when it came to the second appointment, she decided not to go:

> He had told me that he did not think Jon was depressed, that he showed no obvious signs of depression at their last meeting. Why does a person kill themselves if they are not depressed? How far could I trust this man's judgement if he could make such a catastrophic error? How did he feel about it? Was Jon just a statistic to him? He didn't say.

Meetings between the survivors and the victim's psychiatrist or therapist sometimes take place, but the purpose of such encounters is not always clear, and can be an uneasy and uncomfortable experience, as Carole discovered. On a more positive note, though, such meetings can provide both parties with the opportunity to talk together about the suicide; Francesca, for example, had four meetings with her daughter's (private) psychotherapist where they were able to talk about Patricia and about what had happened. The victim's therapist or psychiatrist will have their own feelings and reactions to the suicide, though, and Dunne (1987b) sensibly recommends that the victim's former therapist should not be the person who offers ongoing support to the survivors.

Some survivors may have difficulty in obtaining help when it is needed simply because the service is oversubscribed. This can be the case with the NHS where psychotherapy services tend to be heavily oversubscribed, but private therapists and counsellors often have waiting lists too. Although Janice had seen someone at her local women's counselling and therapy centre on an emergency basis (see p. 151), there was a waiting list for longer-term therapy. As a result, she had to look elsewhere – and eventually found a private therapist (see p. 159).

Even when survivors have found someone who they hope will help them, they may discover that professionals can find it hard to cope with their own feelings about death: 'Even professional helpers ... often defend themselves so thoroughly against the savage pain and anguish of loss through bereavement that they avoid facing it and are thus unable to support the necessary task of mourning' (Pincus 1974: 48). When the death was suicide, members of the helping professions may find it even more difficult to live up to their name. Marie, who is both a survivor and a trained psychiatric social worker, feels that 'suicide is such a painful and difficult area, it is understandable that even the professionals seem to find it difficult to help'. When she returned to work after her husband's suicide, she found that, with one exception, if she started talking about Oliver's death, her social work colleagues would all disappear.

But to return for a moment to the survivors' problems. The Toronto Support Program (Rogers *et al.* 1982) and the Memphis Crisis Intervention Center (Battle 1984) both found it difficult to make contact with male survivors, and in both cases, over three-quarters of the survivors they were supporting were female. Perhaps the men did not see themselves as needing support, although since more men than women commit suicide, there may, of course, be more female survivors – such as spouses – seeking help. It is more likely, however, that men will find other ways of coping with their bereavement (see pp. 109–10).

Experiences with general practitioners

Whereas in the past, the Church would usually have been seen as the main source of comfort and help, it is now more likely that the bereaved will turn to their general practitioner. Research has shown that people who have recently been bereaved tend to consult their family doctor more often than before the death occurred (Parkes 1986). Suicide survivors are no exception; most of the people I met had had some contact with their general practitioner, however fleeting, although the sort of help they had been offered varied considerably.

According to Parkes, members of the medical profession are 'acquainted with the reality of death', and this, he adds, 'should make it possible for the bereaved to talk to them about this taboo topic' (1986: 192). However, by no means all family doctors will be that comfortable when faced with the relatives of a suicide victim. Many survivors sensed their GP's unease, and talked of how their doctor seemed unsure what to say; Heather's experience was not atypical:

> He just was hopeless, and he's a nice person and he just hadn't a clue.... He came in. He was sorry. He sat in the garden, he had his case with him, and he offered us drugs, naturally, and we said 'What we want is help, we don't want drugs. Can you put us in touch with somebody who'll help us?' And he said, 'I don't know of anybody ... the best thing you can do is talk to each other' ... and that was it. So we came a bit unstuck with the GP ... he didn't give us any comfort or help.

Survivors are commonly offered medication by their doctor, although some people had already made up their minds, before visiting the surgery, that they did not want to take any drugs. Sometime before her daughter's suicide, Pat had become dependent on tranquillisers, but had managed to wean herself off them – with little encouragement from her doctor who she described as 'a bit pill happy'. When she went to see him after Caroline's death, however, she found his approach more helpful:

He said, 'I'm not going to give you any pills, because there are no pills for grief', and he was right really. It's something you've got to get through.... He was very good ... what he did say was 'My door is always open. You can come and see me whenever you want, any time, just come, the door is open.'

Very few of the survivors I met had used medication, except perhaps to help them get through the first few days. For some people whose relative had died as the result of an overdose this was a particularly sensitive issue. Susan remembers the thoughtless advice she received after her husband's death, when well-meaning friends urged her to take sleeping tablets, even though they knew that Richard had overdosed on barbiturates.

But apart from medication, what sort of support can general practitioners offer to survivors of suicide? Are they able to offer counselling, or, if they lack the relevant skills, are they able to refer patients on to more appropriate sources of help? Do they hold up-to-date information on local or national bereavement organisations? The answer would seem to be, it depends on your particular doctor. Heather's doctor (see p. 156) had no idea where she could find help, but Carol, on the other hand, was told about Compassionate Friends. When it comes to counselling, some survivors were fortunate in being registered with a practice which had a counsellor attached, but others had a doctor who they felt was ill-equipped to deal with emotional problems of any kind.

Doctors, like others in the helping professions, can be the target of survivors' blame. At the same time, they may be blaming themselves for the fact that their patient committed suicide; all this can make the patient–doctor relationship somewhat uneasy, as Marie discovered. Although she felt that perhaps their doctor could have done more for her husband, she found herself reassuring him that he had done all he could, and telling him he was not to blame – when what she actually wanted to do was change to another doctor in the practice.

Use of counselling and psychotherapy services

Although only a minority of survivors will use this sort of help, it can be an important source of support, and a means of working through some of the complex emotions associated with suicide bereavement.

Counselling and therapy services are still rather thin on the ground in Britain, although the general level of provision is gradually increasing, and, with the advent of 'advice' phone-ins on radio, more people are beginning to understand its potential benefits. In addition to counsellors and therapists who are trained to work with a range of problems, the number of bereavement counsellors is increasing, many working through local CRUSE branches.

As has already been mentioned (Chapters 9 and 11), survivors frequently discover that family and friends have difficulty in offering adequate support; other people may be overwhelmed by their own feelings of grief, or simply not comfortable with the idea of talking about suicide. This can make it hard for survivors to find someone with whom they can share their feelings. A counsellor or psychotherapist, on the other hand, can allow the bereaved to express their thoughts and feelings openly without the survivor having to worry about how the other person is coping (Osterweis *et al.* 1984); as Staudacher suggests: 'you can be allowed to feel the way you do – not talked out of it' (1988: 220). Christine, who started seeing a bereavement counsellor shortly after her husband's suicide, found it helpful to talk about Graham's death, 'and not feel it upset [him]. I mean, it still upsets my friends and relatives – and I can't really discuss it with them.'

Guilt can be a response to any bereavement, but is more common and may be felt more intensely with suicide (Hauser 1987). However, survivors may find it hard to mention their guilty feelings to family and friends – who may have their own views on who was to blame anyway. The listening which a counsellor offers can enable survivors to explore their sense of guilt, and test the reality of their feelings in a safe and non-judgemental atmosphere (Worden 1983; Osterweis *et al.* 1984). Eileen, whose twin daughters had both taken their own lives, found that like many parent-survivors, she blamed herself continually for not having been a better mother. Sessions with a counsellor enabled her to reach a somewhat different perspective on her guilt, and to begin to feel, as she says, 'that every parent does what they feel best at the time'.

As well as blaming themselves, survivors may feel other people hold them responsible for the death. Counselling can help survivors examine the validity of these feelings, to see whether other people really do see them as guilty or whether this is something they are projecting on to others. After Brian's wife took her own life, he began to wonder whether his two grown-up sons perhaps held him responsible in some way for Judy's death, but he did not dare discuss these thoughts with anybody else. It was only when he started seeing a counsellor that he could explore this issue – and realise that his guilt was unrealistic.

Non-communication between family members is not uncommon; after both Marjorie's sisters had committed suicide, she became increasingly upset when her mother, Eileen, refused to talk to her about the twins and their deaths. After another member of the family had pointed this out to her, Eileen decided to seek help from a counsellor; this not only helped her to deal with her guilt, but enabled her to begin talking with her daughter about the twins' deaths. Counselling can help open – or reopen – channels of communication which may have become blocked.

The sheer intensity of the survivor's feelings can be frightening – both for the survivor and for those around them. Counselling or therapy offers a setting in which the survivor can feel safe to face the sort of feelings which, elsewhere, may seem potentially overwhelming. As Ursula said at the beginning of this chapter, she needed to talk to someone outside the family, and she felt safe with a counsellor.

One way of dealing with potentially overwhelming feelings is to put a lid on them, and pretend they do not exist. Melanie, who started seeing a counsellor two months after her husband's suicide, found counselling helped her get in touch with her buried feelings. 'Initially I was just so distant', she says, 'I don't think I could quite think it was real.' For Janice, sessions with a Gestalt therapist offered a very direct means of getting in touch with her emotions; although she found the Gestalt method rather confrontational, she felt it was right for her because, as she admitted, 'I'm very good at just talking and not letting the emotions out'.

Survivors are frequently coping people; that is how they see themselves, and how other people tend to see them too. (Perhaps they survived because they were the ones in the family who coped.) The trauma of suicide can threaten anyone's coping strategies, but for someone who has always coped, acknowledging their possible need for support can be difficult. Jane has been seeing a psychotherapist since her brother's suicide, but she admits that reaching the point of accepting that she needed help was not easy: 'I think my unconscious took me there because I needed it, but I went protesting.' Even after she started her therapy, relinquishing the coping role did not come easily:

> Once I was there it took me many many months to say 'I'm fed up with coping', to acknowledge that that was what I was doing.... It kept coming out that I was really angry about being this coping person ... out is coming all the anger that I've bottled up all those years.

In Jan's case, it was many years before she could begin to acknowledge that she no longer had to go on coping as she had done since her father's suicide when she was thirteen. Over the years, she has worked on many issues relating to her father's suicide, but during a recent osteopathy session, when her head was being cradled, she was surprised to find herself sobbing uncontrollably. It was only afterwards that she realised she could allow someone else to do the holding, and that she could let go. The child whose mother had died when she was ten, and whose father killed himself three years later had grown into the adult who, as she says, had always told the world, 'I'll manage, I'll show you, I'll do it all on my own.'

When the bereavement occurred in childhood, it can be as many as twenty or thirty years before the survivor finds help. But even adults may not immediately recognise their need for help. As Dunne points out, some survivors look for help straight after the suicide, while 'other survivors seek therapy only after many months or years of living with a host of unpleasant conditions and feelings' (1987b: 196). Kevin and Jan, who experienced parental suicide as children (see Chapter 9), have both benefited from therapy as adults. Now in his mid-thirties, Kevin has been in therapy for the past year; twenty years after his mother committed suicide, when his sister had a major breakdown and attempted suicide, he realised that he needed to find help:

> My sister's illness triggered a lot of emotions in me ... my life was becoming more and more intolerable because of the gap between thinking and feeling.... You can actually only go on for a certain period of time not feeling ... and it's a sense of me needing to move on ... [to] grow and to become real and complete ... and it's very difficult to actually get involved in relationships and be a real person if there are some major gaps ... and bits which have been frozen for a very long time.

Kevin can acknowledge how much he has been helped by therapy, but he still resents the fact that it is something he has *had* to do. For

Jan, too, it felt as though there was no real choice about entering therapy – she had to confront her past: 'It's a kind of blight that I know I have to deal with.... It does feel for me about survival to have dealt with some of these issues.' For some people, the legacy of suicide can literally feel like a matter of life or death, of surviving or not surviving.

Self-help and mutual support

As Jennifer said at the beginning of this chapter, she really needed to talk to somebody who had been through a similar experience. However, self-help or mutual support which focuses specifically on suicide bereavement is very limited in Britain, with the notable exception of the Shadow of Suicide (SOS) network in The Compassionate Friends and a few local suicide bereavement groups (see Appendix A).

Because, at present, the SOS parents' network is virtually the only provision of this kind for survivors of suicide, what follows looks at one particular group of survivors – parents of suicide victims – although many of their experiences could well apply to other survivors. The level of contact which these parents had had with others similarly bereaved varied considerably but included: joining Compassionate Friends and receiving their newsletter; being in touch with other parents by letter and/or telephone; meeting with another parent on a one-to-one basis; attending meetings locally; and attending the national gatherings of the Shadow of Suicide group which are held from time to time.

After their daughter's suicide, Robert and his wife had searched for help for some time before they came across the SOS network; Robert has vivid memories of Pat's first contact with another parent survivor, and the difference this made:

> there was a sort of relief on her face, that she'd actually found someone, because so many people say, 'I know how you must feel', and really I wanted to hit them, and say 'You can't possibly know how I feel. There is no way you can know how I feel.'

As previous chapters (8 and 10) have described, when one member of the family commits suicide, survivors may feel that their entire family is abnormal, stigmatised, and different from other families. Meeting fellow-survivors can often help families like this to see themselves in a less negative light. After her son's suicide, Heather attended a national gathering of SOS; for her this was:

> a real life-saver. I couldn't believe that all those people were so nice ... and their children had died.... I'd felt we must be a horrendous family to have had a child who could be so unhappy, but they weren't horrendous, so it followed that I wasn't.

Like a number of other parents, Heather had also been helped by reading Anne Downey's book about her son's suicide in which she describes her pressing need to find other people who had gone through a similiar experience:

> you really believe for a while that you are the only one to whom it has happened. There is a great desire in the beginning to find someone else who has gone through this traumatic experience. It is an almost desperate searching as though you have some rare disease for which there is no cure.... It does not seem to matter what state they are in so long as they are able to tell you that the same thing happened to them.... You become one of the many instead of one alone. (1987: 93)

As she points out, survivors will be in different states, partly because everyone grieves in their own way, but also because some survivors will be further down the road. Pam, who, together with her husband, has supported many other parents in the ten years since their daughter's suicide, has found that newly bereaved parents can benefit considerably from meeting others whose loss was less recent. 'It's nice', she says, 'just to meet somebody who says "OK, we've been through it, and look, we're still alive, and I didn't think I would live through it."' This is one of the benefits of mutual aid: parents can act as support models for one another, and having been helped by less recently bereaved parents, many survivors appreciated the opportunity that SOS gave them to help other parents in turn. They wanted to be able to contribute something as well as receive.

Like the experiences of some of those who were in therapy, meetings of survivors could also provide a setting where it was safe to acknowledge and talk about feelings which could not easily be expressed elsewhere. As Irene commented: 'people can say things they'd never say to the husband or wife or whoever's at home. [You] can admit to suicidal feelings which you can't at home.' This is borne out by Appel and Wrobleski who, from their involvement with support groups, have found that survivors 'can experience unconditional caring and support for the expression of whatever feelings may be plaguing them' (1987: 223).

Whatever the cause of death, the bereaved may question why the death happened and whether they could in any way have prevented it. Mutual support groups can provide a place where it is acceptable to air these thoughts and feelings, knowing that those who listen will understand why survivors need to do this. As Carol discovered: '[they] understood what I was going through ... and why I was going through it ... and the sort of search for the whys and the if-onlys'. Self-help and mutual support groups can provide a listening ear for the sort of searching which Carol was going through; but other survivors can also help them see that perhaps they do not need to go on shouldering responsibility for the death, and that anyone can miss what were understood to be clues or threats when it was too late. With the help of other parents, survivors can learn to be more self-forgiving, and more realistic about the limits of their responsibility for the death.

But do survivors always need to be in separate support groups, or can they be helped just as much by attending ordinary bereavement groups? The evidence (mainly from research undertaken in the USA where survivor support is more widely developed) is contradictory (Dunne 1987b). Battle states that: 'suicide survivors have unique problems and should not be placed in support groups for people facing their own loved one's natural death' (1984: 45). On the other hand, placing survivors in the same group can have its difficulties too. Billow found that where survivors with different relationships to the dead person (e.g. parents, siblings, spouses) met together, 'members vied with one another for first place in the competition for whose anguish was worse' (1987: 210). In the end, it may be a question of individual preference. Brian has found the meetings of an ordinary bereavement group to be very supportive. Some of the people quoted earlier in this chapter, though, felt very strongly that they would only meet with other survivors. This is an important issue because it will have a bearing on the way survivor support should develop in the future (see Chapter 15).

Moving on

Bereavement is a process which people move through and, if all goes well, emerge from at some point; Chapter 14 will look at some of the ways in which survivors begin to come through their grief and pick up the threads of life again. One marker on the road to recovery may be when survivors decide they no longer need to be involved in a bereavement group. According to Parkes, one of the functions of such groups is to act as 'a bridge between the world of the bereaved and the community' (1986: 195). An organisation like CRUSE, he suggests, is there 'for transition rather than a perpetual refuge' (p. 195).

Nancy was helped by The Compassionate Friends, and she in turn has supported other parents. For the last few years she has been secretary of her local group, but now she feels ready to relinquish her involvement in the world of bereavement, and has resigned as secretary: 'It's time I moved on ... one doesn't want to be a member for a long, long time ... I no longer need to talk about Clare.'

For other survivors, a decision to terminate therapy may be a sign that they are ready to move on. This does not necessarily mean that their grieving has come to an end, but the feelings are probably less intense, and occurring less frequently. Janice decided to stop seeing her therapist about a year after her mother's death:

> It was time for me just to get on with my life, but to be aware that I was still going to get upset, and if I did that was OK, and I could cry, and I could be feeble sometimes about it, and I shouldn't just clam up about it.

Good support should offer help with the immediate tasks of mourning, but it should also equip the survivor to cope in the future, when grief re-emerges, as it inevitably will from time to time, even though the feelings will be less strong and less painful.

This chapter has been mainly concerned with the support offered by general practitioners, counsellors, therapists, and fellow survivors. Earlier chapters touched on the role of other helpers, and in particular the clergy (Chapter 8) and the survivor's social network (Chapter 9). But although more fortunate survivors will find the help they need, this will not always be the case. Chapter 15 will look at some of the ways in which we may, in future, provide better support for survivors.

Chapter thirteen

Facing the feelings

There are lots of aspects that are exactly the same [as other bereavements], but there are also aspects that are different. (Ursula)

I thought he loved us too much to actually do that to us, because it's such a cruel thing to do.... So you get all these dreadful mixed-up feelings, and it's a different sort of bitterness from somebody who dies of other types of disease. (Susan)

It's a relief, because somebody like that, they're an emotional burden on you, you can't run away from it ... she was a worry.... I'd give anything to have her back, have her here, but that's not really the choice. (Dick)

'Grief', writes Parkes, 'is a process, not a state', and he identifies four stages in that process: 'numbness, the first stage, gives way to pining and pining to disorganization and despair, and it is only after the stage of disorganization that recovery occurs' (1986: 27). This concept of stages provides a valid and useful framework for understanding the process of grieving, so it is unfortunate that the idea has sometimes been misinterpreted or misunderstood. Parkes does not claim, for example, that people pass neatly through each stage, completing the first before moving on to the second and so forth, nor that each stage will last for a fixed period of time. As he makes clear: 'there are considerable differences from one person to another as regards both the duration and form of each stage' (1986: 27). There are rarely distinct phases, and one may overlap with another.

Previous chapters have focused mainly on issues which relate to the first and second (and occasionally the third) stages of mourning, and Chapter 14 will look at how survivors move towards and beyond the final phase. This chapter, meanwhile, is predominantly concerned with the third stage, the phase characterised by 'disorganisation and despair'. The format of this chapter, with its outwardly neat categorisation of feelings, may appear to contradict the complicated process of mourning. For the purpose of communication, some semblance of order is unfortunately necessary; but at the same time, it is important to remember that, like the stages of grieving, feelings do not come in neat packages either. Grief is complex and often chaotic; sometimes a single feeling will predominate, while at other times it can feel, as one survivor said, 'like a bag of every emotion under the sun'. It is also the case that 'good grieving' does not require survivors to experience every feeling mentioned here – guilt is not obligatory, anger may not be present. What this chapter aims to do, though, is to point to the normality of these feelings. Suicide bereavement can leave people feeling very abnormal.

The survivor's inner dialogue

It may seem strange to have a separate chapter about feelings when so much of the rest of this book is about feelings. Emotions such as guilt and anger have already been mentioned at various points so why another chapter? Up to this point, most of the discussion has been about the survivor's experiences in relation to the rest of the world – the public rituals of funerals and inquests, relationships with family and friends, and contact with support services. This chapter, on the other hand, is more concerned with the grieving which survivors must do on their own – in what Marris has called 'the ultimate privacy of grief' (1978: 153). As Pincus reminds us: 'without an ongoing interaction with [the dead person] ... the whole painful and complicated process of separation has to be worked out entirely by the survivor alone' (1974: 46).

As survivors talked, their stories often took on the form of a dialogue, a questioning, a searching which they had undertaken alone, and were now recounting for the listener's benefit. It is the dialogue they are now unable to have with the other person. Frequently it seemed to represent the survivor's attempt to work through some of the most painful legacies of suicide – the guilt, the anger, the search for understanding. Susan's thoughts are typical of this sort of dialogue – actually a monologue:

I could have forced him to have treatment, I suppose, but I chose to let him choose, and I suppose for that I might feel guilty, but I don't ... but if I had realised he was going to commit suicide, perhaps I would have done; I mean, what happened was that I never thought that he would actually leave us like that – I thought that he loved us too much.

In that brief monologue, there are questions of power and control ('I could have forced him'), about the other person's rights and autonomy ('I chose to let him choose'), about testing the reality of guilt ('I might feel guilty, but I don't'), about wisdom with hindsight ('had I realised'), a denial of the possibility of suicide ('I never thought he'd leave us'), and a sense of being rejected by the victim ('I thought he loved us too much'). As Marris has suggested: 'the process of grief seems to be the working out of conflicting impulses ... [and] this conflict is crucial to an understanding of grief and mourning' (1978: 28).

Some survivors had written down their thoughts and feelings – often in the form of 'letters' to the dead person; Anne Downey (1987), for example, wrote her book *Dear Stephen* as a letter to her dead son. After her brother's suicide, Jennifer found that writing had helped her: 'I wrote down things simply because I wanted to at the time, and it got it out of my head.' Other survivors had expressed their feelings in poetry. Storr, in his recent book *Solitude*, suggests that the creative act of writing 'is one of the ways of overcoming the state of helplessness.... It is a coping mechanism, a way of exercising control as well as a way of expressing emotion' (1989: 129). For survivors of suicide, often grappling with devastating feelings of shock and horror, writing may be, as Storr suggests, a means of exercising a measure of control over what may otherwise feel potentially uncontrollable. C.S. Lewis's book *A Grief Observed* became a bestseller but that was not the author's original intention. Written after his wife's death from cancer, it was something he needed to do: 'partly a defence against total collapse, a safety valve' (1966: 50).

Staudacher (1988) suggests there may be several potential benefits in keeping a journal or diary: because it is a private activity, previously denied aspects of the survivor's relationship with the victim can be safely expressed; obsessive thoughts when written down may lose some of their obsessive quality; and survivors may find they are recording thoughts of which they were not previously aware.

The same as other bereavements?

As previous chapters have indicated, survivors of suicide are faced with additional stresses including the central fact that the death was self-inflicted, but will their patterns of grieving be any different? Certainly many of the feelings described in this chapter are likely to strike a familiar chord with other bereaved people. As Ursula said at the start of this chapter, though, it is both the same and different, a point echoed by Barbara Porter, co-facilitator of a survivor support group, who sees suicide bereavement as 'like other bereavements, but more so'.

Survivors of suicide may have certain things in common with several different groups of bereaved people; like those bereaved as the result of murder, for example, the death was sudden, untimely, and often violent. Robert described his daughter's suicide as a triple burden: 'the sudden death, the sudden death of a child, and the sudden death of a child by suicide'. Many survivors feel they carry an additional burden, and Shneidman describes how: 'the person who commits suicide puts his psychological skeleton in the survivor's emotional closet – he sentences the survivor to deal with many negative feelings.... It can be a heavy load' (1972: x).

Returning for a moment, though, to Parkes's stages of grief; survivors often seem to remain in a state of numbness which characterises the first stage of grieving for far longer than other bereaved people. Suicide is always sudden, and often violent, and prolonged shock is, therefore, a normal reaction. Brian, for example, described his mourning as 'dreadfully slow, with a numbness that must have gone on for nine months or a year'. Ursula also found getting through to the feelings took a long time: 'Although you know all these things, I don't think you really start feeling them for an awful long time.'

When the numbness wears off, however, the weeks or months of pent-up feelings can lead to an intense period of grieving. Carol returned to her teaching job only a few weeks after her son's suicide; perhaps this stopped her from dwelling too much on what had happened, but it was six months later when her real feelings of grief broke through:

> for six months I'd cried, but not really cried, if you understand what I mean ... I cried on the surface, but not properly crying, and I sort of survived and survived and survived, and it was a

week in June ... I completely went to pieces ... I couldn't stop crying.... It was almost as if the protective layer was coming off.

The intense guilt experienced by some survivors can make grief less easy to resolve than with other bereavements. Stephanie was faced with a particularly horrific suicide when a close friend set fire to herself in front of her children. This was, she realised, a particularly difficult legacy. 'If it was in order to reproach us all', she wrote, 'then perhaps it worked, as such deaths are impossible to work through as normal grief.' It may take survivors a long time to work through such powerful emotions as guilt and anger.

Guilt and the if-onlys

The guilt doesn't go away. I don't believe it will ever go away.... I keep rationalising, and everybody says, 'of course you're not guilty', but of course you are; well, I believe I am, because who else was supposed to sort it out, and decide that he needed help? (Heather)

If only I'd phoned him up then, if only I'd forced him to speak to me when I met him ... he said he felt terrible; if only I'd said to him, 'for heaven's sake tell me about it'; if only I'd forced myself. (Suzy)

Guilt is a common bereavement reaction (Worden 1983; Parkes 1986), but the intensity with which it is experienced – and the ways it is dealt with – may be different with self-inflicted death. Cain and Fast have suggested that because suicide is such a deliberate, intentional act 'the ferocity of guilt in the survivors of suicide is particularly striking' (1972b: 149). The way Carol described her guilt shows how strong these feelings can be: 'I thought I was a wicked, evil woman who had brought Alan's death upon myself – that I was the reason for it. I was guilty, I was wrong ... I thought I was evil, and I cried and cried.'

The survivor's guilt can take many forms, and focus on many different things, depending on the individual's circumstances, and the relationship they had with the dead person. Where the death was apparently out of the blue, survivors may berate themselves for not having noticed anything was even wrong; if suicide was known to be a possibility, survivors may blame themselves for not being there to stop it happening. Whatever the guilt is about, the net result may be what Behrens refers to as 'an unending list of if-onlys' (1988: 97). Survivors like Janice can find themselves caught up in a constant and repetitive dialogue:

> I think after the asking 'why' it was probably the guilt bit ... going over and over and over it, again and again – the Friday night phone call, to her, and the fact that I hadn't gone down to see her when I said I was going, and that I'd put it off quite a few weeks, and the sort of irony of the fact that I'd written her a letter that arrived [after she died] – and just sort of blaming myself and thinking of what I could have done and if onlys – if only the GP hadn't retired, if only I'd sent her that present which I meant to and never did – or if only I'd been more generous with her and had her to stay more often.

If these 'if onlys' could be cancelled, and the clock turned back, the dead person would return to life. Many people carry round these lists of 'if onlys', and letting go of them can sometimes be difficult. In an attempt to punish themselves, survivors may choose to live permanently with their guilt, convinced that that is what they deserve for having been a bad parent or husband or whatever. After his wife's suicide, John embarked on what he describes as 'a kind of self-imposed exile' which lasted two years; he felt responsible for Averil's death, and even reached the point where he began to wonder whether he had actually wanted her to die. By deciding that they are personally responsible for the suicide, though, survivors are actually claiming that they had considerable power over the victim, as Carole eventually realised:

> I think that's partly what the guilt is wrapped up in – that I want to take all the responsibility for Jon's life ... in fact he passed beyond my responsibility, and he had a wide circle of friends and other relationships which would have had just as much bearing on the outcome as my relationship to him.

In situations like this, survivors are continuing a power struggle which may have been happening before the suicide (see p. 58). But as Staudacher (1988) points out, the death is not within the realm of the survivor's control or power.

Mutual support, counselling, and therapy can all provide the chance for survivors to examine their guilt in a more realistic light (see Chapter 12). Staudacher (1988) suggests that friends or relatives can also help the survivor with this task. Occasionally, the survivor has reality thrust upon them – as Isabel discovered. A practising Catholic, she regularly went to confession, where she would talk about her guilt over Eric's suicide, until one day, nearly two years after his death, she suddenly heard the priest telling her he was fed up with hearing about this, would she please not mention it again because she'd done what she could, and as far as he was concerned, that was the end of the matter!

Guilt is a very common response to suicide, but not all survivors are going to feel responsible for the suicide. When Wrobleski (1986) asked 158 survivors about their feelings of guilt, 34 per cent said that they felt 'moderately guilty', and 39 per cent felt 'very guilty'. However, 14 per cent claimed to feel no guilt at all, and the remaining 13 per cent felt only mildly guilty; as she points out (1984–5), society assumes that survivors will automatically feel guilty, an assumption which these findings, at least, show to be untrue.

Anger

> I was furious with her. I've never been so angry with anybody in my life until the day she died.... How dare she leave me in this bloody horrible world ... that she made wonderful for me ... that she helped me to love in ... and then she left me. How dare you do this? Why did you do it? (John)

Anger is a common respose to loss; it can stem from frustration or bitterness that the death was not preventable, or it can be the rage of abandonment (Worden 1983). Lukas and Seiden suggest that with suicide, anger can have a threefold origin: 'It is a rage at being rejected, at being abandoned and at being accused' (1987: 56). Such rage can be extremely powerful as Carole discovered:

> After the continual weeping in the summer came fits of rage. I threw my body around and grovelled in anguish. I took to hurling things around, and beating myself continually against walls. I would pound my fists into beds and pillows, screaming with rage.

The survivor's anger may be directed towards a number of possible targets including the dead person, other family members (Chapters

9 and 10), friends (Chapter 11), or professionals (Chapter 12). The victim may be blamed for having cheated the survivor. After a friend's suicide, the poet Rilke (1957) wrote of feeling as if a door had been slammed in his face. Survivors may resent the fact that they had no choice in the matter, but it is they, and not the victim, who are left to cope with the aftermath. Susan recalls the bitterness she felt after her husband committed suicide:

> I did feel bitter at what he'd done.... Why should he think that I was strong enough to carry on without him ... and I really did resent what he'd done to his son. I mean, it was a dreadful thing to do, wasn't it ... it sounds awful, as though one's a horrible person but I resented [his suicide] ... it was sixteen years I'd supported him and this is what he's left me with.

Anger which is directed towards the dead person can leave the survivor feeling particularly guilty. After her daughter Julie's death, Phyllis would find herself angrily 'telling' her how the suicide had ruined her life, but then apologising to her afterwards. As Vollman and colleagues point out: 'in the event of suicide ... anger towards a dead person is widely felt not to be legitimate, and is only experienced with great discomfort' (1971: 102). After her son's death, Heather found it difficult to allow angry feelings to emerge:

> He's left us in a real mess ... and I think well, if he left us in a real mess, what kind of a mess was he in? He must have been in a worse mess, and I can't really be angry.... We said at the beginning, if he was to walk back in that door we'd all let him have it ... yes, we've been cross with him, but I feel more basically very, very sad for him.

Coping with anger can be difficult; survivors may oscillate between guilt and anger – unsure whether it is the victim or themselves they should be feeling sorry for, unsure who is to blame. Anger and guilt may become confused. Melanie spent much of the first year blaming herself for Ian's death, but then her feelings changed:

> I just wanted to scream how unfair it was ... because I was the one that went away because I wasn't coping very well, and yet he was the one who killed himself; but it was typical of him in a way because he couldn't bear me to have any attention to myself ... so in a way, by killing himself, he gave himself a lot more attention.... Ian had a lot of choices and he gave me no choice at all.

Allowing feelings of anger towards the suicide victim to emerge may be difficult, but resenting the rest of the world can also be uncomfortable. Since their daughter's suicide, Robert and Pat have found it particularly hard to attend family celebrations, because as Pat said: 'It's very difficult to join in their joys.... We do get resentful at times because they seem to have everything, and we can't have that.'

Rejection

I could not cope with the idea that Jon really wanted to die, so I kept pushing it to the back of my mind. It was too much of a blow to my ego for me to think that a child of mine would want to die, that my love was not enough to keep him alive. (Carole)

> Hell is a sort of underground bog.
> There are no landmarks. In it
> Those we have loved and failed
> Turn their backs for ever.
> 'The Guide', U.A. Fanthorpe (1982)

According to Hauser: 'In every suicide, there is a component of rejection' (1987: 65) or, in Mark's words, 'if a person rejects life, they reject you'. 'Why did they do this?', becomes 'why did they do this to me?' Some survivors will react with anger to the victim's implied rejection of their love, but to others it will be proof of the fact that they are totally unlovable. In Irene's case, this feeling that nobody cared about her led her to attempt suicide:

I didn't care about the grief I was leaving because I didn't expect that there would be any. I thought we'd used it all up on Bill, and I didn't particularly care what anybody thought about me and yet ... I needed somebody to tell me that I was worth it.

To regain their sense of self-worth, survivors like Irene badly need reassurance that they are capable of loving and being loved; Eileen remembers feeling 'rather good' when her surviving daughter told her how much she now enjoyed her mother's love and attention; it helped to counter her feelings about not having been a good parent to her twin daughters who had taken their own lives.

Survivors may be left feeling wholly inadequate; whatever they did, and however much they tried to help, even that was rejected, and was not enough to keep the other person alive. For Brian, who had supported his wife through three years of mental ill-health and suicide attempts, this sense of inadequacy was one of the most painful aspects of her death: 'You obviously weren't adequate as a person, you weren't providing a good enough life, a happy enough environment or whatever, to make a person's life worth living – and that I found very hard.' It can be difficult for survivors to reach the point of acknowledging that however much they had done, perhaps this could never have been enough to keep the other person alive.

Bereavement can bring feelings of tremendous insecurity; it can, Parkes suggests, 'undermine one's faith in the world as an ordered and secure place' (1986: 103). The survivor may feel that it is only a matter of time before something equally dreadful happens again – and if it does, the world can seem even more precarious. When she was seventeen, Bridget had to cope with two suicides within five months, when one of her sisters and then her father took their own lives. As a result, she says:

> I was really dangerously worried for everybody I was close to after that ... [worried] that my brothers might kill themselves or be alcoholic ... or my [other] sister would go mad.... I was really terrified and always thinking that another bad thing was going to happen.

Although these fears have diminished somewhat over the seven years since the suicides occurred, Bridget's sense of insecurity remains; she still sometimes finds herself suddenly panicking about someone in the family, and will have to telephone them and reassure herself they are all right. This sense of insecurity can also make it hard for trust to operate in any of the survivor's relationships – 'they can't trust their world and the people in it ever to treat them fairly again' (Lukas and Seiden 1987: 38). As a result, survivors may hold back from other people because, as Maureen says, 'you're frightened to think too much of anyone in case [they are] gone again'.

The experience of bereavement has been compared to losing a limb (Parkes 1986), and survivors may literally feel as though a part of themselves has been forcibly amputated. This may occur with spouses – who have lost their 'other half' – and with parents who have lost the child who was a part of them before birth. After her son's death, Pauline described it as feeling:

as if I was on a railway, and my leg had been cut off by a train, and I had to get up and there was no support, there's nothing, and you have to get up and go, and how can you?

Other survivors talked of feeling that they had 'lost a limb', or been 'cut in half', and of 'a great huge chunk of your life that has gone'. As Pauline and the others discovered, trying to get around with a missing limb and no crutches is not terribly easy.

Stigma

I felt as if I had leprosy – it's a terrible feeling ... I wanted the ground to swallow me up. (Pauline)

As will be clear from previous chapters, feelings of shame and stigma are not uncommon among survivors of suicide. Although this is by no means a universal reaction (Shepherd and Barraclough 1976; Rudestam 1987), when such reactions do occur, they can be very powerful, as Miriam's experience demonstrates: 'I felt I was sort of stained by an atrocity which had made me accursed – so that I felt I was a sort of pollutant.' The fact that her husband had committed suicide left Melanie feeling not only undeserving of sympathy, but different from other widows: 'I wasn't a proper widow, he hadn't been run over by a bus or had a heart attack.' Society no longer treats suicide victims as criminals, but survivors may end up bearing the stigma on their behalf.

In his book on the nature of stigma, Goffman (1968) discusses how people who feel stigmatised see themselves as being very different from the rest of society – the 'leprosy' which Pauline described above. Maureen felt that her son's suicide meant she no longer even belonged to the human race:

I look at my next-door neighbour, and I feel I am not one of you any more – I'm not a normal person any more. I'm different. I've got nothing in common with anybody, my whole outlook has changed, the way I live has changed and I feel alienated ... as if I belong to a different planet, with my own kind ... but I don't want to belong to people of this grief ... I don't want to be with all of these sad people ... even my friend, good as she's been, I'm not on the same wavelength any more.

Like many in her position, it was hard for Maureen to feel she was on

the same planet as other people; survivors of suicide may always retain something of that sense of differentness, but recovery may be
beginning at the point when they feel they are returning from that
'different planet' and rejoining the human race.

Relief

> We had years and years of listening to Patricia going round in
> circles – over and over the same ground – and sometimes I felt I
> was going mad, because it's such a circular thing, depression ...
> and it was very wearing and very hard, so that's a relief, not to
> have all that.... I wouldn't have wanted to have years and years
> more of her being depressed and living at home. (Francesca)

> I thought, well obviously he was in a lot of pain, and he's not in it
> any more. I sort of felt, he's safe now. (Christine)

Newly bereaved people often experience a sense of relief, especially
if death was the culmination of a long or painful illness. Relief, in
these circumstances, is an acceptable reaction; the person is no
longer suffering, everyone feels relieved that that is the case, and
they will often say so to each other. Survivors of suicide may experience similar feelings of relief (Solomon 1981). Andrew had looked
after his wife through several years of her mental illness and heavy
drinking so when she committed suicide: 'There was sadness – but
really an overwhelming feeling of peace.' When someone takes their
own life, however, relief can be less straightforward than with other
deaths. Survivors may be unsure whether they are relieved for the
victim or for themselves. When her daughter took her own life,
Ursula was left with the feeling that perhaps it was a relief for Josie
– but perhaps for the rest of the family too:

> It was something at the back of my mind, I'd been fearing. I'd
> been dreading [it] for a long, long while ... and in a sense, as I
> pulled up to the house and saw the ambulance, I almost hoped
> she was dead because she so desperately wanted to be; the
> thought of dragging her back so that she could attempt again
> was even more horrific than her being dead.... It was a positive
> thing she did, a conscious decision ... so in a sense, although I
> felt awful, there was also a tremendous sense of relief.
> Something that had been going on for years was over, and

something else began of course that was just as difficult.

As Ursula recognised, what was to follow would not be any easier. It is rare for survivors to feel straightforward, unmitigated relief. Even when the survivor had expected to feel relieved, this does not always happen, as Janice discovered when her elderly mother died. Their relationship had often been troubled, and Janice had often thought her death would be a relief. Because her mother committed suicide, though, her feelings were more complicated:

> because of having to cope with the way she died I think it wasn't a relief – and I just missed her, I still miss her terribly, I miss the 'phone calls, I miss the letters, even though, when she'd been alive, sometimes I dreaded the 'phone calls, and sometimes the letters came through the letter-box too often.

When Solomon (1981) interviewed ninety suicide survivors, nearly a third expressed feelings of relief, but some also admitted to a sense of guilt about feeling relieved. Even when there is relief, the survivor can still want the person back, as Mark discovered after his daughter took her own life: 'strictly within the terms of selfishness, life has been better which is a paradox, isn't it? My life is better, but of course I would rather have her here than not.'

Even if the survivor does not experience the suicide as an unmitigated relief, there can still be a sense of confusion: who am I hurting for, and do I have the right to feel so hurt about what the other person did when they were in such pain? For Peter, the pain of Susie's suicide was mingled with a feeling that perhaps he was being selfish:

> there's an element of me that's very hurt and very angry with Susie for committing suicide, because I feel betrayed, I suppose, in some sort of self-centred way. But if that was the only option Susie felt she had, then I really have to come to terms with that for Susie, and it's no good just loving her for me. I have to love her for her.... I don't think she accounted for how we might feel, but I don't think she was in a position to account for that – the desperation was absolute.

Unravelling these complicated and sometimes conflicting feelings can be hard work for the survivor.

Suicidal feelings

> For some reason I felt cheated when he committed suicide ... I was the one who wanted to die, and for some reason I felt I couldn't do it because he'd beat me to it. (Irene)

> Certainly one goes through periods of almost taking your own life because you say, well, what's the point? I mean, that *was* my life. I didn't really see staying alive for the boys as being an issue ... I couldn't see that they needed me; my life had ended almost with her life. (Brian)

Suicidal thoughts are not uncommon during the early months of bereavement, although serious suicide attempts and actual suicides are less common (Bowlby 1985). It has been claimed, however, that survivors are a greater suicide risk; Lukas and Seiden (1987), for example, quote claims that the suicide rate among survivors is between 80 and 300 per cent higher than for the general population. McIntosh (1987a), on the other hand, cites a review of fourteen studies, only six of which found an above-average risk among family and friends of suicide victims.

Lukas and Seiden use the term 'bargains' to describe the different ways in which survivors will cope with the death, and the 'saddest bargain', they suggest, is when the person says 'because you died, I'll die too' (1987: 103). There are a number of reasons why someone may choose this response. The bereaved may believe that death will reunite them with the dead person; death may also be seen as putting an end to their feelings of misery (Parkes 1986). Although Heather never reached the point of seriously contemplating suicide, she can remember feeling that she wanted to:

> In the beginning it upset me a lot that I couldn't commit suicide, because I wanted to go with Alastair, and I felt that I had to go with him ... but I couldn't leave [her daughter], you see, that was my dilemma. That caused me a lot of anguish because I knew I couldn't go with him.

During a radio programme on suicide, Colin Murray Parkes made the point that: 'to some extent, suicide has to be learned'. Sometimes the very fact that someone close to the survivor has committed suicide can make a previously impossible idea suddenly seem possible; the unthinkable can become thinkable. Ann can still remember something that happened to her fifty-two years ago, on the day her brother committed suicide:

> I was walking somewhere – I suppose going to my lodgings; I remember just pausing to cross the road, and a bus was just coming up, and the thought went through my mind – shall I just walk out? I had absolutely no feeling in me, and I thought to myself, well, I might just as well be under that bus.... It was just the feeling that I'd lost all feeling for life really.

As Jane said, after her brother's suicide, 'It's a real option which it wouldn't be to a lot of people', a point echoed by Behrens, whose book, *The Monument*, was written after the suicides of his younger brother Justin, and of Justin's mistress: 'I've found out that suicide is infectious', he wrote. 'If you have suicidal instincts and somebody in your immediate circle kills himself, it's hard not to think, whether consciously or not, "he had the courage to do it – why shouldn't I?"' (1988: 194).

Even when survivors are not actually contemplating suicide, they can display a complete indifference to death. In a manner reminiscent of the Hiroshima survivors (see p. 13) who had experienced 'a jarring awareness of the fact of death' (Lifton 1969: 481), the idea of dying no longer seemed quite so alien. As Jennifer found after her brother's suicide, it was not that she actually wanted to die but more a sense that it really would not matter if she did. For Robert, dying would, he felt, provide a welcome release:

> Death doesn't mean that much, it really doesn't. It would be a release from the pain of grieving to be perfectly honest – not in the sense [of] wanting to take your own life, but [it] wouldn't be nearly as painful as it was before Caroline died.

At other times, survivors will behave in potentially self-destructive ways (Lukas and Seiden 1987), and may be quite indifferent to danger (Kast 1988). In the very cold winter following her husband's suicide, Irene deliberately neglected herself, ending up with bronchitis and frostbitten ears: 'I was hoping to get pneumonia, to be honest. I was hoping that I would be so ill that I would die.'

Other reactions

As previously mentioned (Chapter 9), survivors may worry about whether the suicide was a sign that insanity runs in the family. But apart from those fears, the sheer pain and intensity of grieving can make survivors feel they must be going mad. At other times it is the sort of irrational behaviours, common in any bereavement (Worden 1983), which can be a source of considerable distress. After her daughter's suicide, Pat twice found herself driving away from petrol stations without paying the bill, leading her to fear she might start shoplifting.

In some cases, survivors find rituals for coping with the loss which, though often a positive way of coping with feelings, can seem bizarre or even mad to themselves – and to other people. Wrobleski describes how 'survivors have so-called crazy thoughts, ideas and actions which bewilder and frighten them' (1984/5: 177); but apparently abnormal feelings can be a normal reaction to a major trauma such as suicide bereavement. In the months after her son's death, Heather continually wanted to buy things for Alastair, so she would buy his favourite foods, take them up to the local forest where he had died, and throw them around. It was something she needed to do, and as she said, throwing Jaffa cakes around could also be quite fun really! She was only worried in case anyone saw her doing this.

Physical reactions to bereavement have been well documented in the general bereavement literature (e.g. Worden 1983; Raphael 1985; Parkes 1986), although Worden believes their significance is often overlooked. For some survivors, the pain of bereavement was experienced physically as well as emotionally; several people had suffered from severe chest pains – perhaps the symptom of a broken heart? For some people, like Lois, this physical pain was intense: 'sometimes the pain has been so bad that I've felt I would pass out. I've never had such pain as I've had from his death.' Worden makes an interesting point about pain: *Schmerz* – the German word for pain – has, he says, a broader definition than the English term, and includes 'the literal physical pain that many people experience and the emotional and behavioural pain associated with loss' (1983: 13).

Major trauma often affects a person's sexual feelings. Both Parkes (1986) and Raphael (1985) point out that the impact of bereavement on a person's sexuality can vary widely; some people may feel a total lack of interest in sexual activity, while others will feel an increased need for this form of intimacy. Two survivors who mentioned this reaction, had both experienced a complete lack of interest in sexual activity in the months following the suicide.

Although few of the survivors I met had used any medication, except possibly to help them through the first few days (p. 157), at least half a dozen people mentioned having been through a phase where they had depended fairly heavily on alcohol, usually in the early months after the suicide. Sometimes this was because they had decided that alcohol was preferable to medication. (Perhaps it is also a more socially acceptable 'drug' than pills?) Mainly, though, it was seen to offer possible relief, however short-lived, from the intense pain of their bereavement, as well as the possibility of sleep without recourse to sleeping pills.

In his book on grief counselling, Worden poses the question, 'When is mourning finished?' but suggests it is 'a little like asking how high is up?' (1983: 16). As Marie discovered, for the survivor of suicide, the tasks of mourning can be particularly hard to complete: 'it's too overwhelming, too much; there's too much in the way of feelings. It's just too awful, the whole thing, the feelings, the violence.' Later, though, she wrote:

> I am relieved to find my own life is calmer and the pain not so intense all the time – generally [I] feel more at peace with myself. Now I can recall [how] Oliver was able to speak of the happiest years of his life during our too-short marriage without being overwhelmed by a confusion of unhappy and guilt-laden feelings.

The lessening of pain, and the return of happy memories can be two markers on the road to recovery, and this is the subject of the next chapter.

Chapter fourteen

Finding a way through

*For Simon to commit suicide was almost beyond my endurance.
Yet nevertheless, we do endure, and we do laugh, and we do go on
contributing to our family and friends, and that, I suppose, is the
miracle. (Lois)*

*I count myself lucky in an odd sense, because I'm repairing
damaged goods, and confident of being repairable. (Kevin)*

In the weeks and months following a suicide, survivors may feel that
they can never learn to live with the aftermath of such a traumatic
event. But gradually a way through may begin to seem possible. Two
and a half years after his sister's suicide, Peter can look back and see
how things have changed:

> It has got better, and it's got calmer, and life's gone on, and one
> finds one's way through.... I don't believe you get over it, but I
> just think you learn how to accommodate it, and how to deal
> with it, and how to cope with it.

The fifty people I interviewed were at very different stages of bereavement: over half had been bereaved for less than three years –
some of these for less than a year – while one person had been a
survivor for over fifty years (see Appendix B). The number of years,
though, does not tell the whole story: people move through the process of bereavement at their own pace, healing takes place at different rates, and two people who have been bereaved for the same
length of time will not necessarily be at the same stage.

Sometimes survivors can look back and see the different stretches
of road along which they have travelled, recognising the points when
they seemed to reach a new stage. Brian can recall three distinct

phases in the two years since his wife's suicide:

> first of all it's deadfully slow ... there's a numbness that must
> have gone on for nine months or a year.... Then I think one
> comes out of the numb period, and that's hard too, because as
> you thaw, you think more, and you realise, you question. Then I
> think ... for me there was a degree of acceptance ... [that] that's
> it, she isn't coming back; it's a phase of my life that has passed
> now. I've got to try and build something for the future.

In Ursula's case, her stages of mourning are charted in a series of
dreams which she has had in the three years following Josie's death:

> Initially I had several dreams where I was quite cross with her ...
> not because of [the suicide] but reliving events in the past ... and
> I've had one or two dreams of saying to myself, 'Gosh, what will
> she do now?'..... But more recently I've had dreams, and she's
> been there and I've said, 'Oh, it's wonderful to see you', and yet
> I've known she's died ... it's as if even whilst dreaming I've not
> allowed myself the luxury of pretending [she was alive].

Dreaming is often intense after a death (Parkes 1986), and a se-
quence of dreams of the kind Ursula described is not unusual. Kast
(1988) suggests that this may be the means by which the unconscious
is guiding the bereaved through the process of mourning. Ursula's
dreams served a further purpose: they pointed to the inescapability
of Josie's death. The suicide had happened, and the clock could not
be turned back. As Jane realised, life would be different in future:
'There's one thing I do know, and that is that I will never be the same
again.' As Heather found, you have to learn to live with what's happened to you and once that is accepted,

> once you realise that that's what you have to do, then you begin
> to do it. At the beginning, you hope that it will go away and that
> you'll be back to normal one day, but you won't ... but you can
> learn to live with a different world and that's what I'm now
> trying to do.

In the midst of their grief, though, one of the things which comforted
some survivors was the feeling that if they could cope with this – and
survive – then they could cope with anything. It was not that they
believed nothing terrible would ever happen to them again, but
rather a sense that nothing could ever *feel* so bad; if disaster struck

again they would be equipped to cope with it. In Melanie's words: 'In a way it gives you a certain kind of strength, and I feel that whatever else happens to me, it wouldn't be so awful.'

Time scales of grieving

As already mentioned (Chapter 11), after a time, survivors may find that the victim is no longer mentioned; other people may assume that they are no longer grieving, and decide that it is best not to raise the subject. But there is no finite period after which the person will automatically pick up the threads of normal living again, and how people respond to the loss will depend on a range of different factors including the manner of their death (for example, anticipated, unexpected, violent, peaceful), their relationship with the person who died (for example, close, distant, warm, hostile, ambivalent), and the sort of support available to them.

Nevertheless, survivors can still find that after a certain time, others will expect them to have recovered. After her brother's suicide, Bushy Kelly wrote: 'somehow there is a belief that there is some magical date after which you are supposed to be normal, yourself again' (1989: 16). But survivors themselves may think they should stop grieving by a specific date. Janice had read somewhere that this was one year after the death: 'I was really impatient with myself, thinking it was time I got over this.' But, as she discovered, 'It was obvious that I hadn't ... and that probably I think that's something that is sort of there for ever really.'

Staudacher (1988) claims that the grief of suicide survivors will last longer than with other deaths. While this is by no means always the case, suicide bereavement has certain features which can lengthen the process; survivors may become stuck in an endless and fruitless search for the definitive answer to why the suicide occurred; or they may decide that they were responsible for the death and will punish themselves by continuing to grieve. As Shneidman found, in his work with survivors: 'some people offered help wished to maintain their suffering out of expiation. They felt they deserved punishment' (1975).

When Parkes studied a group of widows he found that half of them experienced 'a feeling of "numbness" or "blunting" ... [which] lasted for a few hours to a few days' (1986: 84). Worden also refers to this state as lasting 'for a brief period of time' (1983: 32). With suicide, however, survivors may feel numb for weeks or even months (see also Chapter 13). As Isabel discovered, though, 'At the beginning everyone comes round, and they think the bereavement is only going to last a couple of months, and [that you] will pull yourself together – and you're left stranded.'

The struggle towards acceptance

> When the pain is bad, it's as bad as it ever was, and I still get on my knees and say 'Why can't you come back?' – I mean, a totally illogical thing to say, but I still say, 'Please, let her come back.' (Pat)

Acceptance was a word frequently used by survivors; it often seemed to hold the key to their recovery and survival. It meant acknowledging the finality of death, and recognising that they would not see or speak to the person again. All bereaved people are faced with this task of accepting the reality of their loss (Worden 1983), but for suicide survivors there were other aspects too: a need to accept the wounding that had occurred, and to work through some of the particular legacies of suicide (see also Chapter 13).

Being able to let go of the dead person can be particularly difficult for the survivor of suicide; there may be unanswered questions (see Chapter 6), and the survivor will cling to the hope of continuing a dialogue with the person who died; if the survivor feels guilty about the death, there may be hopes of a second chance, an opportunity for restitution. Whatever the reason, as long as the survivor refuses to accept that the person is not coming back, all their energies will be channelled in that direction (Worden 1983), and they may become stuck in their grieving, unable to move on; Heather realised the danger of this when, eighteen months after Alastair's death, she said: 'I want him back. That's bad; I want to let go of that – it's useless, a complete waste of energy, It wears me out.'

But letting go does not necessarily mean losing the person altogether. As Jean discovered, when the survivor can accept that the relationship in its previous form is no longer possible, a new feeling of closeness may emerge:

> A lot of people said to me, 'You'll come to terms with it.' I thought, I can't possibly come to terms with it. They talked about acceptance. I do know she's dead now, and that took me a long time ... to say – 'she's dead and she's not coming back'.... I

had this mad feeling that the doctors were going to do
something, that next week she [was] going to get better and
come home.... But I do know that she's dead now, and I have
been able to feel her close to me which is something I didn't for
a long time.... I must have been angry with Anna or I couldn't
understand her, because she was miles away from me. I thought,
I'll never get close with you ... and I do feel her close now.

Jean wondered whether her anger was possibly causing some kind of
block, and getting these sorts of feelings into perspective may be a
necessary task if the survivor is to emerge satisfactorily from mourning. After her brother's death, Jennifer questioned whether she
could have done more to help Tim; should she have offered to sort
out his business problems, she asked herself? She had known he was
having financial problems and that people owed him money. Recognising and accepting the limits of her responsibility was an important
stage in her recovery:

Twelve months later you begin to realise ... how much you could
have done, and how much difference it would have made
anyway.... You start to see things a bit more reasonably – that
you can't possibly live someone's life for them.... You start
forgiving yourself a bit, because you can't do someone else's
jobs for them unless they ask you to do them.

Survivors often talked in terms of learning to live with what had happened, of accepting that the hurts which had been inflicted would
never really disappear. Pam described this as feeling one is 'bruised
for ever'. However unrealistic it may be, human beings still tend to
see perfect happiness as their inalienable right. For people like Pat,
being a survivor meant surrendering that expectation: 'I cannot imagine that we will ever be totally happy again. We might experience
happy times, but I can never be totally happy again because I've lost
Caroline.' Similarly, John commented: 'I don't expect to be happy
again, but I expect peace – and that's what I ask for now ... as peaceful
a life as possible and just [to] be content with what I have.'

Gains and losses

I think back on Alan as somebody who ... brought the greatest
joy into my life, the greatest pain into my life. He was my first

child, and therefore the greatest joy I think any mother can have, and I think his death was the hardest thing, the greatest pain I've had to suffer. And he has also brought me the greatest understanding of what life is about. (Carol)

The way down is also the way up.... Surviving a beloved person can become, at least for some, a time of growth and of becoming more fully human.... [The survivor] may discover the values and capacities which he did not know of in himself. (Seligman 1976)

No one chooses to be bereaved, and suicide bereavement can seem a particularly pointless and unnecessary loss; nevertheless, it can bring gains as well as losses. Drawing on her work as a psychotherapist with bereaved people, Kast suggests that recovery can sometimes depend on whether the survivor is able to see the possible gains:

I have observed that the sense of meaning ... could be experienced, once they became aware of the fact that the death of the mourned one not only took a great deal away from them, but had also brought them a great deal. (1988: 66–7)

Sometimes, what was lost or never achieved in the relationship with the person who died, can be gained elsewhere, as Dick realised: 'Maybe I could have sorted things out more with Sally; then she was dead, and I couldn't ... but I can do it with other people – I don't have to have that failure with everybody.' For Dick, the fact that Sally had chosen not to continue with her life made him more aware of the need to live his own life more fully: 'I was glad I was alive ... it made me appreciate a lot of things I'd taken for granted before.... Her death shook me up in terms of looking at my life.' Since Sally died, he has moved to a job he finds more worthwhile, has committed himself to a permanent relationship, and has recently become a father for the first time.

Staudacher suggests that 'commonly, a survivor has less interest in social functions or materially oriented activities, and an increased interest in those areas of life concerned with human values such as love, compassion, assistance to others' (1988: 49). This was reflected in comments made by a number of survivors who described how their attitudes towards other people had changed since the suicide. They talked of becoming 'more compassionate', of being 'more aware of other people's feelings', and of 'realising that other people are vulnerable'. Their own tragedy had made them more sensitive to the needs of those around them. Others described how the suicide had made them understand the relative unimportance of material objects, because as Carol said, 'people are important, not things, not possessions, and I think that it's important that you get this over to people – that they matter'.

Some survivors had decided to use their experiences in a positive way by supporting other bereaved people; in Suzy's case her decision to train and work as a bereavement counsellor was 'the bonus ... of my father's death'. Some people had become counsellors with their local CRUSE groups, whilst others had become active members of the SOS network in Compassionate Friends (see Appendix A). As Raphael points out, it is not unusual for people to become involved in bereavement support activities as a direct result of their own losses; our own bereavement 'allows us to empathise with the distress of others and to offer comforts and consolation' (1985: 404).

Existing relationships may be changed by the suicide too. When one member of the family dies, those remaining may become closer to one another (Tatelbaum 1981). Ursula has noticed that, since Josie died, the rest of the family have become more caring of one another, because, as she says, 'I think it's up to us to make sure that there is something positive as an end result.'

Survivors may decide on major life changes, and a switch of career – often into one of the helping professions – is not uncommon (Staudacher 1988). Since his wife's death, Brian has decided he will probably take early retirement from his job in the business world, and move into something involved with helping people. 'Material things', he says, 'have lost their value. Life itself – the quality of life – has taken on a much increased importance.' Carole has also recently decided to leave teaching and retrain for a new career. Other survivors had taken up new hobbies and developed new interests.

Career changes of this kind can be part of inner change and growth which some survivors will experience as a direct result of the suicide. Ian's death has led Melanie to rethink her whole life – though as she says, 'it was a very hard way to find out':

> I think I've grown as a person in the last four years, because I've really had to sort out how I feel about a lot of things – not just his death, but our relationship, how I feel as a mother, what I'm going to do with my life – it's made me question an awful lot, whereas I'd just have stumbled on before.

Previous chapters have touched on some of the losses which stem from the one overarching loss of the person who died. Many survivors talked of a loss of security – of losing trust in the world, in other people, or in themselves:

> Personal disasters involve the personal experience of loss.... They involve a loss of belief in the security of the personal and sometimes physical world, and in one's own immortality. These losses must be grieved in the adaptation to personal disaster. (Raphael 1985: 351)

Survivors talked of feeling 'less confident and less happy', of being 'more anxious and apprehensive', and of having 'a tremendous fear of rejection and a lack of confidence in handling life'. This sense of rejection was not uncommon (see pp. 173–5). However, even losses can include elements of gain, as Francesca discovered:

> I've learned that I'm not queen of the world ... I don't know it all. I'm not as good as all that. I think it's made me a little less pleased with myself than I was.... I always felt I could do practically anything, and knew all about people.... It's important too to know that I'm as vulnerable as the next person from time to time, and that's something I need to recognise rather than always being the strong person and able to cope with absolutely anything.

Memories

> When I think about him now, I think more about his life than dwelling on his death, although you're obviously aware of that even whilst you're thinking, because that doesn't go away.... It's a step forward from the beginning, when all you can think about is the death. (Jennifer)

After the suicide, survivors will often mentally retrace the events leading up to the death. Where the manner of death was particularly violent, or if the survivor discovered the body, they may be obsessed with memories of what they saw or imagined. Even when this is not the case, in the early stages of bereavement, the dead person may only be remembered in the context of their suicide, and sometimes these painful memories will persist, as Pauline discovered: 'In the beginning it's all that day, isn't it? I suppose I went over that for nine or ten months – well a year, I suppose. Now I'm beginning to think differently [but] it's still there, it comes back.' As Pam said, 'suicide fouls up the memories'.

The survivor may feel that the act of suicide has negated or even destroyed everything that went before, including the happy times. When Susan's husband committed suicide, it seemed to her 'as if he had destroyed everything that we had done and had together ... and it was difficult to think of the good times'. These feelings about the death may have to be faced and worked through, though, before other – perhaps better – memories of the victim can emerge. Jane found that, although it took some time, she was eventually able to regain positive memories of her brother.

> In my mind, in my inner being, I have a picture of him.... I think what I carry with me is a sense of his essential being which was very big in every sense, laughing a lot, very good-natured, and enjoying himself, and that's good.... All the rest is over; [good memories] were hard to hold on to at first, they came and went, but the horror kept [them] away for a bit.

There may be other barriers; overwhelming feelings of grief and loss may need to abate before the good times can be recalled. Two years after his wife's death Brian was still unable to recall any of the happy times he and Judy had shared, and he wondered whether this was because there was, as he put it, 'still a kind of trapped grief there'. Persistent guilt may also cut the survivor off from happy memories, as Maureen found:

> I can remember him as a young man, and the laughs, sometimes the bad things, but I've shut out his childhood, I can't bear to think [about it].... I feel I didn't give him enough cuddles as a little boy but ... as my doctor said, that's a normal thing to feel because you're trying to turn the clock back ... so that I didn't tell him off and didn't smack him.... So I find I can't look at photos of him as a child because it just tears me apart; if I see a little boy, a little ginger-haired boy, I just want to pick him up and bring him home and start again.

Strange as it may apear to others, survivors can sometimes find it easier to think about the difficult times; in that way the loss may feel more bearable, as Pam realised: 'I used to try and remember her when she was down and unhappy with herself and inside herself, and then I could understand perhaps, and I could live with her not being with us.' Three years after her daughter's suicide, Ursula still felt distant from Josie; she knew that Josie used to cuddle her, but she could not remember what that actually felt like, and she wondered whether perhaps remembering would be too painful.

Worden suggests that one of the signs of mourning coming to an end is when the survivor is able to think of the dead person – but without pain: 'There is always a sense of sadness when you think of someone that you have loved and lost, but it is a different kind of sadness – it lacks the wrenching quality it previously had' (1983: 16). Almost a year after her daughter's death, Francesca was beginning to recapture some of the 'rare moments of Patricia's happiness' – but they were mingled with sad memories.

A wasted life?

Would-be suicide victims are no longer tried in the courts, but when someone commits suicide survivors are often on the receiving end of other people's criticisms of the victim (see Chapter 11). But do survivors make these sort of judgements too? Do they see the victim's life as a waste, do they see the suicide as a wrongful act? Or do they place the dead person on a pedestal? According to Worden (1983), suicide survivors often tend to have a distorted image of the dead person, seeing them as either all good or all bad. Certainly a tendency to idealise may sometimes contrast with the victim's own lack of self-worth. Peter admits that perhaps he does rather venerate Susie but, as he sees it, she was 'a very remarkable person who just never understood how remarkable she was'.

Because of the traumatic and untimely nature of the death, the rest of the victim's life, and particularly the more positive aspects, can be almost completely overlooked, but for some survivors it was important to recognise that the victim's life had included some significant achievements; Dick's sister, for example, had made an important contribution to the national campaign for lead-free petrol, and to him, Sally's life had to mean more than the mental illness which had overshadowed her last few years:

> I suppose I like to think of her ... as all right. The later
> memories can overlie that, but we shouldn't forget that her life
> wasn't all awful ... the last five years probably were a lot of pain

and suffering, but she did have twenty-five years [before that], and I think it's something you can lose sight of.

I was told about many different contributions which the victims had made to other people's lives: the doctor whose patients had found him a deeply caring man; the researcher who had undertaken valuable work with handicapped children; and the writer whose books had been well received. Frances's contribution was particularly poignant; because she was in a coma for some time before she died, her parents were able to give permission for her organs to be used for transplant surgery. Her death literally enabled others to live.

Survivors talked of ways in which the victim had enriched their own lives; Brian described how Judy had taught the family to share her love of art and music; she had also taught Brian how to fold fitted sheets! In Andrew's case, his wife had worked in order to support him through medical school, enabling him to train for the career he had always wanted to pursue and which has been such an important part of his life. One of the most touching tributes came from Stephanie, whose aunt had committed suicide. She wrote:

> In my teens I was gawky and incoherent, unbearably shy and lacking in confidence. I was small and undersized and mousy. My aunt Dorothy was blond, tall, and voluptuous and articulate. She did, however, the most important thing for me. She made me feel I was attractive and worth listening to. She was a role model for years.

The funeral can be an opportunity for celebrating the person's life and their achievements (Chapter 8), but not all survivors can contemplate the idea of celebration so soon after the suicide. Josie was cremated on Christmas Eve, and Ursula had not even been able to face people coming back to the house afterwards. Three years later, though, she decided she wanted to celebrate Josie's life and organised a gathering of family and friends, 'to celebrate Josie and her uniqueness', because, as Josie's father said: 'in her short life she made her mark'.

Anniversaries

For many bereaved people, the thoughts and feelings experienced at the time of the death may recur at the time of the anniversary;

'anniversary reactions' are mentioned frequently in the bereavement literature (e.g. Tatelbaum 1981; Bowlby 1985; Raphael 1985).

But for many survivors, the time leading up to the anniversary of the death was even more difficult than the day itself. Jennifer found the run-up to Tim's first anniversary very hard: 'as we came up to the first anniversary it felt so big and awful ... but the day wasn't as bad as the weeks before'; it felt almost worse than the time of the death itself, when she had been numbed by shock: 'you're not thinking straight anyway, and twelve months later ... you're beginning to think again'.

Anne Downey has pinpointed another possible reason for the overwhelming feelings of dread which often seem to precede the actual anniversary:

> there are now only twelve days to go before the first anniversary of your death.... I cannot sleep at night and am in a terrible state of anxiety. I know what is happening. I am reliving all the events of those final weeks except that *now I know the outcome*. Because there is no way of changing anything, I feel like an observer tied in chains and unable to do anything. (1987: 90; my italics)

Her situation is reminiscent of the dreamer who, in the throes of a nightmare, cannot stop the dream by waking up.

For some survivors, anniversaries posed a particular problem because they did not know the real date when the death had occurred (see Chapter 4). When someone had been missing for some time, there was often only an estimated date, decided by the pathologist or the police. In some cases, survivors could accept that, but others were convinced that it was wrong, and so were left with the confusion of an 'official' date, and the date when they felt sure the death had occurred.

Although, at a national level, December and January are not the peak months for suicide, nearly a third of the fifty survivors I met had an anniversary which was around Christmas or New Year. At a time generally associated with celebration, these survivors annually faced a reminder of their loss, and for parent survivors, the missing son or daughter at the Christmas table often felt particularly painful.

Where the suicide is carried out in anger, the victim may even choose a date they know will be especially hurtful to the survivors. Melanie's husband Ian had threatened to kill himself if she did not return by a certain date. When she refused, he carried out his threat in a way she now realises was deliberately intended to cause the most hurt possible – he killed himself on her birthday.

Survival

> I think now I've accepted her death ... I think I have let go. At the time it didn't seem as though I'd ever be happy again ... every morning waking up was an awful struggle, to get out of that awful black pit every morning, but then, eventually, you find it's not like that and you can be normal again. (Nancy)

The Chinese symbol for 'crisis' is the combination of the symbols for both 'danger' and 'opportunity' (Jones 1987: 141). The Chinese recognised many centuries ago a concept which others have more recently developed and labelled crisis intervention theory. 'Crisis', wrote Erikson, 'is a turning point, a crucial period of increased vulnerability and heightened potential' (1971: 96). Danger and vulnerability, opportunity and potential – are all evoked by and present in crises. Suicide bereavement represents a major crisis, but one from which the bereaved can emerge as survivors, and that, as Lois said at the beginning of this chapter 'is the miracle'. But it also forces people to make choices; the bereaved person, Seligman suggests, 'may remain the victim of an irredeemable loss, or he may emerge from darkness into dawn and become the survivor' (1976: 135).

Living with the aftermath of suicide can mean having to accept that one has been badly wounded and that scars will remain – and occasionally hurt. 'There is a sense in which mourning can be finished', Worden suggests, 'and then there is a sense in which mourning is never finished' (1983: 17). Three years after her husband's suicide marked a turning point for Melanie: 'I really thought, I'm all right basically; some things still hurt, but basically I'm all right.' Her bereavement had been particularly painful and difficult, but becoming a survivor meant choosing not to let Ian's final angry gesture ruin the rest of her life. Similarly, as Jan found, it is for the survivor to choose whether or not they will become a victim – like the person who died.

> OK, my life has been difficult and I've got to take responsibility for making it different, and that's a lot of my struggle – to see that as my responsibility, and not to expect other people to fix it, and not to be a victim – and I do struggle with that day by day.

No one goes round seeking out suffering, and when the suicide occurs, the survivors may understandably seek an escape route from its aftermath; as Dick realised, though, escape is not always possible, and the impact of the death has to be faced: 'You've got to live with it, and however much you went out, or you drank, or you watched telly, or whatever you did ... it was there. I think that was the most difficult thing.'

Feeling 'all right', 'learning to live with it', 'living with a different world', realising one day that you feel 'normal again' – each person discovers how to live with their particular loss. Some of the people in this book were still struggling to accept their identity as survivors; others had reached the point where they accepted what had happened, and had incorporated the experience into their lives; they had learned that they could live with it – and still live. The pain had not always gone away, but they had become true survivors. In Seligman's words, they had become 'the prospective carriers of life and hope' (1976: 135).

Part three

Looking to the future

Chapter fifteen

Meeting the needs of survivors

This book aims to draw attention to a group of people who have remained largely hidden, and to examine some of the reasons why this is so. Is it because survivors choose to hide themselves? Or does society choose to avoid them? I believe that the act of suicide is still viewed with such horror and discomfort by many people that they can only face the survivors with extreme discomfort. On the other hand, the sense of stigma and shame frequently experienced by those bereaved by suicide can make it hard for them to face the world. The resulting collusion helps to ensure that the needs of survivors are swept under the carpet.

Because survivors have been largely ignored, their particular needs have not always been recognised. The fifty people whose stories are told here represent a minute fraction of the total number of survivors in Britain. However, even from the experiences of this small group, it is clear that there is no such thing as the typical survivor, and needs will vary from person to person. But despite this, there are some common threads, which suggest that they could often be supported in a more appropriate, and more sensitive fashion.

Suicide bereavement can severely challenge a person's coping resources – grief work is hard work; but it is also a natural process. As Susan Wallbank, counsellor at CRUSE headquarters, explains: 'the role of those who support the bereaved – offering advice, support, and reassurance when it is needed – is comparable to that of the midwife; both are there to support a natural process'. However, because suicide can involve such powerful and complex emotions, survivors may find it hard to believe that they are going through a normal – and indeed necessary – process. They may feel there is something intrinsically wrong with them, that they are somehow 'sick' or abnormal, although, according to Barbara Porter, a counsel-lor and co-facilitator of a suicide bereavement group: 'we are not dealing with people who are neurotic, but with people who have suf-fered a severe trauma'.

Need is an all-embracing word, but most survivors will have a number of different needs; sometimes practical information and ad-vice will be sought, while at other times they will want support and comfort. Needs are likely to differ at different stages in the bereave-ment process. Survivors will have varying ways of meeting their needs; some find themselves able to draw on their own inner re-sources for coping; they may also have the support of family and close friends. Others will decide they want help from people who are not directly involved in their loss. Many will be supported by a com-bination of all these coping strategies. Just as there is no one way of reacting to suicide, so there is no single optimum way of providing support. A range of different helping strategies is needed.

As previous chapters have shown, when a suicide occurs, survivors often come face-to-face with many different people: ambulance crews, members of the police, pathologists, coroners' officers, under-takers, clergy, and journalists – to name but a few. Their involvement is often unsought, sometimes unwelcome, but frequently necessary. All, however, have the potential to help – or to harm – the survivor. This chapter suggests some ways in which survivors might be helped more effectively.

The proposals in this chapter draw on a number of different sources. Many of the survivors I met had suggestions to make about how their own needs could have been met more satisfactorily; they usually knew what had helped them (and what had not), and they were clear about wanting a better deal for future survivors. People working in the bereavement field who were in contact with suicide survivors also had suggestions to make. Finally, in spite of differen-ces in culture and tradition, there are some useful lessons to be learned from survivor support programmes operating in other coun-tries – notably in Canada and the USA.

The immediate needs of survivors

Suicide is a major crisis, and what happens to survivors in the period immediately following the death can be crucial in determining how well they will cope with the bereavement. Indeed, Richman goes as far as to suggest that, at this point, 'the future fate, and even the very lives of some survivors may be determined' (1984: 141). The crisis of bereavement, by its very nature, throws survivors into a state of disorganisation which requires them to change and adapt to the loss. But if survivors receive appropriate help in those early days, though the feelings of grief that follow may be no less intense, this may set them on the path of healthy mourning and adaptation to their loss.

In the period immediately after the death, families often gather together, but will tend to disperse again immediately after the funeral. This gathering of the family can provide an opportunity for all those most directly affected to share the fact that one of their number has committed suicide, and it is at this point that the seeds of healthy mourning can be sown. As earlier chapters have shown, family myths and secrets can all too easily develop if communication between survivors is distorted or non-existent, but if survivors are well supported at this time, families can confront the truth about the manner and circumstances of the death. If communication is as open and honest as possible, if painful feelings of anger, guilt, or blame can begin to be faced and shared at this point, the development of unhealthy or blocked mourning may be prevented.

In the days immediately following the suicide, survivors will often have to cope with particularly stressful experiences such as the post-mortem, and the police investigations. Sometimes there are difficult decisions to be made: whether or not to see the body, who should be told outside the family, and exactly what information other people should be given about the manner of death. In many instances, survivors will be able to make these decisions and cope with these events with little or no outside help. It is worth remembering that the aim of professional help should be to support and not supplant people's existing support networks. Families may need the support of people who are less directly affected such as close friends, but at this point they may not need help from people outside their immediate circle.

In the first few days, survivors can feel overwhelmed by the sheer numbers of people around them. The house may be full of relatives and friends, as well as police and undertakers. The idea of anyone else coming into the house – and especially a stranger – may be more than they can cope with at this stage. They may feel so wounded and vulnerable that they only want to hide from other people. Alternatively, they may feel too numbed to know whether or not they want help. At this point, survivors can still be told what help is available. Then whether or not they decide to follow this up is their choice. Just knowing that help is available may be sufficent to enable them to cope.

But regardless of whether survivors decide to ask for outside help at this stage, they are required to deal with a number of people who may be in a position to offer help of one sort or another. Those on the 'front line' include the police, the coroner's officer, the undertaker, and members of the clergy. General practitioners are also likely to have contact with survivors shortly after the death.

These 'first responders', as Dunne and his colleagues describe them (1987), will regularly be in contact with bereaved people, but may be less used to dealing with survivors and less comfortable with suicide deaths. As Shepherd and Barraclough concluded, after studying the needs of widows and widowers bereaved by suicide: 'members of the "helping professions" ... have no grounds for complacency ... greater sensitivity is clearly required' (1979: 72, 73). If first responders are to offer the right sort of help to survivors, even if it is only to be on a short-term basis, this will have definite implications for training and support (see pp. 211–13).

There may be very specific ways in which people outside the survivor's immediate circle can usefully offer support. Shepherd and Barraclough (1979) cite two examples: a health visitor who went with the widow to identify her husband's body; and a child care officer who accompanied a widow to the inquest. The support of an uninvolved person on such occasions can free the survivor from having to worry about how other people in the family are coping. At other times, all that may be needed is for someone to ensure that the survivor has a friend or relative with them – to check that the survivor's own support network is functioning.

The police and the coroner's court

The police and the coroner's officer are usually among the first on the scene when a suicide occurs, but their role differs somewhat from that of the clergy or the family doctor; they are there primarily to investigate the circumstances surrounding the death.

The first task for the police is often to break the news to the nearest relatives. Communicating bad news is never easy; indeed, it is sometimes claimed that because of its unpopularity, the job is usually given to the newest (and therefore least experienced) members of the force. Whether or not this is always so, initial training programmes need to prepare the police not only for dealing with the technicalities of investigating sudden deaths, but for coping with the relatives of suicide victims as well.

Writing from an American perspective, Danto (1987) makes a number of useful proposals, which could equally well be applied in Britain. First, he suggests, members of the police need to be more aware of the likely reactions of survivors, including the possibility that anger and hostility may sometimes be directed towards them. Second, survivors need an explanation from the police about why their investigations are necessary, including the fact that any suspicion of foul play must be ruled out. Third, the police should be in a position to refer survivors to appropriate national and local organisations for help.

The increasing emphasis in police training on self-awareness, communication, and general interpersonal skills should result in the police being better equipped to deal with cases of suicide. However, investigating sudden death can still be a stressful aspect of their work, and dealing with the results of violent death and with the distress of relatives can challenge even trained and experienced members of the force; their own needs for support should not be forgotten. Police authorities are beginning to take this on board, but support and counselling services in most areas are still highly inadequate.

In theory, the police and the coroner's officer each have specific and separate responsibilities when dealing with sudden deaths. Coroner's officers are responsible for organising removal of the body, and arranging for the post-mortem to be carried out. It is also part of their job to keep relatives informed about what is happening – where the body has been taken, for example – and to advise families about any arrangements they need to make. They should also liaise closely with the police, ensuring that all necessary investigations have been completed before the full inquest. The role of the police is primarily to investigate – to obtain statements from relevant people, and collect any further evidence required for the inquest.

However, because the coroner's officer may have little face-to-face contact with the family – often only liaising with them by telephone – relatives may expect the police to provide them with information and advice, a situation which Phil Clements of the

Metropolitan Police Training School believes can cause problems: 'We are there to ask questions and to investigate the death', he argues, 'and that can sometimes conflict with the relatives' need to find out more about the suicide, since both are then wanting to ask the questions.' Given this somewhat confused situation, the respective roles of police and coroner's officers need clarification, and relatives need to know who they can reliably turn to for information and advice.

It has been suggested that coroner's officers could develop a more supportive role; in practice, some officers already do spend time helping relatives, but it is not a recognised part of their job, it may conflict with the investigatory aspects of their work, and they may simply not have the time to sit and talk with relatives. To circumvent these difficulties, Morris (1976) has proposed that a local authority social worker should be attached to each court, to act as the coroner's welfare officer, and provide crisis assistance to relatives. Their intervention, he suggests, would be primarily short-term, assessing the situation, offering whatever advice and counselling is called for, and, where appropriate, referring people on to other organisations who can offer longer-term support. Survivors would be offered a visit as a matter of routine, but would be free to refuse if they felt it unnecessary, or did not wish to see the welfare officer. In the fourteen years since Morris wrote that article, no action has been taken to implement his proposals, which is unfortunate, since the idea has much to commend it. However, if local authority social services departments are unwilling or unable to take this on, the voluntary sector could perhaps consider developing a service of this kind on a pilot basis.

In the mean time, there are other practical steps which could be taken, which would ease the survivors through the inquest system. Shepherd and Barraclough (1979) have suggested that coroner's courts should issue a leaflet explaining the purpose and nature of the enquiry, providing information about inquest procedures, and telling relatives how the death certificate can be obtained. From the experiences of some survivors in this book, there is certainly a need for such a leaflet since people often went into court having little or no idea of what was likely to happen (see Chapter 7). Survivors also need to understand their rights in relation to inquest procedures: they should be aware that they are entitled to appeal against the verdict, and that suicide notes addressed to them are their property and should not be retained by the court once the inquest has been completed. At present, the onus is largely on relatives to find out these things for themselves – which they are unlikely to do. The information needs to be in writing since people in shock or under stress tend not to remember everything that has been said to them. It would also be helpful if coroner's officers were routinely available to meet with relatives immediately before the inquest to explain the procedures to them.

It has been proposed that the present inquest system should be reformed, so that in the majority of cases, the inquest would be dispensed with altogether (HMSO 1971; Barraclough and Shepherd 1976; Chambers 1989). However, no changes are imminent, and while the current system remains in operation, the suggestions made above would go some way towards meeting the needs of survivors more satisfactorily, and in a more humane way than at present.

Suicide and the Press

Apparently, the most popular news items in the national daily Press are stories about ordinary people which have a tragic angle, 'a prescription which accounts of suicide fill exactly', Shepherd and Barraclough point out (1978: 286). But how do relatives feel when they read these sort of headlines: 'It's sixth time lucky for suicide bungler' (*Sun*, 5 April 1989). or 'Death wish boss rams blazing restaurant' (*Daily Mirror*, 30 December 1986)? Are the interests of the media and those of survivors necessarily incompatible?

Although only a minority of survivors will be faced with reports in the national newspapers, local newspapers, read by a very high proportion of the population, frequently carry stories about local suicide victims – mainly based on press attendance at the coroner's court. A study by Shepherd and Barraclough of coverage in one provincial evening paper revealed that, even at the local level, reporting is often selective in its approach. Suicides involving younger victims received greater attention than those of older people, and the more violent the suicide, the more likely it was to be reported; 'non-violent and middle-aged suicides', they concluded, 'do not command priority' (1978: 286).

This distorted coverage not only presents an inaccurate picture to the public at large, but calls into question whether press reporting can or does have an educative function. Dunne-Maxim, whose brother committed suicide and who now co-ordinates a survivors' project, believes that the interest of the media and of survivors need not be mutually incompatible, and that the Press can educate the public about suicide. 'The media and the survivors', she suggests, 'can work co-operatively in a way which is healing for the family, helpful for society, and still "sells newspapers"' (1987: 47).

However, if reporting is to become more accurate, and is to present a less partial or distorted view of suicide, this will require the active involvement of survivors and of the bereavement organisations who support them. Dealing with reporters on the doorstep may be unwelcome, but if survivors are able to talk to the Press, perhaps with the support of a close friend to hand, they may not only prevent inaccurate statements being made, but may also succeed in injecting a more positive focus to the story; they can perhaps tell reporters something of the positive qualities or particular achievements of the person who has died so that coverage presents a more rounded picture of the victim. For Dunne-Maxim, her own experience of doing this when her brother committed suicide was, she writes, 'a very significant factor in my grief resolution' (1987: 47).

National and local bereavement organisations can also contribute to improved press reporting. If they can establish good contacts with relevant journalists and reporters, they will be in a good position to encourage articles and programmes which explore in greater depth than news stories can some of the key issues relating to suicide. Those working with survivors can make it clear that they would be available to provide informed comment on individual cases, if called upon to do so.

It has been suggested (Barraclough and Shepherd 1977) that members of the Press should be excluded from inquests, a measure which would make press coverage much more unlikely. In Scotland, which does not have the same inquest system, suicide stories rarely feature in the Press. It is debatable, however, whether this form of censorship should be exercised, solely to protect relatives. Writing in *The Guardian*, Sarler (1987) raised this issue after photographs of two suicide incidents had appeared earlier that year in the national Press. One showed a woman jumping off the cliffs at Beachy Head, and the other a man diving from a crane in a London park. Questioning whether intrusion of this kind into matters of private pain could be justified in terms of press freedom and the public's right to know, Sarler rejected legal measures as a possible solution, concluding that: 'this is not an issue of censorship, [but] it is an issue of taste and judgement'. Fortunately publication of such pictures is relatively uncommon; the Beachy Head picture was taken by a passing tourist, and in the second case, the man had asked the Press to attend because he wanted to draw attention to a political grievance. Banner headlines and sensationalised accounts, though, are quite common.

Public interest and private grief may never be comfortable bedfellows. However, if survivors and bereavement support services are willing to enter into a dialogue with the media and, as a result, can bring about more sensitive, accurate, and positive reporting of suicide, this may help to prevent those lapses into inaccuracy, bad taste, and sensationalism which occur at present.

Longer-term needs

It would be wrong to assume that all survivors of suicide will either need or want long-term help. Where the victim had a history of longstanding or intractable difficulties, the suicide may be seen as an acceptable solution and a relief by the survivors. Others, though not necessarily experiencing the suicide as a relief, may receive all the help and support they need from family members and close friends. However, informal support is not always sufficient, and survivors may decide to seek further help.

Although specialist services for survivors of suicide are somewhat sparse in Britain (see Appendix A), there is a growing network of local bereavement support groups (mainly run by CRUSE and The Compassionate Friends), as well as organisations offering counselling and therapy for a range of problems. However, information about these various sources of help is rarely made available to survivors on a routine basis. A clearly written leaflet or pamphlet is needed which would include details of both local and national organisations. Copies should be made available in all coroner's courts, and in other places where survivors are likely to be found, including doctors' surgeries, undertakers' premises, hospital casualty departments, mortuaries, and crematoria. Survivors would be able to take the leaflet home, and if they subsequently decided to seek help, then they would have the information readily to hand. Finding help would not be the lottery that it so often is at present.

Some survivors will seek help immediately, while others will find that it is only when the shock begins to wear off – weeks or even months later – that they feel the need for support. In some instances, survivors will apparently have adjusted to their loss at the time, only to discover years later that there are unresolved issues relating to the suicide. They may have sought help for what they thought were unrelated problems, only to discover that unresolved grief is at the root of their difficulties (Dunne 1987b).

Whatever sort of help survivors look for, and whatever their particular difficulties, a key task of those supporting them is to give survivors the opportunity to tell their story; 'the crucial thing', Lukas and Seiden suggest, 'is having the opportunity to be heard. To talk and be heard' (1987: 156). But each person's story will be different, and help must be offered in ways which recognise and support the uniqueness of each person's grieving. For one person the overriding issue will be a need to search for answers to why the suicide occurred, while for another person this may be totally irrelevant and unnecessary. Guilt can be a major issue for one survivor, but not for the next. In whatever form it is provided, support needs to be sufficiently flexible to accommodate these differences.

When considering how support for survivors should be developed, a number of other issues need to be considered. Can survivors best be helped in groups, or is one-to-one support more appropriate? Should survivors be encouraged to join ordinary bereavement groups, or do they always need to be catered for separately? Should those who offer help be survivors themselves, and can people who have not been bereaved by suicide support survivors? Should support be organised on a self-help basis, or should professionals always be involved?

Can non-survivors offer support?

Some survivors would answer with an emphatic 'no', believing that unless someone has been through a similar experience they cannot possibly be of any real help. Many survivors do feel their situation is different from that of other bereaved people. When the BBC screened an Open Space film about survivors – *Shadow of Suicide* – many of the callers to the phone-in which followed said they wished there was an organisation specifically for people bereaved by suicide.

There is a sense in which only someone who has been through a suicide bereavement can know what it feels like, but Barbara Porter, who has co-facilitated a suicide bereavement group for the last four years, believes that non-survivors can play a valid supportive role, a view shared by Billow who, from her involvement with support groups, has concluded that: 'a mental health professional need not be a survivor of suicide in order to bring survivors together' (1987: 213). If non-survivors are to become involved in this area, though, they must be aware of their own feelings and attitudes about suicide. For example, bereavement counsellors and other helping professionals can be as shocked as anyone else by suicide, but they need to find this out before embarking on support work with survivors.

Volunteers with the Toronto Survivors Support Program (Rogers *et al.* 1982) include both survivors and non-survivors. The project involves teams of two trained volunteers meeting for eight structured two-hour sessions with individual families who have suffered a suicide bereavement, and who have referred themselves to the project for help. These families are subsequently invited to attend four bi-weekly groups where they meet with other survivors. The project has found that the inclusion of survivors among their volunteers is useful, since some families specifically request assistance from a survivor. As Rogers and her colleagues (1982) point out, though, this should not be the sole criterion when matching families and volunteers; it is equally important, both when matching volunteers with each other and with the families who are seeking help, to take into account their individual personalities, approaches, and needs.

Can survivors join ordinary bereavement groups?

The short answer is 'yes'. There is nothing to stop survivors of suicide joining a group whose members have been bereaved by non-suicide deaths. Indeed, because there are so few survivor groups, if they want to join a group rather than be helped on a one-to-one basis, they may have no choice at present. However, certain factors have to be taken into account.

One of the main reasons why bereaved people join groups is to share their experiences with others in a similar situation. For survivors of suicide, this can be difficult; telling other people about how someone died on a railway line or jumped from the top of a building can meet with expressions of shock and horror which may only serve to reinforce the survivor's own feeling that this is indeed something shocking and horrid. On the other hand, if the group consists of fellow survivors, although they may not find it particularly easy either to hear about the circumstances of the suicide, their reactions are likely to be less powerful and less negative.

Other features of suicide bereavement can make it difficult for survivors to be in the company of other bereaved people. A sense of stigma and shame may inhibit them from joining ordinary bereavement support groups where they may feel they are going to be judged in some way, or even blamed for the suicide. If survivors feel they were responsible for the death, they may feel undeserving of any support, or, at the very least, less deserving than people whose relatives have died from other causes. The implied rejection in suicide can lead survivors to conclude that they are indeed different from other bereaved people whose relatives apparently did not choose to leave them.

For these and other reasons, many survivors decide not to attend ordinary bereavement groups, but some do, and find they are able to get the help and support they need. Others will prefer to have individual counselling sessions where they will not have to meet other bereaved people. However, it is dangerous to assume that all survivors can automatically be grouped together, when the only common factor among them may be that everyone is going through a suicide bereavement. Other factors, such as the relationship to the dead person (parent, sibling, spouse, and so on), the age of the victim, and the personality of the survivor, may be equally relevant.

Voluntary, professional, or self-help?

Current provision for survivors – and for the bereaved in general – is provided in all three forms at present. The Compassionate Friends, for example, is a self-help movement (with professional advisers), while CRUSE has both volunteers and professionals in its local groups. Suicide bereavement groups tend to use professionals, although not necessarily in a leadership role. Barbara Porter, for example, sees her role as that of a facilitator who can enable group members to offer mutual support; she does not see herself as the leader of a therapeutic group.

The Toronto support programme (see p. 209) is an interesting example of how professionals and volunteers (including survivors) can work collaboratively to provide a service. Rogers *et al.* stress the benefits of this approach, and disagree with the commonly held view 'that voluntary services using self-help concepts ... are relatively easy to operate and require little if any funding' (1982: 447). They have learned from experience that good programmes require adequate professional assistance and consultation, help with the training and support of volunteers, and the resources to fund at least a part-time director. They have also found that the involvement of professionals enhances the project's credibility and results in a greater number of referrals.

Despite the relatively recent development of self-help groups in the USA, the principles on which they are based are not new; they have been used for some time by groups such as Alcoholics Anonymous. While self-help groups undoubtedly have an important and useful role to play, difficulties can sometimes arise. Survivors may join who have needs so great or so intense that other members of the group can feel swamped, and unable to help. Survivors may have problems linked to the suicide which are particlarly difficult to resolve, or the bereavement may have raised other more long-standing difficulties. As in any group, one person can dominate or manipulate the group, making it difficult for anyone else to talk and be heard. This is where the involvement of facilitators with groupwork skills can be advantageous, as they can use their skills to resolve these types of problems; since the facilitators are not there to talk about their own experiences they are also able to give their complete attention to the rest of the group. Not surprisingly, the emotional temperature in such groups can become very high, and in Barbara Porter's experience, the facilitator also has a key role to play in holding and containing the group so that participants feel safe to express their feelings.

Other survivors will decide to seek professional help, and may turn to a psychiatrist, counsellor, or psychotherapist (see Chapter 12). Sometimes they will find their GP or local member of the clergy has the necessary skills and is willing to offer help. They may prefer to talk about their bereavement with just one other person, and they may feel the need for a trained listener. In some cases, the bereavement will trigger a much wider and deeper re-appraisal of the survivor's life, and they may decide to use counselling or therapy to explore possible future life changes.

Training and support for the supporters

Whether help is being offered by trained volunteers or qualified professionals, and regardless of whether they have personal experience of suicide bereavement, those providing support need to have some understanding of the range of possible reactions of suicide survivors. They need to be aware, for example, that anger is a common response to suicide, and that hostility can sometimes be aimed at those offering help or support.

They will also need to develop a real awareness of their own attitudes towards suicide, and the particular reactions and emotions it may arouse in them. Unless helpers have gained this self-awareness, their attitudes and feelings about suicide can seriously inhibit their ability to help the survivors. If, for example, someone believes deep down that people are usually 'driven to suicide' by their relatives (a not uncommon belief), they may find it hard to empathise with survivors who are asking for help to deal with their guilt. Knowledge and self-awareness are equally important tools for those in a helping role.

There are other reasons why self-awareness is important. On some occasions, would-be helpers may need to recognise that they are unable to meet a particular request for help. For example, the doctor or therapist who is feeling angry or guilty because a patient has committed suicide may need to accept that he or she cannot work with the surviving family. What that person may be able to do, though, is to find someone else who is in a better position to help the survivors. Some people may discover that, for various personal reasons, survivors are not a group of people they can work with effectively.

Survivors quite frequently go on to become supporters of other bereaved people, whether as part of a self-help network such as SOS, or by becoming bereavement counsellors. Indeed, they can have much to offer, but unresolved issues may surface at times, and any unfinished business needs to be dealt with either during initial training or in ongoing support or supervision sessions (Rogers *et al.* 1982). Those survivors who become helpers also need to be aware of the dangers of overidentifying with those they are helping.

Working with suicide survivors is often very draining; good listening is hard work, and being alongside people who are in pain can feel very painful. The helper can sometimes feel very helpless; when the survivor's distress is particularly acute, it can be hard for those supporting them to recognise that the best they can do is simply to be there for the survivor. Survivors may also look to them for an explanation of why the suicide occurred, and it can be hard to admit that probably no one has the answers. Where the suicide has left the survivor feeling particularly rejected, they may need to test out whether the person helping them is also going to abandon them, and this testing-out can be very demanding at times. The establishment of proper support mechanisms should be a priority for all groups, whether voluntary or professional. If this aspect of the service is ignored, the result may be burn-out and a consequent high turnover of helpers.

One-to-one or group support?

Some of the benefits of suicide bereavement groups have been described elsewhere (see Chapter 12), but groups are not everyone's cup of tea, and by no means all survivors will want to join one. Some of those who decide to join a group may find it does not meet their particular needs, in which case they should, wherever possible, be directed towards a more suitable form of help; in other cases, people may simply leave the group without giving any particular reasons. According to Wrobleski (1984–5), there is a 40 per cent dropout rate from survivor groups in the USA; a few are people who feel they have received all the help they need after attending the group once or twice. Others, she suggests, are people who when faced with potential pain will seek to repress their feelings. Participating actively in a group can mean allowing the painful feelings to emerge, and for some survivors that may be too confrontational and threatening.

In practice, survivors do not necessarily have to choose between groups or individual support. Indeed, one may lead on to the other. Appel and Wrobleski suggest that survivors 'who may need additional mental health services are more likely to seek and accept professional help as a result of participation in this type of group' (1987: 229). After attending a group, some survivors may decide they could benefit from individual counselling or therapy sessions. This may be because they feel unable to deal with certain issues in the group; alternatively it may be because, as mentioned above, the bereavement has raised other issues not directly related to their loss which they wish to work on further.

Postscript

Inevitably a book of this kind can do no more than begin to open up such a huge topic. I am conscious of the fact that there are many matters which have not been dealt with here. For example, none of the survivors I met belonged to ethnic minority groups. Nor have I included anything of the experiences of gay men and women survivors. I have only been able to raise other issues very briefly.

I am aware of gaps in what I have written – but gaps exist in services too. Survivors may read this book, but where will they go for help when they have read thus far? If they are lucky they will find someone to whom they can tell their story, someone who will be the listener that they need. If they do not find this, then they should press for a local suicide bereavement group to be set up.

But I hope the story of suicide bereavement is not one of unmitigated gloom. This is a book about one of the most devastating losses which human beings can face, but I have endeavoured to show that it also carries a message of hope – that survival is possible:

> There is no growth without pain and conflict; there is no loss which cannot lead to gain. (Pincus 1974: 278)

Relevant organisations

British Association for Counselling
1 Regent Place
Rugby
CV21 2PJ
Tel. 0788 578328 (Information line)
0788 550899 (Office)

Although it does not provide counselling services directly, BAC is able to provide callers with information on how to obtain access to a counsellor in their local area. Publications include an Information Sheet entitled 'What is Counselling?' and 'A Client's Guide to Counselling and Psychotherapy'. Telephone enquiries can be made, although BAC prefers to receive enquiries in writing (with stamped addressed envelope, please).

The Compassionate Friends
53 North Street
Bristol
BS3 1EN
Tel. 0272 539639 (Helpline)
0272 665202 (Administration)

The Compassionate Friends is a nationwide self-help organisation of parents whose child of any age (including adult) has died from any cause. TCF offers personal and group support and befriending (but not counselling). There is a quarterly newsletter, a postal library and a range of leaflets. TCF contact list includes SOS (Shadow of Suicide) contacts in some parts of the country.

CRUSE
Cruse House
126 Sheen Road
Richmond, Surrey
TW9 1UR
Tel. 081 940 4818
    081 332 7227 (Cruse Bereavement Line)

CRUSE Bereavement Care is a national organisation which offers help to all bereaved people through its local branches and national office. It has nearly 200 branches offering individual counselling as well as social support and advice on practical matters relating to bereavement. Wherever possible, enquirers will be directed to their local CRUSE branch. Where no local branch exists, head office offers a link with a counsellor by letter or by telephone via the Bereavement Line. CRUSE has a wide range of publications on various aspects of bereavement. There is *Cruse Chronicle*, a newsletter for members, and *Bereavement Care*, a journal for professionals who work with the dying and the bereaved.

Jewish Bereavement Counselling Service
Visitation Committee
Woburn House
Tavistock Square
London WC1H 0EZ
Tel. 071 387 4300 ext. 227 (Office hours)
    081 349 0839 (24-hour ansaphone)

The service offers counselling and support to members of the Jewish community who are bereaved. People are visited in their own homes by trained volunteer counsellors. At present, the Jewish Bereavement Counselling Service operates mainly in North West and South West London and in Redbridge (Essex).

Lesbian and Gay Bereavement Project
Vaughan M. Williams Centre
Colindale Hospital
London NW9 5HG
Tel. 081 200 0511 (Office)
081 455 8894 (Helpline, see below)

The project offers telephone counselling for lesbians and gay men bereaved by the loss of a same-sex partner, or otherwise affected by bereavement. A member is on duty every evening from 7 pm to midnight, and can be contacted via the helpline number listed above. The project also publishes a will form and can often find suitable clergy or secular officiants for funerals. Speakers and discussion leaders can be provided for any group concerned with issues relating to death and dying.

London Association of Bereavement Services
London Voluntary Sector Resource Centre
356 Holloway Road
London N7 6PN
Tel. 071 700 8134

LABS is an umbrella organisation for over 70 bereavement services and associate members in the Greater London area. They can assist enquirers with locating their nearest bereavement service.

NAFSIYAT
278 Seven Sisters Road
London N4 2HY
Tel. 071 263 4130

NAFSIYAT is an inter-cultural therapy centre offering a range of different psychotherapies. The majority of its current users live in the London Borough of Islington, but referrals (including self-referrals) can be accepted from elsewhere. NAFSIYAT has worked with individuals, couples and families from many different ethnic groups. The centre is able to offer some consultation and assessment services to professionals in other services. The centre also offers counselling and psychotherapy training.

National Association of Bereavement Services
20 Norton Folgate
London E1 6DB
Tel. 071 247 1080 (Referrals)
071 247 0617 (Administration)

NABS is a support organisation for bereavement services and acts as a referral agency by putting bereaved people in touch with their nearest most appropriate local services. It was founded in 1988 to bring together individuals and groups who are actively involved in the care of the dying and bereaved. NABS promotes networking, training and professional standards. It produces a quarterly newsletter and holds an annual training conference.

The Samaritans
10 The Grove
Slough
Berkshire
SL1 1QP
Tel. 0753 532713
Local branches are listed under S in the local directory

The Samaritans operate in the UK and the Republic of Ireland. They are available at any hour of the day or night to befriend those passing through personal crisis or in imminent danger of taking their own lives. Their telephone service, which is confidential and free of charge, operates every day of the year. There are around 200 branches throughout the UK and Ireland which are staffed by 23,000 volunteers. Anyone wishing to contact them may do so by telephoning or by calling in at their local branch. In addition to the telephone service, all local branches are able to offer face-to-face befriending during the daytime.

Information on people interviewed for the book

Name of survivor	Age at time of suicide	Victim's name	Relationship of victim to survivor	Victim's age at time of death	Date of suicide
Andrew	50	Gwen	Wife	47	1972
Ann	23	Giles	Brother	19	1936
Betty	58	Jonathan	Son	26	1985
Brian	50	Judy	Wife	48	1986
Bridget	17	Catherine	Sister	20	1982
		n.a.	Father	55	1982
Carol	47	Alan	Son	21	1985
Carole	46	Jon	Son	21	1986
Christine	42	Graham	Husband	35	1987
Colin	48	Helen	Ex-lover	40?	1979
David	39	Paul	Son	20	1987
Denise	4	n.a.	Father	25	1963
Dick	33	Sally	Sister	30	1984
Eileen	53	Sheila	Daughter	30	1976
	59	Donna	Daughter	36	1982
Francesca	57	Patricia	Daughter	29	1987
Frank	45	Josie	Daughter	21	1985
Harry	50	Frances	Daughter	22	1977
Heather	42	Alastair	Son	18	1987
Hilary	18	n.a.	Mother	48	1953
Irene	53	Bill	Husband	55	1984
Isabel	51	Eric	Husband	52	1977
Jan	13	n.a.	Father	58?	1963
Jane	37	Christopher	Brother	41	1984
Janice	40	n.a.	Mother	75	1986
Jean	52	Anna	Daughter	20	1987
Jennifer	29	Tim	Brother	30	1987
Joan	44	Lesley	Sister	42	1977
John	54	Averil	Wife	44	1984
Kevin	10	n.a.	Mother	42	1963
Liz	29	Tony	Brother	32	1984

Information on people interviewed for the book

Name of survivor	Age at time of suicide	Victim's name	Relationship of victim to survivor	Victim's age at time of death	Date of suicide
Lois	48	Simon	Son	21	1987
Marie	61	Oliver	Husband	72	1985
Mark	68	Patricia	Daughter	29	1987
Martin	14?	n.a.	Mother	mid-50s	1950?
Maureen	39	Paul	Son	20	1987
Melanie	28	Ian	Husband	37	1984
Miriam	46	Ben	Son	20	1987
Nancy	53	Clare	Daughter	20	1980
Nick	30	n.a.	Mother	64	1983
Nicola	23	Caroline	Sister	20	1987
Pam	46	Frances	Daughter	22	1977
Pat	45	Caroline	Daughter	20	1987
Pauline	62	Michael	Son	40	1987
Peter	32	Susie	Sister	21	1985
Phyllis	45	Julie	Daughter	19	1986
Robert	47	Caroline	Daughter	20	1987
Sharon	15	Paul	Brother	20	1987
Susan	41	Richard	Husband	43	1973
Suzy	32	n.a.	Father	59	1985
Ursula	45	Julie	Daughter	21	1985
Wendy	31	n.a.	Father	74	1981

References

Alexander, V. (1987) 'Living Through My Mother's Suicide' in E.J. Dunne, J. McIntosh, and K. Dunne-Maxim (eds) *Suicide and its Aftermath. Understanding and Counseling the Survivors*, New York and London: W.W. Norton.

Alvarez, A. (1974) *The Savage God: A Study of Suicide*, Harmondsworth: Penguin.

Andress, V.R. and Corey, D.M. (1978) 'Survivor Victims: Who Discovers or Witnesses Suicide?', *Psychological Reports*, 42: 759–64.

Appel, Y.H. and Wrobleski, A. (1987) 'Self-Help and Support Groups: Mutual Aid for Survivors' in E.J. Dunne, J. McIntosh, and K. Dunne-Maxim (eds) *Suicide and its Aftermath. Understanding and Counseling the Survivors*, New York and London: W.W. Norton.

Atkinson, J.M. (1978) *Discovering Suicide. Studies in the Social Organization of Sudden Death*, London: Macmillan.

Augenbraun, B. and Neuringer, C. (1972) 'Helping Survivors with the Impact of a Suicide' in A.C. Cain (ed.) *Survivors of Suicide*, Springfield, Illinois: Charles C. Thomas.

Barraclough, B.M. and Shepherd, D.M. (1976) 'Public Interest: Private Grief', *Br. J. Psychiatry*, 129: 109–13.

—— (1977) 'The Immediate and Enduring Effects of the Inquest on Relatives of Suicides', *Br. J. Psychiatry*, 131: 400–4.

—— (1978) 'Impact of a suicide inquest', Letter in *The Lancet*, 1978; ii: 795.

Battle, A. (1984) 'Group Therapy for Survivors of Suicide', *Crisis: International Journal of Suicide and Crisis Studies*, no. 5, 1: 45–58.

Behrens, T. (1988) *The Monument*, London: Sphere.

Bernhardt, G.R. and Praeger, S.G. (1983) 'After Suicide: Meeting the Needs of Survivors', paper presented at the Annual Convention of the American Personnel and Guidance Association, Washington, DC, March 1983.

Billow, C.J. (1987) 'A Multiple Family Support Group for Survivors of a Suicide' in E.J. Dunne, J. McIntosh, and K. Dunne-Maxim (eds) *Suicide and its Aftermath. Understanding and Counseling the Survivors*, New York and London: W.W. Norton.

Bowlby, J. (1985) *Attachment and Loss, Volume III. Loss: Sadness and Depression*, Harmondsworth: Penguin.

Cain, A.C. (ed.) (1972) *Survivors of Suicide*, Springfield, Illinois: Charles C. Thomas.

—— and Fast, I. (1972a) 'Children's Disturbed Reactions to Parent Suicide: Distortions of Guilt, Communication and Identification' in A.C. Cain (ed.) *Survivors of Suicide*, Springfield, Illinois: Charles C. Thomas.

—— and Fast, I. (1972b) 'The Legacy of Suicide: Observations on the pathogenic impact of suicide upon marital partners' in A.C. Cain (ed.) *Survivors of Suicide*, Springfield, Illinois: Charles C. Thomas.

Calhoun, L.G., Selby, J.W., and Faustich, M.E. (1980) 'Reactions to the Parents of the Child Suicide: A Study of Social Impressions', *J. of Counselling and Clinical Psychology*, 48, 4: 535–6.

——, Selby, J.W., and Selby, L.E. (1982) 'The Psychological Aftermath of Suicide: An Analysis of Current Evidence', *Clinical Psychology Review*, 2: 409–20.

——, Abernathy, C.B., and Selby, J.W. (1986) 'The Rules of Bereavement: Are Suicidal Deaths Different?' *J. Community Psychiatry*, 116: 255–61.

Cardinal, M. (1984) *The Words to Say It*, London: Pan.

Carstairs, G.M. (1973) Foreword in E. Stengel, *Suicide and Attempted Suicide*, Harmondsworth: Penguin (revised edition with revisions).

Chambers, D.R. (1989) 'The Coroner, the Inquest and the Verdict of Suicide', *Med. Sci. Law*, 29, 3: 181.

——, and Harvey, J.G. (1989) 'Inner Urban and National Suicide Rates: A Simple Comparative Study, *Med. Sci. Law*, 29, 3: 182–5.

Chesser, E. (1967) *Living with Suicide*, London: Hutchinson.

Colt, G.H. (1987) 'The History of the Suicide Survivor: The Mark of Cain' in E.J. Dunne, J. McIntosh, and K. Dunne-Maxim (eds) *Suicide and its Aftermath. Understanding and Counseling the Survivors*, New York and London: W.W. Norton.

Conley, B.H. (1987) 'Funeral Directors as First Responders' in E.J. Dunne, J. McIntosh, and K. Dunne-Maxim (eds) *Suicide and its Aftermath. Understanding and Counseling the Survivors*, New York and London: W.W. Norton.

Danto, B. (1987) 'Recommendations for Police Officers and Physicians' in E.J. Dunne, J. McIntosh, and K. Dunne-Maxim (eds) *Suicide and its Aftermath. Understanding and Counseling the Survivors*, New York and London: W.W. Norton.

Davenport, D. (1989) 'A Past and a Future Too' in T. Philpot (ed.) *Last Things: Social Work with the Dying and Bereaved*, Wallington, Surrey: Reed Business Publishing/Community Care.

Dorpat, T.L. (1972) 'Psychological Effects of Parental Suicide on Surviving Children' in A.C. Cain (ed.) *Survivors of Suicide*, Springfield, Illinois: Charles C. Thomas.

Downey, Anne (1987) *Dear Stephen ... A Letter Diary Written to Stephen by His Mother*, London: Arthur James.

Dunne, E.J. (1987a) 'A Response to Suicide in the Mental Health Setting' in E.J. Dunne, J. McIntosh, and K. Dunne-Maxim (eds) *Suicide and its*

Aftermath. Understanding and Counseling the Survivors, New York and London: W.W. Norton.

—— (1987b) 'Special Needs of Suicide Survivors in Therapy' in E.J. Dunne, J. McIntosh, and K. Dunne-Maxim (eds) *Suicide and its Aftermath. Understanding and Counseling the Survivors*, New York and London: W.W. Norton.

—— and Dunne-Maxim, K. (1987) Preface in E.J. Dunne, J. McIntosh, and K. Dunne-Maxim (eds) *Suicide and its Aftermath, Understanding and Counseling the Survivors*, New York and London: W.W. Norton.

——, McIntosh, J., and Dunne-Maxim, K. (eds) (1987) *Suicide and its Aftermath. Understanding and Counseling the Survivors*, New York and London: W.W. Norton.

Dunne-Maxim, K. (1987) 'Survivors and the Media: Pitfalls and Potential' in E.J. Dunne, J. McIntosh, and K. Dunne-Maxim (eds) *Suicide and its Aftermath. Understanding and Counseling the Survivors*, New York and London: W.W. Norton.

——, Dunne, E.J., and Hauser, M.J. (1987) 'When Children are Suicide Survivors' in E.J. Dunne, J. McIntosh, and K. Dunne-Maxim (eds) *Suicide and its Aftermath. Understanding and Counseling the Survivors*, New York and London: W.W. Norton.

Erikson, E.H. (1971) *Identity: Youth and Crisis*, London: Faber & Faber.

Fanthorpe, U.A. (1982) *Standing To*, Calstock, Cornwall: Peterloo Poets; *Selected Poems*, Peterloo Poets and King Penguin (1986).

Finney, A. (1988) 'When death haunts the track', *The Independent*, 12 December.

Goffman, E. (1968) *Stigma: Notes on the Management of Spoiled Identity*, Harmondsworth: Penguin.

Gordon, R. (1985) 'Growth Through Loss: A Jungian View of Loss' (CRUSE Academic Paper No. 4), Richmond, Surrey: CRUSE.

Gorer, G. (1965) *Death, Grief and Mourning in Contemporary Britain*, London: Tavistock.

Grollman, E.A. (1984) 'First-Line Help Following A Funeral' in N. Linzer (ed.) *The Will to Live vs. The Will to Die*, New York: Human Sciences Press.

Handke, P. (1976) *A Sorrow beyond Dreams*, London: Souvenir Press.

Hauser, M.J. (1987) 'Special Aspects of Grief after a Suicide' in E.J. Dunne, J. McIntosh, and K. Dunne-Martin (eds) *The Aftermath of Suicide. Understanding and Counseling the Survivors*, New York and London: W.W. Norton.

Henley, S.H.A. (1984) 'Bereavement following Suicide. A Review of the Literature' (CRUSE Academic Paper No. 1), Richmond, Surrey: CRUSE.

Hildebrand, J. (1989) 'Working with Bereaved Families' in T. Philpot (ed.) *Last Things: Social Work with the Dying and Bereaved*, Wallington, Surrey: Reed Business Publishing/Community Care.

HMSO (1971) *Home Office Report on Death Certification and Coroners*, Cmnd. 4810, London: HMSO.

—— (1984) *Coroners Rules 1984*, Statutory Instrument No. 552, London: HMSO.

James, K. (1988) 'Overdose of suicide', *Guardian*, 1 June.

Johnson, W. (1982) *The Care of the Suicide Survivor: A Model for Funeral Home Personnel*, Montgomery County, Ohio: Suicide Prevention Center.

Jones, F.A. (1987) 'Therapists as Survivors of Client Suicide' in E.J. Dunne, J. McIntosh, and K. Dunne-Martin (eds) *Suicide and its Aftermath. Understanding and Counseling the Survivors*, New York and London: W.W. Norton.

Kast, V. (1988) *A Time to Mourn. Growing through the Grief Process*, trans. Diana Dachler and Fiona Cairns, Einsiedeln, Switzerland: Daimon Verlag.

Keir, N. (1986) *I Can't Face Tomorrow. Help for Those Troubled by Thoughts of Suicide*, Wellingborough, Northants: Thorsons.

Kelly, B. (1989) 'In the Face of Death' *Open Mind*, June/July 1989, 16: 16.

Kingston, M.H. (1981) *The Woman Warrior: Memoirs of a Girlhood amongst Ghosts*, London: Pan.

Lake, T. (1984) *Living with Grief*, London: Sheldon Press.

Lewis, C.S. (1966) *A Grief Observed*, London: Faber & Faber.

Lifton, R.J. (1969) *Death in Life: Survivors of Hiroshima*, New York: Vintage Books.

Lindemann, E. and Greer, I.M. (1972) 'A Study of Grief: Emotional Responses to Suicide' in A.C. Cain (ed.) *Survivors of Suicide*, Springfield, Illinois: Charles C. Thomas.

Litman, R.E. (1970a) 'Management of Suicidal Patients in Medical Practice' in E.S. Shneidman, N.L. Farberow, and R.E. Litman (eds) *The Psychology of Suicide*, New York: Science House.

—— (1970b) 'Immobilization Response to Suicidal Behavior' in E.S. Shneidman, N.L. Farberow, and R.E. Litman (eds) *The Psychology of Suicide*, New York: Science House.

——, Curphey, T., Shneidman, E.S., Farberow, N.L., and Tabachnik, N. (1970) 'The Psychological Autopsy of Equivocal Deaths' in E.S. Shneidman, N.L. Farberow, and R.E. Litman (eds) *The Psychology of Suicide*, New York: Science House.

Lukas, C. and Seiden, H. (1987) *Silent Grief. Living in the Wake of Suicide*, New York: Charles Scribner's. London: Macmillan (1990).

Lyall, J. (1987) 'Too young to despair of life', *The Independent*, 25 August.

McIntosh, J. (1985–6) 'Survivors of Suicide: A Comprehensive Bibliography', *Omega*, 16, 4: 355–70.

—— (1987a) 'Suicide as a Mental Health Problem: Epidemiological Aspects' in E.J. Dunne, J. McIntosh, and K. Dunne-Martin (eds) *Suicide and its Aftermath. Understanding and Counseling the Survivors*, New York and London: W.W. Norton.

—— (1987b) 'Survivor Family Relationships: Literature Review' in E.J. Dunne, J. McIntosh, and K. Dunne-Martin (eds) *Suicide and its Aftermath. Understanding and Counseling the Survivors*, New York and London: W.W. Norton.

—— (1987c) 'Research, Therapy, and Educational Needs' in E.J. Dunne, J. McIntosh, and K. Dunne-Martin (eds) *Suicide and its Aftermath. Understanding and Counseling the Survivors*, New York and London:

W.W. Norton.

Marris, P. (1978) *Loss and Change*, London: Routledge & Kegan Paul.

Mitchell, S. (1985) *The Token*, London: Futura.

Mooney, B. (1985) *The Anderson Question*, London: Pan.

Morris, A. (1976) 'Wanted: A Coroner's Welfare Officer', *Community Care*, 26 May, 20.

Morse, S.R. (1984) 'Survivors of suicide: the siblings tell their story' (Doctoral dissertation, Boston University, 1984), *Dissertation Abstracts International*, 45: 1025B.

Nichols, R. (1981) 'Sudden Death, Acute Grief and Ultimate Mourning' in Otto Margolis *et al.* (eds) *Acute Grief: Counseling the Bereaved*, New York: Columbia University Press.

Office of Health Economics (1981) *Suicide and Deliberate Self-Harm*, London: Office of Health Economics.

Osterweis, M., Solomon, F., and Green, M. (eds) (1984) *Bereavement: Reactions, Consequences and Care*, Washington, DC: National Academy Press.

Parkes, C.M. (1980) 'Bereavement Counselling: Does it Work?' *Br. Medical Journal*, 281: 3–6.

—— (1986) *Bereavement: Studies of Grief in Adult Life*, Harmondsworth: Penguin (2nd edition): Hardback published by Routledge.

Pincus, L. (1974) *Death and the Family: The Importance of Mourning*, New York: Vintage Books; London: Faber & Faber (1976).

—— and Dare, C. (1978) *Secrets in the Family*, London: Faber & Faber.

Raphael, B. (1985) *The Anatomy of Bereavement. A Handbook for the Caring Professions*, London: Hutchinson.

Resnik, H.L.P. (1972) 'Psychological Resynthesis: A Clinical Approach to the Survivors of a Death by Suicide' in A.C. Cain (ed.) *Survivors of Suicide*, Springfield, Illinois: Charles C. Thomas.

Richman, J. (1984) 'Family Factors in Bereavement Following a Death by Suicide' in N. Linzer (ed.) *Suicide. The Will to Live vs. The Will to Die*, New York: Human Sciences Press.

Rilke, R.M. (1957) *Requiem and Other Poems*, trans. J.B. Leihman, London: Hogarth Press.

Rogers, J., Sheldon, A., Barwick, C., Letofsky, K., and Lancee, B. (1982) 'Help for Families of Suicide: Survivors' Support Program', *Canadian J. Psychiatry*, 27, October: 444–9.

Rosenfeld, L. and Prupas, M. (1984) *Left Alive: After a Suicide Death in the Family*, Springfield, Illinois: Charles C. Thomas.

Rubey, C.T. and Clark, D.C. (1987) 'Suicide Survivors and the Clergy' in E.J. Dunne, J. McIntosh, and K. Dunne-Martin (eds) *Suicide and its Aftermath. Understanding and Counseling the Survivors*, New York and London: W.W. Norton.

Rudestam, K.E. (1987) 'Public Perceptions of Suicide Survivors' in E.J. Dunne, J. McIntosh, and K. Dunne-Martin (eds) *Suicide and its Aftermath. Understanding and Counseling the Survivors*, New York and London: W.W. Norton.

—— and Imbroll, D. (1983) 'Societal Reactions to a Child's Death by

Suicide', *J. Consulting and Clinical Psychology*, 51, 3: 461–2.

Sarler, C. (1987) 'Keeping the horror out of the picture', *Guardian*, 9 November.

Seligman, E. (1976) 'On Death and Survival', *Harvest*, 22: 135–7.

Shepherd, D.M. and Barraclough, B.M. (1976) 'The Aftermath of a Parental Suicide for Children', *Br. J. Psychiatry*, 129: 269–76.

—— (1978) 'Suicide Reporting: Information or Entertainment?', *Br. J. Psychiatry*, 132: 283–7.

—— (1979) 'Help for Those Bereaved by Suicide', *Br. J. Social Work*, 9: 67–74.

Shneidman, E.S. (1972) Foreword in A.C. Cain (ed.) *Survivors of Suicide*, Springfield, Illinois: Charles C. Thomas.

—— (1975) 'Suicide' in A.M. Freedman, N.L. Farberow, and R.E. Litman (eds) *Comprehensive Textbook of Psychiatry*, Volume II, Baltimore, Maryland: Williams and Wilkins.

—— (1982) *Voices of Death: Personal Documents from People Facing Death*, New York: Bantam Books.

—— and Farberow, N.L. (1970) 'Sample Psychological Autopsies' in E.S. Shneidman, N.L. Farberow, and R.E. Litman (eds) *The Psychology of Suicide*, New York: Science House.

Simpson, M. (1979) *The Facts of Death*, London: Prentice-Hall.

Smith, K. (1978) *Help for the Bereaved*, London: Duckworth.

Solomon, M.I. (1981) 'Bereavement from Suicide', *Psychiatric Nursing*, July–September, 18–19.

Staudacher, C. (1988) *Beyond Grief. A Guide for Recovering from the Death of a Loved One*, London: Souvenir Press.

Stengel, E. (1973) *Suicide and Attempted Suicide*, Harmondsworth: Penguin (revised edition with revisions).

Storr, A. (1989) *Solitude*, London: Flamingo.

Tatelbaum, J. (1981) *The Courage to Grieve: Creative Living, Recovery and Growth through Grief*, London: Heinemann.

Todd, S.H. (1981) 'Sibling survivors of suicide. A qualitative study of the experience of adolescent siblings whose brother or sister completed suicide' (Doctoral dissertation, Boston University School of Education, 1980), *Dissertation Abstracts International*, 41, 3165B.

Vollman, R., Ganzert, A., Picher, L., and Williams, W.V. (1971) 'The Reactions of Family Systems to Sudden and Unexpected Death', *Omega*, 2: 101-6.

Wallace, S.E. (1977) 'On the Atypicality of Suicide Bereavement' in B.L. Danto and A.H. Kutscher (eds) *Suicide and Bereavement*, New York: MSS Information Corporation.

Woolf, L. (1969) *The Journey not the Arrival Matters. An Autobiography of the Years 1939 to 1969*, London: Hogarth Press.

Worden, W.J. (1983) *Grief Counselling and Grief Therapy*, London: Tavistock.

Wrobleski, A. (1984–5) 'The Suicide Survivors Grief Group', *Omega*, 15, 2: 173–84.

—— (1986) 'Guilt and Suicide', *Afterwords*, October.

Name index

(*Note*: The survivors are to be found in the Subject index)

Subject index